The Realities of Change in Higher Education

The Realities of Change in Higher Education explores the theory and practice of the everyday reality of change to promote learning and teaching in universities. Drawing on international case studies, it analyses a range of practical strategies to promote change that enhances students' learning.

Structured to flow from analysis of policy level change through to small-scale change at curriculum level, experienced practitioners consider key topics including:

- national policies and strategies
- different leadership styles
- the advancement of teaching and learning through research and scholarship
- how communities of practice may be effective agents for change in higher education
- the relationship between technology and change
- student assessment as a strategic tool for enhancing teaching and learning

With practical advice to enhance the learning experience of increasing numbers of university students, this book will appeal to all practitioners involved in improving learning and teaching outcomes in higher education.

Lynne Hunt is Professor and Leader of Learning and Teaching at Charles Darwin University, Australia.

Adrian Bromage is Pedagogic Research Assistant at Coventry University Centre for Higher Education Development, UK.

Bland Tomkinson is University Adviser on Pedagogic Development at the University of Manchester, UK.

The staff and educational development series
Series editor: Professor James Wisdom

A Guide to Staff and Educational Development
Edited by Peter Kahn and David Baume

Inspiring Students
Edited by Stephen Fallows and Kemal Abmet

The Management of Independent Learning
Edited by Jo Tait and Peter Knight

Managing Educational Development Projects
Effective management for maximum impact
Edited by Carole Baume, Paul Martin and Mantz Yorke

Motivating Students
Edited by Sally Brown, Steve Armstrong and Gail Thompson

Research, Teaching and Learning in Higher Education
Edited by Peter Knight

Reshaping Teaching in Higher Education
Linking teaching with research
Edited by Alan Jenkins, Rosanna Breen and Roger Lindsay

Resource-Based Learning
Edited by Sally Brown and Brenda Smith

Teaching International Students
Edited by Jude Carroll and Jeanette Ryan

SEDA is the Staff and Educational Development Association. It supports and encourages developments in teaching and learning in higher education through a variety of methods: publications, conferences, networking, journals, regional meetings and research – and through various SEDA Accreditations Schemes.

SEDA
John Foster House
36 Gordon Square
London
WC1H 0PF
Tel: 020 7380 6767
Fax: 020 7387 2655
Email: office@seda.ac.uk
Website: www.seda.ac.uk

The Realities of Change in Higher Education

Interventions to promote learning and teaching

Edited by Lynne Hunt, Adrian Bromage
and Bland Tomkinson

Routledge
Taylor & Francis Group

LONDON AND NEW YORK

First published 2006 by Routledge
2 Park Square, Milton Park, Abingdon, Oxon OX14 4RN

Simultaneously published in the USA and Canada
by Routledge
270 Madison Avenue, New York, NY 10016

Routledge is an imprint of the Taylor & Francis Group, an informa business

Typeset in Times by
GreenGate Publishing Services, Tonbridge, Kent
Printed and bound in Great Britain by
The Cromwell Press, Trowbridge, Wiltshire

British Library Cataloguing in Publication Data
A catalogue record for this book is available from the British Library

Library of Congress Cataloging-in-Publication Data
The realities of educational change in higher education : interventions to
promote learning and teaching / edited by Lynne Hunt, Adrian Bromage
and Bland Tomkinson.
      p. cm. – (Staff and educational development series)
    Includes bibliographical references and index.
    ISBN 0-415-38580-6 (pbk. : alk. paper) – ISBN 0-415-38581-4 (hard-
back : alk. paper) 1. Education, Higher. 2. Educational change. I. Hunt, Lynne,
1948- II. Bromage, Adrian, 1964- III. Tomkinson, Bland, 1944- IV. Series.

LB2322.2.R43 2006
378.1–dc22
                                                          2006008734

ISBN10: 0-415-38581-4 (hbk)   ISBN13: 978-0-415-38581-7 (hbk)
ISBN10: 0-415-38580-6 (pbk)   ISBN13: 978-0-415-38580-0 (pbk)
ISBN10: 0-203-96965-0 (ebk)   ISBN13: 978-0-203-96965-6 (ebk)

Contents

Illustrations

Contributors

Dr Adrian Bromage, currently Pedagogic Researcher at Coventry University's Centre for Higher Education Development, maintains practical and collegial research support and webpages for the iPED Research Network. He is involved in the Economic and Social Research Council-funded Enhancing Teaching-Learning Environments project. Adrian's interests include ontological and epistemological questions regarding virtual reality, online teaching, social research methods, beliefs and attitude change.

Gavin Moodie is Principal Policy Adviser and Law Tutor at Griffith University, Australia and a regular correspondent for the Australian's higher education supplement. He has published over 40 refereed papers and chapters on higher education and its relations with vocational education, the subject of his doctorate. Gavin is a referee for Higher Education and was joint editor of the *Journal of Higher Education Policy and Management.*

Lesley Parker holds a Personal Chair in Higher Education at Curtin University of Technology, in Western Australia. She was appointed Planning Director of the Carrick Institute for Learning and Teaching in Higher Education following nearly eight years as Senior Deputy Vice-Chancellor and Vice-President at Curtin. Her research interests and leadership in educational reform span all sectors of education. Lesley has published widely in the areas of structural curriculum change, professional development of educators, and gender equity.

Professor Craig McInnis is Higher Education Policy Advisor to the Deputy Vice-Chancellor (Academic) at the University of Melbourne, having been Director of the Centre for the Study of Higher Education. Craig has published widely, including studies of the first year experience in Australian universities, the impact of part-time work on students, and assessment policy and practice. He is currently working on strategic governance and management of learning and teaching, the future of the academic workforce, and the internationalisation of higher education.

Alison Thair provides operational and strategic advice to further develop, communicate and embed the university's quality approach and culture as Strategic Quality Coordinator at Edith Cowan University, Australia. This role builds upon Alison's previous management and quality expertise in the higher education and professional services sectors.

Professor Patrick Garnett is Deputy Vice-Chancellor (Academic) at Edith Cowan University, Australia, with responsibility for the University's academic profile, quality assurance, strategic staffing, and coordination of the University's approach to pathways, partnerships and precincts. He is a Fellow of the Royal Australian Chemical Institute and a recipient of the Royal Australian Chemical Institute Chemical Education Division Medal.

Dr Susan King has helped shape strategic planning, governance, performance monitoring and quality assurance processes as Executive Director, Governance, Policy and Planning at Edith Cowan University, Australia, including the university's preparations for its Australian Universities Quality Agency audit. This work follows policy and resource management roles in public sector departments at both Federal and State levels.

Professor Lynne Hunt is Leader, Learning and Teaching, at Charles Darwin University, Australia. She has received three university-level awards for teaching excellence and the 2002 Australian Award for University Teaching in the Social Science category. She also won the 2002 Prime Minister's Award for Australian University Teacher of the Year. She received the 2002 Merit Award for Best Paper on Authentic Learning from the Higher Education Research and Development Society of Australasia. She is a HERDSA Fellow and a board member of the Carrick Institute for Learning and Teaching in Higher Education.

Craig E. Nelson is Professor Emeritus of Biology at Indiana University Bloomington, USA, where he helped start both the Scholarship of Teaching and Learning Program and the International Society for the Scholarship of Teaching and Learning. He was the first president of the society. His articles apply the scholarship of teaching and learning to the improvement of learning and teaching. He consults widely on related topics.

Jennifer Meta Robinson, Director of Campus Instructional Consulting at Indiana University Bloomington, USA, consults campus-wide on teaching and scholarly inquiry into learning. She directs the Scholarship of Teaching and Learning program there and is a founding member and vice president of the International Society for the Scholarship of Teaching and Learning. Recent publications discuss problem-based learning, the scholarship of teaching and learning, and community building.

Milton D. Cox, Director, Center for the Enhancement of Learning and Teaching at Miami University, USA, founded and directs the Lilly Conference on College Teaching, is founder and editor of *Journal on Excellence in College Teaching and Building Faculty Learning Communities*. He received the special achievement certificate from the Professional and Organizational Development Network in Higher Education (POD), and the MacDuffee Award for distinguished service to Pi Mu Epsilon, US mathematics honorary.

Wim H. Gijselaers is Professor of Education at Maastricht University, the Netherlands. Wim is chair of the department of Educational Development and Educational Research at the Faculty of Economics and Business (Maastricht University). Besides his research on problem-based learning, cognition and instruction, and expertise development, Wim serves as consultant and is involved with curriculum reform in higher education.

Sigrid Harendza, is Assistant Professor for internal medicine/nephrology at the Faculty of Medicine, University of Hamburg, Germany. Sigrid worked as postdoctoral fellow at UCSF, San Francisco, and received her MME degree at the University of Bern, Switzerland. Besides clinical work, research, and curriculum reform at Hamburg Medical School, she teaches educational management in the MME program in Germany.

Conor Vibert is Associate Professor of Business Strategy at the Fred C. Manning School of Business of Acadia University in Wolfville, Nova Scotia. His research interests focus on the application of the internet to contemporary business issues. He received the 2002 Outstanding Teacher Award for Acadia's Faculty of Professional Studies as well as the 2000 University President's Award for Innovation. He helped develop the Acadia Real Time Case Competition, the Management Interview Series Video Database, and the Acadia Distinguished Business Speaker series.

Craig Place is Manager of the Acadia Institute for Teaching and Technology. He joined Acadia University in 1988 to teach geology. He joined the Institute in 1996 as an Academic Computing specialist. He has developed and delivered international teacher and faculty training programs and has been invited to speak and present workshops on topics of educational technology across North America and in Australia.

Mark Atlay is currently Head of Teaching Quality Enhancement at the University of Luton and Director of the University's Centre for Excellence in Teaching in Higher Education, which is exploring further the implementation and impact of personal development planning and employability on the curriculum. He has been responsible for coordinating and supporting the University's skills initiative and responding to national initiatives such as those on progress files and personal development planning.

Frank Lyons has been developing work-based learning at the University of Portsmouth, UK since 1990. This was recognised with the award of a National Teaching Fellowship in 2003. A lifelong learner at the University, he taught sociology from 1968 to 1990 before becoming Associate Dean, Curriculum, in the Faculty of Technology and then Director of the Centre of Excellence in Teaching and Learning, in 2005. He was Visiting Fellow at Edith Cowan University in Western Australia in 2004.

Dr Mike Bement is Director of Postgraduate Studies for the Partnership Programme at the University of Portsmouth, and in 1991 convened the group that set up the programme. A former engineering designer who moved into tertiary education, his publications focus on learner-managed education, and he is particularly interested in the accreditation of prior and experiential learning. He has delivered keynote speeches on new approaches in engineering education across the globe, and acted as consultant to UK institutions.

Charles E. Engel is Visiting Professor at the University of Manchester; Visiting Academic, Institute of Education, University of London; founding editor, *Education for Health: Change in Learning and Practice;* Member, World Health Organisation Expert Advisory Panel for Human Resources Development; Member, International Advisory Board, Faculty of Medicine, Humboldt University; and was Foundation Head, Discipline of Medical Education and Outcome Evaluation, University of Newcastle, Australia.

Bland Tomkinson is the University Adviser on Pedagogic Development at the University of Manchester, having been Director of the Teaching and Learning Support Centre at the University of Manchester Institute of Science and Technology (UMIST), and Programme Director for the Postgraduate Certificate in Academic Practice. Bland is the author of several book chapters on pedagogic subjects and on managing change, as well as of a number of journal articles and monographs. He co-edited *Critical Encounters: Scholarly Approaches to Teaching and Learning.*

Foreword

Lewis Elton

It is a pleasure to see a new and scholarly work on change in higher education. The title, *The Realities of Change in Higher Education*, accurately reflects the case studies presented in each chapter. These provide practical exemplars for the promotion of learning and teaching in higher education as well as commentary on the process of change. It is a particular pleasure to see my paper on the 'new collegiality' quoted by Adrian Bromage in the first chapter of this collection: I have become more and more convinced of the validity of the model (Elton 2005) that exhorts the infusion of abilities and skills into essentially content oriented curricula[1].

The collegial model was based on the Enterprise in Higher Education initiative of the UK Department of Employment in the 1990s. The important features of this change strategy were to prescribe only in the broadest manner in response to institutional plans. Further, advice was provided by academics and not civil servants and a great deal of mutual trust was generated. These processes were innovative. As a consequence, the danger was that they might not be sustainable. In fact, ten years later, its lessons seem to have been forgotten, to be replaced by mutual distrust between the UK government and its higher education sector and a compliance culture that is proving wholly counter-productive to the advancement of learning and teaching in universities. The programme also failed to redress the prestige balance between teaching and research; a disparity that has been further impaired by successive Research Assessment Exercises in the UK.

Even so, the enterprise programme was a highly effective agent for change (Elton 1994). It led not only to doing things better, but also to doing better things. I am delighted to note that the authors of this volume bring back the lessons learned in the programme. There is a strong and consistent message in all chapters that engagement, collegiality and empowerment are the most effective bases for

---

1 The current estimation of the success of the enterprise programme, as held by different researchers on the basis of the same evidence (total failure because all the enterprise units have disappeared or considerable success because the reason for their disappearance resulted from the absorption of the enterprise ethos and practice into general institutional policy and practice, and not only in 'enterprise' institutions) is an interesting slant on the difficulty of interpreting evaluative evidence.

change in higher education and that this is true internationally. Chapters from the UK, Australia, the USA and Canada share this vision.

The scope of the book includes reflections on policy level change, whole-of-university change, and micro-change at the curriculum level. The strength of the book is that it foregrounds processes for effective change to enhance learning and teaching in ways that interrogate enduring questions about top-down and collegial management in universities. *The Realities of Change in Higher Education* provides a significant contribution to the literature on change management in higher education, not only because it provides practical examples of how to manage change, but also because it is consistent in its promotion of student-centred outcomes. I commend this book to those in the international arena interested in promoting student learning in higher education.

Bibliography

Elton, L. (1994) 'EHE – an agent for change', in P. Knight (ed.) *University wide change – staff and curriculum development*, SEDA Paper 86, Birmingham: SEDA.

Elton, L. (2005) *Could there be a balance between top down and collegial management in universities?*, 4th Annual Conference on Leadership Research, Lancaster, 12–13 December 2005.

Preface

This book documents the theory and practice of the everyday reality of change to promote learning and teaching in universities. Its scope is international, taking examples from the United Kingdom, the United States, Australia and Europe. It shows that the reality of change is complex and multi-dimensional. This is reflected in the chapters, which include top-down, middle-out and bottom-up perspectives on change management in higher education. Each intertwines theory and policy with practical outcomes at the university level. Within this framework of complexity, common themes are explored that address the following questions:

- What was the nature of the changes?
- What stimulated the changes?
- Who were the change agents?
- How was the change process planned?
- What model of change was adopted?
- What were the outcomes of the changes?
- What facilitated change?
- What were the obstacles to change?
- What are the implications of the case study for change management in higher education?

With contributions by experienced practitioners from a range of academic backgrounds, *The Realities of Change in Higher Education* explores key topics including:

- national policies and strategies
- different leadership styles
- the advancement of teaching and learning through research and scholarship
- how communities of practice may be effective agents for change in higher education
- the relationship between technology and change
- student assessment as a strategic tool for enhancing teaching and learning.

Each chapter is self-contained and may be read in isolation from the others. However, the book is structured to flow from an analysis of big-picture, policy-level change in higher education to small-scale change at the curriculum level. Flow is a key metaphor because it illustrates that change is a process: what happens at the beginning has repercussions and consequences for what emerges at the end.

This first chapter provides a generic, theoretical overview of change management that guides analysis in subsequent chapters. In chapter two, Moodie provides the big picture of policy level change. The title, 'No money: no change', reveals the core argument that insufficient funding renders impotent policy-initiated change. Governments in the Western world are now seeking greater accountability for expenditure on higher education and they are using funding to set the direction of change. Chapter three provides a case study of how this happens through Parker's analysis of the new Australian Carrick Institute for Learning and Teaching in Higher Education. In chapter four, McInnis shows how organisations, such as Carrick, actually do influence change. He describes a national initiative to promote learning and teaching through improved assessment practice. Government initiatives to assure quality in higher education have also had learning and teaching outcomes. Thair, Garnett and King describe these in chapter five, which explores the trickle-down effect of quality assurance processes in one university.

Subsequent chapters are organised to move from changes that are managed across the university to change that occurs at the curriculum level. In chapter six, Hunt provides an account of the change management role of university teaching and learning centres. In chapter seven, Nelson and Robinson present a case study of whole-of-university change inspired by the advancement of the scholarship of learning and teaching. This chapter shows the influence on teaching and learning of the American Carnegie Foundation, as does chapter eight, in which Cox explores the role of communities of practice in change management. In so doing, he spotlights the importance of bottom-up change management processes in American higher education. In chapter nine Gijselaers and Harendza, drawing on experiences of change in Germany, address values and behaviour as an important reality of change in universities. Chapter ten draws on a Canadian example of technology-led change across one university. In this chapter, Vibert and Place move from managing change to championing it.

Chapters eleven to thirteen draw on British experience to document curriculum change. In chapter eleven, Atlay explores the complexity of change in his account of the introduction of graduate attributes into the curriculum. In chapter twelve, Lyons and Bement introduce work-based learning and direct attention to the importance of partnerships in the change management process. Finally, in chapter thirteen, Engel and Tomkinson discuss the barriers to change in their account of the introduction of interdisciplinary curricula for global sustainability. We hope that the appeal of this book is that it critically evaluates how academics actually handle change, what works and what doesn't. Its reflective approach and practical advice on how to enhance the learning experience of increasing numbers of university students should appeal to administrators, academic staff, educational developers and anyone involved in improving learning and teaching outcomes in higher education.

Lynne Hunt
Charles Darwin University, Australia

Adrian Bromage
Coventry University Centre for
Higher Education Development, UK

Bland Tomkinson
University of Manchester, UK

Chapter 1

The management of planned change

An interdisciplinary perspective

Adrian Bromage

Introduction

This book on the realities of change in higher education arguably sits within a generic literature on change management that is concerned with the meta-analysis of cumulative case studies to provide practitioner guidelines. Buchanan and Huczynski (2000) describe several such 'cook-books' from the world of commerce, while educationalists have over the years also shared their 'recipes', for example Miles *et al.* (1988), Elton (1994) and Jones and Anderson (2001). Some of the literature aims to increase local control over the innovative processes, for example Guba and Lincoln (1989), Elton (1994) and Mabey and Mayon-White (1993). Not all of this summarising literature can claim to be empirically or theoretically grounded, although it is not unreasonable for practitioner theory to take a generous inferential span or reserve the right to be speculative. The present volume seeks to include in this literature a consideration of such guidelines in the context of real-life change management in the significant industry that higher education has become.

The analysis of change in large-scale organisations such as universities can draw on the arguably broadly consistent body of conventional wisdom that exists within the generic change management literature. This book takes a deeper view, adopting a case study approach in order to highlight the realities of change in higher education, a setting with several specific contemporary issues that must be addressed, including varying levels of governmental control and intervention; mergers between institutions which may have differing vaunted purposes and cultures; the uptake of information and communications technologies; globalisation and internationalisation; professional cultures and quality control across a sector; and student priorities including equity and diversity.

The focus is on changes that are intended to promote learning and teaching. Universities have traditionally been called centres of learning; however, their emphasis has for the past two centuries been on research, following the establishment of the University of Berlin by Wilhelm von Humboldt in 1810. Nowadays taken for granted, this was at the time controversial and widely resisted, most prominently by Newman (1959). With the so-called massification of higher education, governments around the world have refocused their attention and policy on initiatives to support student learning. The Dearing Report (1997) in the UK, The Nelson Report (2004) in Australia, and the European 'Bologna Declaration' of 1999 (European Ministers of Education 2003) all bear testimony to this trend. This book seeks to explore the space created by such policy initiatives, in order to understand how different higher education organisations have taken up the challenge to promote learning and teaching and the kinds of issues that they have faced in doing so. This particular chapter seeks to set the scene by exploring practical advice for those who would implement planned change, with an emphasis on behaviours associated with success.

The generic literature on managing planned change

The generic practical literature on managing planned change has since the early 1990s arguably developed in parallel with the rise of information and communication technologies, frequently in the context of moves towards flatter and more responsive organisational structures. Paton and McCalman (2000) note that at around this time the literature began to emphasise the importance of communication in the context of volatile operating environments. Parallels will be drawn with educational change management literature, and this convergence will be examined in relation to some established philosophies of change.

There is wide agreement in the generic change management literature that good planning enables the change process to be controlled during its execution. Hopkins and Ainscow (1993) and Fullan (1993) see change as a process that needs to be carefully considered, however accelerated the time-lines, if it is to be assimilated into an institution's culture. The first step is the establishment of clear objectives (Whittles and Lovell 1994). Many recommend a service-user focus; anticipating clients' needs in order to design added value into the service in question. In a similar vein, writers addressing change management in higher education argue that it must be driven by educational criteria (Laurillard 1993). Monitoring and evaluation are also held to be important. A detailed plan normally features a timetable of goals and milestones, which the change process must be evaluated against, a process that is crucial for both assessing and reinforcing the success of the change process (Whittles and Lovell 1994).

Another consideration is the change model deployed. Feeny and Ruddle (1997) identify several such models, outlining the circumstances they are suited to. They present these different styles of innovation in a two-times-two, or dichotomous, model that addresses change that is' incremental' or 'step' in its movement, and either 'directive' or 'organic' in its orientation. 'Incremental-directive' change is centrally driven and does not rely on bottom-up learning or client feedback. It suits successful organisations within stable, operating environments. 'Incremental-organic' change entails ongoing, organisation-wide, client-focused, evolutionary learning, and suits successful organisations within uncertain operating environments. 'Step-directive' centrally-driven radical change works best in clearly identifiable units within an organisation, although it is unlikely to carry stakehold-ers' hearts and minds with it. 'Step-organic' transformation entails centrally initiated projects that are intended to facilitate 'transformational change', the development of new working practices involving many stakeholders across the organisation. It suits the most challenging circumstance – a poorly performing organisation within an uncertain operating environment.

There is a strand in the literature that analyses the change process itself, exploring its various stages and their attributed characteristics. Change is typically seen as long and discontinuous, made up of very small changes in stakeholders' behaviour and attitudes. Consequently, change agents are advised to prepare plans and strategies to 'un-stick' the process if it stalls. Duck (2001) describes, in somewhat emotive terms, a predominant pattern of change comprising five broad stages. The unattractive sounding 'Stagnation' phase describes the organisation performing poorly and lacking a clear focus. During 'Preparation' it is realised that things must change, perhaps triggered by client feedback or external scrutiny, and a plan is devised. 'Implementation' tends to be characterised by hard work for little immediate gain. 'Determination', the next in sequence, is seen as the crucial stage, in which change agents must counter stakeholders' resistance to change arising from doubts raised by the difficulties of implementation. Finally, 'Fruition' sees the process gradually begin to deliver positive results, and step-change begins to turn into continuous improvement as stakeholders use their developing capability and confidence.

It is no surprise, then, that human factors feature strongly in the generic literature. It is generally acknowledged that defensible changes and strategies should be ethical and fair, and set within a context characterised by high levels of trust between all stakeholders (Lovell 1994; Paton and McCalman 2000). Similarly Hopkins and Ainscow (1993), writing on change in higher education, offer the generalisation that change is typically facilitated by organisational cultures that are characterised by a consensus of values, willing collaboration and an orderly, secure environment where stakeholders are encouraged to take on leadership roles. However, consensus can never be assumed; it has long been recognised that a certain amount of resistance is to be expected; for example, Bennis et al. (1969) hold that the potential for conflict between stakeholders holding different views is a critical issue for planned change. Others suggest that conflict and resistance is in some cases justifiable, and can be a positive force in the context of open discussion (Paton and McCalman 2000: 49).

There are clear implications for the role attributed to change agents. Many authors implicitly adopt a top-down view, albeit asserting that senior managers should act as the 'champions' of change, developing and maintaining an innovation-supporting culture (Simpson 1996), and behaving as 'leaders' rather than 'managers' (Kotter 1990). There is wide agreement that such leaders should recognise that stakeholders' motivations are likely to differ. Lovell (1994) argues that managers must understand and take account of stakeholders' adaptive behaviour during organisational change, while Manning (1994) holds that those leading change must be able to understand and deal with stress, both their own and that of other stakeholders. Similarly, educational change leaders should 'walk the job' to understand the work environment and demonstrate their commitment to change (Jones and Anderson 2001). Effective communication at all levels is held to be crucial to the success of planned change. Change agents are generally advised to consult, involve, inform and provide feedback to all colleagues with a stake in the changes (Dutfield and Eling 1994a). The basic rules are to listen to others, to provide adequate information and involve stakeholders in the change process, and to encourage goal-directed behaviour.

These issues raise questions concerning how individual stakeholders respond to change. Lovell (1994) characterises stakeholders' adaptive modes in terms of a 'Wild West' metaphor, perhaps to capture the 'frontier' feeling that often accompanies change, although this labelling perhaps carries too many emotional overtones. 'Explorers' are highly motivated to initiate change, while 'Pioneers' are willing to support change. The majority of stakeholders, however, can be characterised as 'Settlers', unwilling to make the first moves, yet able to survive under novel conditions. Finally, 'Outlaws' lack the will or skills to change and strongly support the status quo, yet gradually acclimatise to change, although with considerable stress. Similar contentious language appears within more recent change management literature, for example, von Münchhausen and Scherer (2003) talk of 'saboteurs' protecting vested interests or avoiding demanding work by deploying delaying tactics. Interestingly, it is hard to reconcile language of this kind with their proposed counter-measures – honest communication and justification of the proposed changes, and careful planning for and clearly defined monitoring of the change process. It can only be assumed that terms such as 'outlaw' and 'saboteur' are deployed as a means to engage emotionally with those charged with the responsibility of managing change.

The nature of these recommendations is arguably rendered comprehensible in terms of the wide agreement that responding to change is essentially a learning process. For example, Dutfield and Eling (1994b) characterise likely sources of stakeholders' resistance to change and outline strategies to overcome them. They are: stakeholders' lack of trust in managers and differing perceptions of events, to be addressed through 'force and support'; protection of their self-interest, to be overcome with 'participation and negotiation'; and finally their insecurity or fear of change, to be overcome with 'education'. Relevant training that recognises stakeholder preferences for different learning styles (Coffield et al. 2004) should be built into the process. Furthermore, additional training and communications may be required to resolve the inevitable resistance of some stakeholders to change; where colleagues need to be persuaded, arguments should be supported with high–quality evidence (Institute of Management Foundation 1998; 1999).

'Ownership' is a central metaphor in this literature. Stakeholders must be encouraged to participate in the management of change (Armstrong and Stephens 2005), sentiments echoed in Fullan's (1993) 'eight lessons of the new paradigm of change' in educational contexts and Blackwell et al.'s (2001) study of teaching circles. The argument that people will accept the case for change if they are able to personalise it and relate it to their own work is nothing new. For example, Pettigrew (1985), who takes a 'contextual processual' perspective on planned change, concludes that a linear progression from plans to implementation is rare, and the key to success is the extent to which the proposals are perceived to be 'legitimate', justifiable within their context. To establish legitimacy, change agents must relate the organisation's 'inner context' (its structure, culture and the historical events that shaped them) to its 'outer context' (factors in the wider environment such as client demands, competitors' behaviour and technological developments). This notion has been present in management theory for many years, for example, in Deming's (1982) 14 principles of management, intended to revitalise industry in the USA in the face of global competition, although what sets Pettigrew's work apart is that the conclusions reached have an empirical and theoretical basis.

In broad terms, this generic body of literature strongly implies that change management must be sensitive to its cultural context. This resonates to an extent with what Buchanan and Huczynski (2000) term a 'psychologistic' perspective on change management, placing stakeholder's perceptions, motivations and empowerment as central. This perspective is discernible in contributions by key writers on change management such as Handy (1993), who comments:

> To 'manage change' is wishful thinking, implying as it does that one knows not only where to go and how to get there but can persuade everyone else to travel there. To 'cultivate change' is something different, suggesting an attitude of growth, of channelling rather than controlling, of learning not instruction.

On the other hand, the issues dealt with in the generic literature raise questions that go beyond the psychologistic perspective, invoking the relationship between organisational structures and personal agency.

There exist generic models of change that more explicitly consider this relationship. The 'organisational development' approach, developed during the 1960s by writers such as Beckhard (1969), assumes that conflict between individuals, groups and the organisation can and must be resolved. Buchanan and Huczynski (2000) describe its key concepts as 'force field analysis' (Lewin 1952) of factors driving and restraining a proposed change, action research and planned intervention, consultation and negotiation, and team building and inter-group development. However, this approach carries the implicit assumptions that change is episodic, and the wider operating context of the organisation relatively stable.

More recent theorists have developed models that are intended to be highly responsive to a dynamic operating context. Lovell's (1994) model is an example that is particularly relevant to this chapter, given what has been said about the generic change literature. It is perhaps unique in taking an out-and-out phenomenological stance, emphasising the importance of considering employees' perceptions of the causes of their powerlessness when moving towards being a change-ready organisation. Lovell explicitly recognises that employees ultimately decide what work gets done and are in the best position to respond rapidly to clients' changing needs and demands.

Lovell identifies three levels of employee empowerment and their likely outcomes. The first, a basic level where staff are consulted, often fails when they realise that their suggestions are being dismissed without explanation. The second sees staff involved in job design, which can lead to the creation and maintenance of autonomous work groups. The third involves staff in the performance of their entire organisation, which necessitates a culture very different to a control-oriented one, featuring a flattened organisational hierarchy where information and control is shared horizontally. It will be argued that similar themes are also evident in recent literature that explores the processes of change management in higher education.

Theorising change management in higher education

There has been a tendency in recent years for literature on change management in higher education to view the change process as multifaceted and uncertain, and thus extremely challenging, and to focus on stakeholders' reactions to change rather than the 'levers' for controlling change (Fullan 1993; Trowler 1998; Trowler et al. 2003). Within this general trend, there is an emerging debate about the need for greater attention to discipline-specific rather than generic purposes and practices (Evans and Abbott 1998; Healey 2000; Pace and Middendorf 2004; Riordan and Roth 2005). Indeed, Healey and De Stefano (1997) argue that those managing change should not attempt to replicate a given reform measure itself, but instead seek to replicate the conditions that facilitated its success.

To understand why educational change should be discussed in this way, it is necessary to explore the nature of this body of literature in more depth. It arguably spans Pettigrew's (1985) distinction between an organisation's 'outer' context (its encircling environment) and its 'inner' context (its structure and culture and the historical events that have shaped them), the latter chiming to some extent with Parlett and Hamilton's (1972) 'learning milieu'. Furthermore, just as in the generic literature, the relationship between structure and agency is placed under scrutiny. A key example is Trowler's (1998) study of 'NewU', a relatively young institution with a vocational bias, which begins with the kind of analysis of massification put forward by Scott (1998) and others, but then goes on to look at institutional culture and subcultures. Others such as Becher (1989; 1990) and Clark (1987) explore such issues within long-established universities, institutions with a strongly academic tradition. This, too, is the context for Rothblatt's (1968; 1976) exploration of the correspondence between educational culture and conduct over time.

Trowler (1998) offers the evidence that academics' educational values, social background and life experiences act to condition and restrain the policies of senior managers, and that stakeholders both 'enact' and actively reconstruct organisational cultures. Trowler argues that models of change with a top-down 'managerial' and mechanistic emphasis on the efficiency of the 'levers' to pull to bring about a strategic or cultural vision tend to under-theorise and render invisible issues of how subaltern academics exercise power as a part of the 'dialectic of control' within universities. This is significant, as it may manifest itself as obstruction or subversion of policy imposed 'top down' by change agents. He further argues that such models devalue the links between organisational culture, its encircling social context and the change processes.

Trowler holds that the process of implementing educational policy must be understood holistically, not only in terms of local cultural and ideological struggles but also constraints that stem from relationships with encircling socio-economic and political conditions. The latter point sees Trowler effectively calling for an understanding that contextualises the change process both within and beyond the local 'learning milieu', while echoing arguments in the generic literature, such as those advanced by Pettigrew (1985), that change agents must legitimise the proposed change by relating their organisation's 'inner context' to its 'outer context'.

There is evidence to support Trowler's view in the wider literature on change management in higher education. Kogan (2000), for example, analysed what he perceived to be a contemporary belief that politically initiated moralities can lead to an improved higher education. He concludes that universities do not relate to their encircling social world as part of a community with a system of common values. Rather, negotiation and exchange is the basis of mutual support between the separate but linked entities of academics' individual identity, its institutional and subject setting and the world beyond.

Arguably, this phenomenon can be discerned in Rothblatt's (1968) examination of how UK universities have responded to changes in wider society. Rothblatt deploys an historical approach, examining the document archives of several institutions of higher education in order to explore the correspondence between educational culture and conduct over time. He concludes that society's plural nature means that relationships between the wider community and a university will be characterised by complex states of agreement and disagreement, and, in consequence, universities undergoing reform may acquire unanticipated and surprising identities and functions. Intriguingly, in a later study Rothblatt (1976) found that what survives of the culture of a university after its transition to a new state are essentially rhetorical preferences.

Specific studies of curriculum innovation make transparent the broad themes of this literature. Fullan (1991) argues that the uptake by school pupils, tutors, principals and other personnel of innovative practices will depend in part on the extent to which they understand and are motivated to try them. Fullan cites as an example Hull and Ruddock's (1980) exploration of pupils' perceptions of innovative classroom practice, which concludes that their existing interpretations of their personal role in the classroom can act as a barrier to change.

Others have reached similar conclusions when introducing higher education students to innovative practices such as communication and information technology-based distance learning (Collis and Meeuwsen 1999; Monaco *et al.* 2000; Ukpokodu 2000) and problem-based learning (Savin Baden 2000).

Overall, the literature raises questions about the relationships between culture, ideology and individual practice. Cohen and Castner (2000) emphasise the importance of creating learning environments that match the needs of students and the cultures of instruction within institutions. Indeed, with regard to curriculum innovation, Evans and Abbott (1998) present empirical evidence which demonstrates that the learning needs of tutors and learners are not uniform either between or within disciplines, and conclude that a plurality of andragogic methods must be supported. Maskell and Robinson (2001) take this theme further, arguing that higher education should aim to help students to develop the particular style of thought practised within an 'elite' (yet presumably not elitist) scholarly community.

Implications for the management of educational change

It has been seen that centre-peripheral models of change management appear to invite comparisons between the belief systems of the donor and recipient organisations, thus raising questions of 'acculturalisation' and of individuals' motivation. Both Trowler (1998) and Clark (1987) view universities as in a state of dynamic tension, with the university pressing its traditions on to clusters of tutors, while tutors' press their values, both academic and personal, on to the university. Their conclusions lend support to those of Bennis *et al.* (1969) concerning educational change, that social dynamics and the intellectual linkage between theory and practice are crucial to its success. Clark believes that these multiple values will push the university in contradictory ways, frequently with tensions between them. One consequence is that any attempt to impose greater uniformity or universal standards will meet difficulties. Clark, echoing Evans and Abbott (1998), argues that what is actually needed is less uniformity, to accommodate variations between subject areas.

Clark's strictures, if treated as predictive, would seem to suggest the likelihood of difficulties for change strategies that seek to inculcate a measure of uniformity. Trowler emphasises the durability of tutors' values and attitudes and how they combine with their agency to influence policy during implementation. He believes this is best captured within a model of 'implementation as evolution', a conclusion broadly consistent with those in the generic literature on change management. Indeed, Jary and Parker (1998) saw the question of the 'ownership' of an innovation as critical to its success.

The implication seems to be that 'bottom-up' models may be appropriate for managing change in higher education. One such example is Guba and Lincoln's (1989) 'fourth generation evaluation', a recursive consultation process between identifiable groups of stakeholders towards an outcome acceptable to all. Guba and Lincoln's model is predicated upon a social constructivist ontology, viewing shared reality as constructed through discursive practices. A more practitioner-centred model is evident in Carr and Kemmis's (1986) call for tutor empowerment in higher education through a form of action research. This approach explicitly acknowledges the influence of academics' beliefs, values and habits on their practice, and owes much to Habermas's (1974) strictures on the conditions under which education can be held to be emancipatory. However, it is arguable that bottom-up approaches will, in a worst-case scenario, tend to yield very conservative changes that are prone to the influence of stakeholding academic's personal agendas, which may not reflect students' needs. For example, Carr and Kemmis's list of the kinds of knowledge that teachers use in their work includes not only professional knowledge and educational theory, but also 'contextual knowledge' about particular groups of learners, 'commonsense assumptions' and 'folk wisdom' about teaching, and finally their personal, social and moral theories and general philosophical outlook. They, too, are likely to reflect what Trowler calls 'presage' – the influence of academics' social backgrounds.

Both Trowler (1998) and Hopkins and Ainscow (1993) conclude that it is necessary to foster tutors' commitment, reflection and involvement within the context of a highly collaborative 'learning organisation'. As to how planned change might manifest itself in such an organisation, we might look to Berg and Östergren's (1977, 1978) argument that successful change management in higher education requires a combination of facilitative top-down pressures and innovative bottom up pressures. In a similar vein, Elton (1994) advocates a model he terms 'new collegiality', a blend of top-down and bottom-up initiatives that emphasise staff development, with the long-term aim of turning universities into change-ready 'learning institutions'.

Arguably, a more extreme version of this stance is evident in Hopkins and Ainscow's outline for a collaborative strategy for curriculum development, which emphasises supporting, intervening in, and researching the processes of change, the goal being to develop an institutional culture that facilitates continuous innovation in response to emergent challenges and opportunities. At this point we see a convergence with the generic literature, in particular, Senge's (1990) 'double loop' or 'generative learning', with its attendant challenge to existing assumptions within an organisation and creation of new perspectives on its operating context. However, Paton and McCalman (2000) caution that the bulk of the generic literature on learning organisations takes a rational stance, neglecting the political and emotional aspects of change that loom so large in the generic practical 'change cookbooks'. Clearly, some kind of balancing act is necessary, and it may be that Pedler et al. (1991) are right to suggest that this model can best be implemented in terms of an important strategic vision rather than something that can be fully realised.

Conclusions

It has been argued that there is a broad convergence between the generic literature on change management and that generated within the higher education sector. There is recognition of the sheer time that change can take, and of how it tends to evolve during implementation against a background of internal politics and developments in the environment beyond the organisation undergoing change. However, it also seems that, if one moves beyond generic guidelines, models of change management that appear to offer the promise of taking account of these issues have their limitations. Indeed, Blackwell and Preece (2001) call for empirical research into the relative effectiveness of such models in large-scale change in higher education, for the benefit of those who would implement change. It is hoped that this book might represent a useful step in this direction.

Where these two bodies of literature diverge is in their tone and focus. The generic literature appears primarily to address managers, while that from the higher education sector focuses in more detail upon stakeholders. This is not to say that the generic literature does not raise or deal with similar issues, rather, the perspective upon those issues differs. This arguably reflects the relative power of subordinate employees in each sector, and the relative opportunities available for them to elucidate their own experience. On the other hand, Hopkins (2002) notes that there is a norm of autonomy in higher education, which, despite a superficially friendly organisational culture, makes achieving consensus difficult, as everyday communication tends to be on a social rather than professional level. This is arguably a consequence of a tendency, noted earlier by Hopkins (1984), for higher education organisations to be characterised by pluralistic cultures that emphasise individual autonomy within horizontal authority structures.

The broad emergent message is that successful change management in the context of higher education is likely to be characterised by mutual education and learning within a collegiate approach, whereby the case for change is made with reference to high-quality evidence, and the opinions of stakeholding academics are taken into account in the spirit of open debate. As to how those managing change should conduct themselves, perhaps the last word should go to Lao-Tzu, Taoist philosopher of the sixth Century (1998), whose advice, despite an of-its-time gender assumption, both neatly summarises the sentiment of the authors referred to within this chapter while implying that the same issues have faced leaders throughout history:

> A leader is best when people barely know that he exists.
> Less good when they obey and acclaim him.
> Worse when they fear and despise him.
> Fail to honor people, and they fail to honor you.
> But of a good leader, when his work is done, his aim fulfilled,
> they will say, 'We did this ourselves'.

Bibliography

Armstrong M. and Stephens T. (2005) *Management and Leadership: A Guide to Managing for Results,* London and Stirling: Kogan Page.

Becher, T. (1989) *Academic Tribes and Territories,* Buckingham: The Society for Research into Higher Education and Open University Press.

Becher, T. (1990) 'The counter-culture of specialisation', *European Journal of Education,* Vol. 25, No.3, 333–46.

Beckhard, R. (1969) *Organization development: Strategies and Models,* Reading, MA: Addison-Wesley Publishing Company.

Bennis, W.G., Benne, K.D. and Chin, R. (1969) *The Planning of Change* (2nd. Ed.), London; New York: Holt, Reinhart and Winston.

Berg, B and Östergren, B. (1977*) Innovations and Innovation Processes in Higher Education,* Stockholm: UHÅ.

Berg, B and Östergren, B (1978) 'Innovation processes in higher education', *Studies in Higher Education* Vol. 4, 261–8.

Blackwell, R., Channel, J. and Wilson, J. (2001) 'Teaching circles: a way forward for part time teaching staff?', *International Journal for Academic Development,* Vol. 6, No. 1, 40–53.

Blackwell, R. and Preece, D. (2001) 'Changing higher education', *The International Journal of Management Education,* Vol. 1, No. 3, 4–14. Available at <http://www.business.heacademy.ac.uk/publications/journal/> (accessed 12 February 2006).

Buchanan, D.A. and Huczynski, A.A. (2000) *Organisational Behaviour: An Introductory Text* (4th ed.), London: Prentice-Hall.

Burke, P. (1990) 'Future Directions for Staff Development – The Staff Development Specialist', in P. Burke, R. Heideman, and C. Heideman (eds.) *Programming for Staff Development: Fanning the Flame,* London: The Falmer Press.

Carr, W. and Kemmis, S. (1986) *Becoming Critical: Education Knowledge and Action Research,* London: Falmer Press.

Clark, Burton R. (1987) *The Academic Life: Small Worlds, Different Worlds*, Princeton New Jersey: Carnegie Foundation for the Advancement of Teaching.

Coffield, F., Moseley, D., Hall, E. and Ecclestone, K. (2004) *Should We be Using Learning Styles? What Research Has to Say to Practice,* London: Learning and Skills Research Centre. Available at <http://www.lsneducation.org.uk/pubs/index.aspx> (accessed: 6 May 2006).

Cohen, J. and Castner, M.H. (2000) 'Technology and classroom design: a faculty perspective', in L. Lloyd (ed.) *Teaching With Technology: Rethinking Tradition.* Medford, New Jersey: Information Today Inc.

Collis, B. and Meeuwsen, E. (1999) 'Learning to learn in a www-based environment', in D. French, C. Hale, C. Johnson and G. Farr (eds.) *Internet Based Learning: An Introduction and Framework for Higher Education and Business,* London: Kogan Page.

Deming, W.E. (1982) *Out of the Crisis,* Cambridge, Mass: MIT Press.

Duck, D.J. (2001) The Change Monster: *The Human Forces that Foil or Fuel Corporate Transformation and Change,* New York: Crown Business.

Dutfield, R. and Eling, C. (1994a) 'Communications during change', in R. Lovell (ed.) *Managing Change in the Public Sector,* Harlow: Longman.

Dutfield, R. and Eling, C. (1994b) 'Managing the individual's resistance to change', in R. Lovell (ed.) *Managing Change in the Public Sector,* Harlow: Longman,.

Elton. L. (1994) *Management of Teaching and Learning: Towards Change in Universities,* London: CVCP.

European Ministers of Education (2003, first published 1999) *The Bologna declaration of 19 June 1999,* Brussels: European University Association. Available at <http://www.eua.be/eua/jsp/en/upload/OFFDOC_BP_bologna_declaration.1068714825768.pdf> (accessed 12 December 2005).

Evans, L. and Abbott, I. (1998) *Teaching and Learning in Higher Education,* London; New York: Cassell Educational.

Feeny, D. and Ruddle, K. (1997) 'Transforming the organisation: new approaches to management, measurement and leadership', *Oxford Executive Research Briefings,* No. 5, Oxford: Templeton College. Available at <http://www.templeton.ox.ac.uk> (accessed 15 May 2004).

Fullan, M.G. (1991) *The New Meaning of Educational Change* (2nd ed.), London: Cassell Educational Ltd.

Fullan, M.G. (1993) *Change Forces – Probing the Depths of Educational Reform,* London: Falmer Press.

Further Education Development Agency (1995) *Developing College Policies and Strategies for Human Resource Development.* London: FEDA.

Guba, E.G. and Lincoln, Y.S. (1989) *Fourth Generation Evaluation,* London: Sage.

Habermas, J. (1974) *Theory and Practice* (translated by J. Viertel), London: Heinemann.

Handy, C. B. (1993) *Understanding Organisations* (4th ed.), London: Penguin.

Healey, M. (2000) 'Developing the scholarship of teaching in higher education: a discipline-based approach', *Higher Education Research and Development,* Vol. 19, 169–89.

Healey, F. and De Stefano, J. (1997) *Education Reform Support: A Framework for Scaling Up School Reform,* Washington DC: Abel 2 Clearinghouse for Basic Education, 10–11. Cited in Fullan, M. (1999) *Change Forces: The Sequel,* London: Falmer: 63–4.

Hopkins, D. (1984) 'Change and the organisational character of teacher education', *Studies in Higher Education,* Vol. 9, No. 1, 37–45.

Hopkins, D. (2002) *The Evolution of Strategies for Educational Change: Implications for Higher Education,* LTSN Generic Centre. Available at <http://www.heacademy.ac.uk/resources.asp (accessed: 15 October 2005).

Hopkins, D. and Ainscow, M. (1993) 'Making sense of school improvement: an interim account of the "Improving the Quality of Education for All" Project', *Cambridge Journal of Education,* Vol. 23, No. 3, 287–304.

Hull, C. and Ruddock, J. (1980) *Introducing Innovation to Pupils,* Norwich: Centre for Applied Research in Education, University of East Anglia.

Institute of Management Foundation (1998) *Checklist 040: Implementing an Effective Change Programme,* Corby: Institute of Management Foundation.

Institute of Management Foundation (1999) *Checklist 068: Motivating Your Staff in a Time of Change,* Corby: Institute of Management Foundation.

Jary, D. and Parker, M. (1998) *The New Higher Education: Issues and Directions for the Post-Dearing University,* Stoke-on-Trent: Staffordshire University Press.

Jones, C. A. and Anderson, M. (2001) *Managing Curriculum Change,* London: Learning and Skills Development Agency. Available at <http://www.lsneducation.org.uk/pubs/index.aspx> (accessed: 6 May 2006).

Kogan, M. (2000) 'Higher Education Communities and Academic Identity', *Higher Education Quarterly*, Vol. 54, No.3, 207–16.

Kotter, J. (1990) *A Force for Change: How Leadership Differs from Managment*, New York: Free Press.

Lao-Tzu (1998) *The Way Of Life According To Lao-tzu: An American Version* (New And Expanded Edition). Translated from the original Classical Chinese by B. Witter. New York: Penguin Putnam Inc.

Laurillard, D. (1993) *Rethinking University Teaching: a Framework for the Effective Use of Educational Technology*, London: Routledge.

Lewin, K. (1952) *Field Theory in Social Science*, London: Tavistock.

Lovell, R. (1994) 'Empowerment', in Lovell, R. (ed.) *Managing Change in the Public Sector*, Harlow: Longman.

Mabey, C. and Manyon-White, W. (eds.) (1993) *Managing Change* (2nd ed.), London: Paul Chapman.

Manning, T. (1994) 'Stress management and the management of change', in R. Lovell (ed.) *Managing Change in the Public Sector*, Harlow: Longman.

Maskell, D. and Robinson, I. (2001) *The New Idea of a University*, London: Haven Books.

Miles, M.B., Saxl, E.R. and Lieberman, A. (1988) 'What skills do educational "change agents" need?: an empirical view', *Curriculum Inquiry*, Vol. 18, No. 2, 157–76.

Monaco, E.J., Jablonka, K. and Stanley, R. (2000) 'An encounter with Proteous: the transformational impact of distance learning', in L. Lloyd (ed.) *Teaching With Technology: Rethinking Tradition*, Medford, New Jersey: Information Today Inc.

Newman, J. H. (1959, first published 1853) *The idea of a university* (1st ed.), New York: Image Books.

Pace, D. and Middendorf, J. (eds.) (2004) *Decoding the Disciplines: Helping Students Learn Disciplinary Ways of Thinking*, San Francisco: Jossey-Bass.

Parlett, M. and Hamilton, D. (1972) *Evaluation As Illumination: A New Approach to the Study of Innovatory Programmes*, Occasional paper no. 9, Edinburgh: Centre for Educational Sciences in the University of Edinburgh.

Paton, R.A. and McCalman, J. (2000) *Change Management: A Guide to Effective Implementation* (2nd ed.), London: Sage Publications Ltd.

Pedler, M., Burgoyne, J. and Mulrooney, C. (1991) *The Learning Company: A Strategy for Sustainable Development*, Maidenhead: McGraw-Hill.

Pettigrew, A.M. (1985) *The Awakening Giant*, London: Blackwell.

Riordan, T. and Roth, J. (2005) *Disciplines as Frameworks for Student Learning: Teaching the Practice of the Disciplines*, Virginia: Stylus.

Rothblatt, S. (1968) *The Revolution of the Dons: Cambridge and Society in Victorian England*, London: Faber and Faber.

Rothblatt, S. (1976) *Tradition and Change in English Liberal Education: An essay in History and Culture*, London: Faber and Faber.

Savin-Baden, M. (2000) *Problem-based Learning in Higher Education: Untold Stories*, Buckingham: SRHE and Open University Press.

Scott, P. (1998) 'Mass higher education: a new civilisation?', in D. Jary and M. Parker (eds.) *The New Higher education: Issues and Directions for the Post-Dearing University*, Stoke-on-Trent: Staffordshire University Press.

Senge, P. (1990) *The Fifth Discipline: The Art and Practice of the Learning Organisation*, New York: Doubleday.

Simpson, V. (1996) 'The hypertext campus project', in TLTSN Case Studies 2: *Managing the Adoption of Technology for Learning*, Leicester: Teaching and Learning Technology Support Network (TLTSN).

Trowler, P. (1998) *Academics Responding to Change: New Higher Education Frameworks and Academic Cultures,* Buckingham: Society for Research into Higher Education and Open University Press.

Trowler, P., Saunders, M. and Knight, P.T. (2003) *Change Thinking, Change Practices: A Guide to Change for Heads of Department, Programme Leaders and Other Change Agents in Higher Education,* York: Learning and Teaching Support Network. Available at <http://www.heacademy.ac.uk/resources.asp> (accessed 10 December 2005).

Ukpokodu, N. (2000) 'The efficacy of an electronic modularized course for preservice teachers: the multicultural educational course', in L. Lloyd (ed.) *Teaching With Technology: Rethinking Tradition,* Medford, New Jersey: Information Today Inc.

von Münchhausen, M and Scherer, H. (2003) *Die kleinen Saboteure: So managen Sie die inneren Schweinehunde im unternehmen*, Frankfurt/Main: Campus Publishing house.

Whittles, T. and Lovell, R. (1994) 'Managing the project', in R. Lovell (ed.) *Managing Change in the Public Sector,* Harlow: Longman.

Chapter 2

No money; no change

The impact of national policies to improve learning and teaching

Gavin Moodie

This chapter opens by considering the effect on learning and teaching of Europe's Bologna process and the United Kingdom's National Committee of Inquiry into Higher Education chaired by Sir Ron (now Lord) Dearing. These set the context for the case study for this chapter, the attempt by the Australian government to improve learning and teaching in higher education as part of its 'Crossroads' review of higher education (Commonwealth of Australia 2002a). The study finds a number of key issues in managing change and posits one ultimate reality of educational change: change in behaviour is greatly encouraged by change in financial rewards.

The Bologna process

The Bologna declaration (European Ministers of Education 2003) of 19 June 1999 is admirably clear, if a little general in its expression; yet there is marked disagreement over its motivation (Amaral and Magalhães 2004: 84; Tauch 2005: 11), implications (Reichert and Tauch 2003: 45) and value (Neave 2002; Amaral and Magalhães 2004: 85). All, however, agree on its significance (Neave 2002: 186). The declaration was signed initially by 29 European ministers of education, and 40 countries are now committed to its broad goal of creating a European higher education area, which extends far beyond the borders of the European Union (Barblan 2002: 84). More countries are expected to join (Reichert and Tauch 2005: 8).

The declaration sets six objectives:

> Adoption of a system of **easily readable and comparable degrees**, ... Adoption of a system essentially based on **two main cycles**, undergraduate and graduate, ... Establishment of a **system of credits** – such as in the ECTS system, ... Promotion of **mobility** by overcoming obstacles to the effective exercise of free movement [of students and staff], ... Promotion of **European co-operation in quality assurance** with a view to developing comparable criteria and methodologies. Promotion of the **necessary European dimensions in higher education**, particularly with regards to curricular development, inter-institutional co-operation, mobility schemes and integrated programmes of study, training and research.
>
> (European Ministers of Education 2003, emphasis in the original)

To an Anglophone, the diploma supplement through which the declaration seeks to promote European citizens' employability appears to be a combination of a degree certificate or testamur and an academic transcript. In addition to the information one would expect in a testamur and transcript, the diploma supplement includes information on the programme's entry requirements, mode of study, duration, and any eligibility it provides for further study and professional status (European Commission 2005). The ECTS through which the Bologna declaration seeks to promote student mobility is the European Credit Transfer System, which was introduced in 1989 as part of the Erasmus Student and Staff Mobility Programme, now part of the Socrates Programme that encourages European educational cooperation in mobility, organising joint projects, establishing European networks to disseminate ideas and good practice, and conducting studies and comparative analyses. Sixty ECTS credits represent the workload of a full-time student during one academic year (European Commission 2004).

The Bologna declaration refers to its antecedent, the Sorbonne joint declaration 'on harmonisation of the architecture of the European higher education system', adopted on 25 May 1998 by the ministers responsible for higher education in France, Germany, Italy and the United Kingdom (European Ministers of Education 2004). The Sorbonne declaration refers to the Lisbon convention of 1997 which, in turn, refers to six previous conventions on the equivalent periods of university study and on the academic recognition of university qualifications dating back to 1956 (Council of Europe 2004). The Bologna process is, therefore, an important part of the broad goal of European integration, which has historical routes in the promotion of student and staff mobility within Europe for mainly cultural benefits (Larsen and Vincent-Lancrin 2002: 11). This suggests that, notwithstanding the suspicion of students and some scholars (Amaral and Magalhães 2004), the Bologna process is not primarily motivated to attract fee-paying students from outside Europe, nor to cut government support for university education to a shorter, initial qualification.

Most of the very considerable attention devoted to the Bologna process in continental Europe has concentrated on the establishment of the two-tier qualification structure of bachelor and master, often abbreviated as BA/MA. This is a radical change for many countries, whose first university qualification could take from five to seven years' full time study (Ostermann 2005: 57; Michelotti 2005: 79; McManus-Czubińska 2005: 149). Nonetheless, Reichert (2005b: 46) observes that:

> ... far-reaching changes are taking place in approaches to learning, with many traditionally teacher-centred systems reflecting upon ways to place the students' needs at the centre of their attention. Such a change of focus is also making itself felt in the internal quality culture regarding teaching, with heightened attention to teaching performance, and feedback being sought from students on teaching and learning processes.

This may be because many European governments attached to the Bologna process reforms that they believed were desirable in any case (Neave 2002: 186; Huisman and Van Der Wende 2004: 352), and which were the trigger and focus for many changes that had already been contemplated within institutions (Reichert 2005b: 41).

However, Reichert (2005a: 28) observed:

> Perhaps surprisingly, given the increased attention on internal quality development, very few institutions in the sample systematically track basic information regarding success-rates and drop-out rates of students. If institutions are going to have strategies to improve teaching and learning, this is clearly a basic information requirement for strategic management and development which is currently lacking.

Reichert (2005b: 40) also reported that her 'visits to several institutions in one country showed that the same national conditions could result in very different institutional actions'. She (2005b: 42) suggested 'that the institutional leadership (be it one person or the leadership team) had a far-reaching effect on the institutional capacity for change, on the readiness to translate national conditions to an institutional plan, and to reconcile conflicting attitudes.'

Reichert (2005b: 46) found that 'there was a considerable gap between the aims of the Bologna reforms as stated in political declarations by the ministers ... and the means and support given by the state to the institutions to realize these aims'. Reichert (2005b: 46) concluded that 'as most of the costs of Bologna reforms have to be borne by the institutions themselves, in times of restricted institutional budgets this means that resources are being taken away from other essential functions of higher education, such as research'. It is not clear why institutions chose to divert considerable effort and resources from research to reforming learning and teaching. As we will see, the UK and Australian governments have not succeeded in redirecting institutions' priorities from research to learning and teaching. It may be that the discretionary rewards for research are not as great in some continental European countries. Nevertheless, it seems that the lack of additional funding has not prevented considerable progress being made with the Bologna process.

While the UK is a signatory of the Bologna declaration, and indeed is a signatory of the antecedent Sorbonne joint declaration, there has been little ministerial interest in the Bologna process (Reichert 2005b: 44). Instead, the UK government has been concerned with its own far-reaching changes to higher education, starting with the National Committee of Inquiry into Higher Education chaired by Sir Ron, (now Lord), Dearing.

Dearing

The National Committee of Inquiry into Higher Education was the first, wide-ranging review of UK higher education for over thirty years since the Committee on Higher Education (1963) chaired by Lord Robbins reported. So it is huge – it has 93 recommendations and the print version is over 1,700 pages (Dearing 1997: para 1), weighing 6.3 kg (Shattock 1999: 10). As Neave (1998: 120) observed, the UK differs from much of continental Europe in its 'astounding compression in one report and at one moment, of a range of issues each crucial in themselves but which, elsewhere, were tackled successively over a period of ten – or in the case of Sweden – twenty years'. Thus, Bologna is a process while Dearing was a report.

Dearing (1997: para 3.95) noted the very considerable increase in UK student numbers of 50 per cent from 1989 to 1994, the cut in public funding per student in higher education institutions by more than 40 per cent since 1976, and the increase in student:staff ratios over the period (Shattock 1999: 11). However, Trow (1998: 96) complained that:

> There is no serious description or analysis of the transformation of the teaching/learning environment as the student/staff ratio has doubled, and as the administrative staff has expanded and expanded again under the burden of accountability documents and reports.

Trow (1998: 103) argued that the very considerable variation in student:staff ratios between institutions and between departments within institutions 'defines the educational reality' for staff and students. If the variations are to be maintained they have different implications for quality and standards, for which different policies would be appropriate. Yet, Dearing recommended the same mechanisms for establishing and monitoring standards and the same extensive and systematic quality assurance for the whole sector, regardless of the variation in student:staff ratios and other circumstances. The committee based its recommendation on monitoring academic standards on its understanding of an Australian process (NCIHE 1997: para 10.62, recommendation 25). However, Australia conducted only one survey of the academic standard of its honours degrees, from (1990 to 1994), its recommendations were not implemented by all universities, and a decade later the Australian government (Commonwealth of Australia 2002b: para 87) correctly observed that Australia lacks a systematic approach to articulating and monitoring standards (Moodie 2004: 38–9).

In a finding that is also most significant, at least for the US and Australia, the committee reported:

> Although the teaching quality assessments (TQA) carried out by the Funding Bodies, which are designed to measure the effectiveness of teaching, have raised the profile of teaching within institutions, the Research Assessment Exercise (RAE) has been a stronger influence and has deflected attention away from learning and teaching towards research. An analysis of the impact of the 1992 RAE in higher education institutions in England suggests that it has devalued teaching because research assessment is closely linked to the allocation of large sums of money, whereas teaching assessment is not.
>
> (National Committee of Inquiry into Higher Education 1997: para 8.9)

The committee (1997: para 8.59) found that 'the necessary recognition of teaching in higher education will only be achieved through a national scheme of teacher accreditation to which all institutions voluntarily commit'. In this context, it recommended (1997: para 8.61, recommendation 14) the establishment of an Institute for Learning and Teaching in Higher Education to accredit training and practice, conduct research and development and stimulate innovation in learning and teaching, and 'confer associate membership, membership and fellowship to recognize superior levels of expertise'. The committee (1997: recommendation 48) also recommended that:

> ... over the medium term, it should become the normal requirement that all new, full-time academic staff with teaching responsibilities are required to achieve at least associate membership of the Institute for Learning and Teaching in Higher Education, for the successful completion of probation.

The UK government (1998) adopted these recommendations and subsequently merged the Institute for Learning and Teaching in Higher Education with cognate bodies to form a Higher Education Academy in May 2004 (Higher Education Academy 2005).

There are three difficulties in Dearing's recommendations to improve learning and teaching in UK higher education that potentially apply more generally to managing educational change. First, the recommendations are almost necessarily addressed to national bodies and institutions, yet learning and teaching is done by scholars (Trow 1998: 97). Bamber (2002: 444) referred to the 'implementation staircase' (Leithwood *et al.* 1974; Saunders 1986) from national body to institution and to various levels within the institution before it reaches the teaching team or individual teacher, which raises the clear risk that policies will be displaced and distorted at each level. Secondly, Trow (1998: 96) observed that the Dearing report:

> ... sharply separates its discussions of finance and funding from its chapters on teaching and learning. This violates the first principles of effective policy analysis, and makes the sections on teaching and learning seem trivial and irrelevant, its recommendations more like empty rhetoric rather than serious reflections on difficult problems. Again and again the report makes recommendations for yet new forms of accountability and assessment without any regard for their costs – and not just their financial costs – to the institutions and people affected. Under those conditions, rhetoric and exhortation fill the gap in resources.

This is not necessarily characteristic of national policies, but it is very common. Third, Trow (1998: 106) argued that 'Such generalized assertions about what must or should happen also do not reflect the actual processes by which decisions are made about teaching and learning in universities, and about the very considerable authority over teaching that still exists in the teaching staff itself'. He (1998: 107) believes that more effective teaching cannot be achieved without the 'support and willing assent of the academic staff' and since this was not considered by the Dearing report it had 'no real concern for implementation'. Possibly for similar reasons, Bamber (2002: 445) preferred changes to norms that take into account 'local cultural and value systems' to attempts to prescribe behaviour.

Dearing's report and the UK government's subsequent decisions on learning and teaching have strongly influenced the Australian government's attempts to influence learning and teaching in higher education in its 'Crossroads' review. However, not only did the Australian government fail to acknowledge its debt to Dearing in its learning and teaching policy, it also ignored Dearing's observation on the realities of educational change and failed to learn lessons on managing change from the Dearing report and its outcomes.

Crossroads: description

In April 2002 the Australian government began a review of higher education with the publication of its overview paper 'Higher Education at the Crossroads' (Commonwealth of Australia 2002a). This was followed by six issues papers on learning, teaching and scholarship; financing higher education; institutional diversity; Indigenous Australians in higher education; governance and management; and the relation between higher education and vocational education and training (Commonwealth of Australia 2005a). The overview paper posited that: 'The notion of "learning productivity" may be a useful way to frame a discussion of the issues related to teaching and learning' (Commonwealth of Australia 2002a: para 94) and its first consultative question about learning and teaching asked: 'What scope is there for increasing the productivity of learning?' (Commonwealth of Australia 2002a: 20). Other questions concerned enhancing the status and quality of teaching, academic standards, quality assurance, a national graduate aptitude test, and the impact of overseas students (Commonwealth of Australia 2002a: 21).

The first issues paper for the Crossroads review, *Striving for Quality: Learning, Teaching and Scholarship*, was published in June 2002. This framed ten questions about academic standards and quality, and a national graduate aptitude test, and seven questions about student assessment, attrition, the recording of student achievement and the efficient use of campuses (Commonwealth of Australia 2002b: 31, 45). The issues paper's focus on 'constructions of academic work and the quality of teaching and learning' included suggestions on the desirability of establishing 'a program to develop and support a scholarship of teaching (like the Carnegie Foundation's Academy for the Scholarship of Teaching and Learning)', establishing 'a national accreditation scheme for higher education teachers', making tenure and promotion decisions 'conditional on completion of an appropriate teacher preparation course or in-service professional development', and making it possible to be promoted to all academic levels for teaching excellence (Commonwealth of Australia 2002b: 53).

However, the measures 'promoting excellence in learning and teaching' announced in the Australian government's policy paper released in May 2003, *Our Universities: Backing Australia's Future*, were far less ambitious than those raised in the issues paper. The government established a National Institute for Learning and Teaching in Higher Education, which it subsequently named for John Carrick, a grandee of the conservative party in Australia and long-time political mentor of the prime minister (Hogarth and Dayton 1997) and a favourite of the minister for education at the time the Institute was established (Nelson 2004). The Institute took over from the Australian Universities Teaching Committee the management of the competitive grants scheme for innovation in learning and teaching, and the coordination of the awards for university teaching, which the government expanded. The Institute also manages a programme for international experts in learning and teaching to visit Australian institutions, develops reciprocal relationships with overseas jurisdictions, and undertakes a number of exhortatory exercises about academic standards, student assessment and improving teaching (Commonwealth of Australia 2003: 28; see also chapter seven). Notably missing from the Institute's role is managing a national accreditation scheme for higher education teachers, which was raised in the government's issues paper and is part of the role of the UK institute, now the Higher Education Academy. This role was strongly opposed by some participants in consultation meetings on the Institute (Schofield 2003: para 3.8).

The government's policy paper observed that 'Although teaching is recognized as a core activity of all higher education institutions, current Commonwealth funding, internal staff promotion practices and institutional prestige tend to reinforce the importance of research performance rather than teaching performance' (Commonwealth of Australia 2003: 28). Apparently to redress that imbalance, at least partly, the government established a learning and teaching performance fund. The government allocates the fund in two stages: stage one determines an institution's eligibility for funds; stage two assesses institutions' performance in learning and teaching (Commonwealth of Australia 2005b). The method and criteria for assessing institutional performance have been controversial. The Australian Vice-Chancellors' Committee (2004) and many universities argued strongly for peer assessment of institutions' portfolios on learning and teaching. However, the minister has, apparently, insisted that institutions' performance in learning and teaching be assessed by a range of quantitative measures.

Crossroads: analysis

The chapter of the overview paper and the issues paper on learning and teaching in the Australian Government's Crossroads review of higher education were mainly about institutional management of learning and teaching: 'learning productivity', academic standards, student attrition, recording student achievement, and a national graduate aptitude test. The government invited responses on accrediting higher education teachers but did not proceed with the suggestion, apparently because it encountered strong opposition. However, the government did partly proceed with proposals to deregulate student fees, to provide subsidised public loans for private fees, to reduce the size of universities' governing bodies, and to greatly increase the amount and detail of government regulation of universities, despite strong opposition.

The most important change in learning and teaching introduced by the Crossroads review is the establishment of the learning and teaching performance fund. In the first year the government allocated the fund by measures of commencing students' attrition and pass rates, graduates' satisfaction as expressed in the course experience questionnaire, (administered to all graduates four months after completing their programmes), and graduates' destinations four months after completing their programme. The Department of Education, Science and Training's bivariate regression on these measures showed that students' and graduates' institutions explained from as little as 0.36 per cent to a maximum of 4.97 per cent of the variation in the measures' scores. Indeed, all of the student demographic and institutional statistical data collected by the department explained from 0.97 per cent to a maximum of 21.53 per cent of the variation of scores – from 78.47 per cent to 99.03 per cent of the variation in scores is unexplained (Department of Education, Science and Training 2004: appendix C). This can, nonetheless, produce statistically valid comparisons between institutions because the differences, while small, are for large populations. However, the method of calculating institutional scores and adjusting for non-relevant factors is very complicated and, in a review for the department, Access Economics Pty Limited (2005) found problems with the Department's method.

The most prominent learning and teaching outcome from Crossroads has been the establishment of the Carrick Institute for Learning and Teaching in Higher Education. The Institute is an expansion of the Australian Universities Teaching Committee and its predecessors dating back to 1991. Johnstone (2002: 143) reported that reviews of the Institute's predecessors found that they had 'played a crucial role in raising the status of teaching; providing recognition and reward to academics who focused on teaching; acting as a kind of template for the introduction of similar schemes within institutions'. However, notwithstanding this improvement in culture, evidence for individual project grants' 'more concrete, practical and widespread outcomes in terms of improved teaching methods and improved quality of learning was less than convincing' (Johnstone 2002: 144). This was due to 'a distinction between dissemination and the adoption of ideas' (Johnstone 2002: 145). There is, as yet, no evidence that the Carrick Institute will overcome this basic difficulty in effecting change.

A minority of participants in consultation meetings on the Carrick Institute for Learning and Teaching in Higher Education:

... were not confident that by itself it would be effective in enhancing the quality of learning and teaching in Australian higher education. They drew attention to the dominance of incentives provided for other activities (notably research), felt that teaching often lacked status within their own university, and were not convinced that their institutions would either wish to – or be able to – place greater emphasis on enhancing teaching quality.

(Schofield 2003: para 32.3)

This is an accurate reflection of the government's real priorities disclosed by its funding decisions. Even with the establishment of the learning and teaching performance fund, the Australian government's rewards for institutional performance overwhelmingly favour research.

When the learning and teaching performance fund reaches its maximum announced level of A$114 million in 2008 it will be only 10 per cent of the A$1,127 million in contestable funds allocated for institutional performance in 2004 – research and research training dominates with A$986 million or 87 per cent of contestable institutional funds. The government allocated A$6 million to institutions under the higher education equity programme in 2004 but only A$2 million of this was for institutional performance (Commonwealth of Australia 2004: 69). The Australian government's allocation to institutions for equity performance is thus a derisory 2 per cent of all contestable funds. This seems to be the ultimate reality of the government's inability to improve learning and teaching in higher education substantially and systematically. Whatever investments of time, effort and resources may be made to improve learning and teaching, they are swamped by the far greater investments in research.

Discussion

While Europe's Bologna process, the UK's Dearing report and Australia's Crossroads review are quite different and were shaped by different times and circumstances, they share three issues. First, in the Bologna process and in the Crossroads review the measurement of the outcomes of learning and teaching is an important issue, in Bologna because it is not happening and in Crossroads because it is happening. Lombardi (2001: 10) expresses a common view amongst senior managers that:

Measuring performance leads to improvement. Absent measurement, politics replace performance as the institutional criteria ... Faculty [i.e. academic staff] performance drives university performance. Measurement of faculty performance against the best leads to improvement. Improvement in faculty performance depends on rewarding measurable high quality and productivity. Absent rewards for measurable performance, politics replace performance.

A second issue, which is shared by all three national policies, is governments' allocation of inadequate resources, if any, to support their policies to improve learning and teaching. This is all the more ironic, if not hypocritical, of the UK and Australian governments, since they failed to redress the dramatic deterioration in their per capita funding rates and, consequently, universities' student:staff ratios, which led to public concerns about the quality of learning and teaching, and the inquiries they launched.

The third issue, closely related to the second, is that policies to improve learning and teaching are overwhelmed by universities' determination to improve their research, driven partly by the very considerable additional rewards governments allocate for research performance. Furthermore, at least in the USA and the UK, universities that perform strongly in research not only attract more research funding than others, but are also funded at a higher rate for teaching than institutions that are expected to concentrate on teaching and community service (Grubb and Lazerson 2004). In contrast with learning and teaching, techniques to improve research performance such as increasing research activity, winning grants, increasing prominent publications, concentrating effort and resources, and improving institutional performance are widely studied and adapted throughout the sector.

This suggests that government policy is most effective in achieving change when it is linked to discretionary financial rewards. The distinction between the dissemination and the adoption of ideas (Johnstone 2002: 145), which limited the widespread adoption of improvements in learning and teaching in Australia, is a problem if the policy seeks to achieve change by persuasion only; it does not seem to be a problem where policies are supported by significant financial outcomes. It also appears that national policies may be displaced and distorted as they are transmitted down Saunders' (1986) 'implementation staircase' to institutions and to various levels within institutions.

It also suggests that the very considerable variation in institutions' implementation of the same national policy that Reichert (2005b: 40) found in the implementation of the Bologna process may be found also within institutions. In fact, considerable variations in practice and quality are evident within institutions, notwithstanding that they adopt policies on learning and teaching, and research that ostensibly apply equally across the institution. This may be due to the effect of institutions' leadership, as Reichert (2005b: 42) suggested, and variations within institutions may, correspondingly, be due to the influence of deans and heads of department. But variations in the implementation of national and institution-wide policies may also be because policies that ostensibly apply equally to institutions and within institutions have very different impacts depending on each institution's and each discipline's circumstances. Trow (1998: 103) argued that Dearing's universal prescriptions on learning and teaching do not take account of the very considerable variation in student:staff ratios between institutions and between departments within institutions that 'defines the educational reality' for staff and students, and one could expand on the differences between and within institutions that might affect learning and teaching. But following Trow, considering only culture, curriculum and pedagogy misses the ultimate reality of achieving educational change: with no money there is no change.

Bibliography

Access Economics Pty Limited (2005) *Review of Higher Education Outcome Performance Indicators,* Canberra: Department of Education, Science and Training.

Amaral, A. and Magalhães, A. (2004) 'Epidemiology and the Bologna saga', *Higher Education,* Vol. 48, No. 1, 79–100.

Australian Vice-Chancellors' Committee (2004) 'Assessing learning and teaching excellence'. Available at <http://www.avcc.edu.au/content.asp?page=/news/media_releases/2004/avcc_media_28_04.htm> (accessed 14 December 2005).

Bamber, V. (2002) 'To what extent has the Dearing policy recommendations on training new lecturers met acceptance? Where Dearing went that Robbins didn't dare', *Teacher Development,* Vol. 6, No. 3, 433–58.

Barblan, A. (2002) 'The international provision of higher education: do universities need GATS?', *Higher Education Management and Policy,* Vol. 14, No. 3, 77–92.

Committee on Higher Education (1963) *Higher Education: Report,* (Robbins, L., chair) Cmnd 2154, London: HMSO.

Commonwealth of Australia (2002a) 'Higher education at the crossroads: An overview paper'. Available at <http://www.backingaustraliasfuture.gov.au/publications/crossroads/default.htm> (accessed 12 December 2005).

Commonwealth of Australia (2002b) 'Striving for quality: Learning, teaching and scholarship'. Available at <http://www.backingaustraliasfuture.gov.au/publications/striving_for_quality/default.htm> (accessed 12 December 2005).

Commonwealth of Australia (2003) 'Our universities: Backing Australia's future'. Available at <http://www.backingaustraliasfuture.gov.au/policy.htm> (accessed 12 December 2005).

Commonwealth of Australia (2004) 'Higher Education' (Report for the 2004–2006 Triennium). Available at <http://www.dest.gov.au/sectors/higher_education/publications_resources/profiles/higher_education_report_2004_2006_triennium.htm> (accessed 12 December 2005).

Commonwealth of Australia (2005a) 'Higher Education Review Process'. Available at <http://www.backingaustraliasfuture.gov.au/review.htm> (accessed 12 December 2005).

Commonwealth of Australia (2005b) 'Learning and teaching performance fund'. Available at <http://www.dest.gov.au/sectors/higher_education/policy_issues_reviews/key_issues/learning_teaching/ltpf/default.htm> (accessed 12 December 2005).

Council of Europe (2004, first published 1997) 'Convention on the recognition of qualifications concerning higher education in the European region' (Lisbon convention), European University Association, Brussels. Available at <http://conventions.coe.int/Treaty/EN/Treaties/Html/165.htm> (accessed 14 December 2005).

Dearing, R. (1997) 'Chairman's foreword', in *Higher Education in the Learning Society,* report of the National Committee of Inquiry into Higher Education. Available at <http://www.leeds.ac.uk/educol/ncihe/> (accessed 12 December 2005).

Department Of Education, Science and Training (2004) Technical Note 1: 'Student outcome indicators of Australian higher education institutions, 2002 and 2003'. Available at <http://www.dest.gov.au/sectors/higher_education/policy_issues_reviews/key_issues/ assuring_quality_in_higher_education/technical_note_1.htm> (accessed 12 December 2005).

European Commission (2004) *ECTS – 'European credit transfer system'*, Brussels: European Commission. Available at <http://europa.eu.int/comm/education/pro-grammes/socrates/ects/index_en.html> (accessed 14 December 2005).

European Commission (2005) 'Diploma Supplement', Brussels: European Commission. Available at <http://europa.eu.int/comm/education/policies/rec_qual/recognition/ diploma_en.html> (accessed 12 December 2005).

European Ministers of Education (2003, first published 1999) 'The Bologna Declaration of 19 June 1999', Brussels: European University Association. Available at <http://www. eua.be/eua/jsp/en/upload/OFFDOC_BP_bologna_declaration.1068714825768.pdf> (accessed 12 December 2005).

European Ministers of Education (2004, first published 1998) 'Sorbonne Joint Declaration', Brussels: European University Association. Available at <http:// www.eua.be/eua/jsp/en/upload/OFFDOC_BP_bologna_declaration.1068714825768. pdf> (accessed 12 December 2005).

Grubb, N. W. and Lazerson, M. (2004) *The Educational Gospel: The Economic Power of Schooling*, Cambridge, Massachusetts: Harvard University Press.

Higher Education Academy (2005) 'Welcome to the Higher Education Academy: Background'. Available at <http://www.heacademy.ac.uk/3115.htm> (accessed 12 December 2005).

Hogarth, M. and Dayton, L. (1997) 'How the climate sceptics got to Howard', *Sydney Morning Herald*, 24 November. Available at <http://www.gaiaguys.net/24.11smh% 20climatehoward%20mislcad.html> (accessed 12 December 2005).

Huisman, J. and Van Der Wende, M. (2004) 'The EU and Bologna: are supra- and interna-tional initiatives threatening domestic agendas?', *European Journal of Education*, Vol. 39, No. 3, 349–57.

Johnstone, R. (2002) 'Educational development projects in Australia: a system-level per-spective', in M. Baume, P. Martin, and M. Yorke, (eds.) *Managing Educational Development Projects*, London: Kogan Page, 141–52.

Larsen, K. and Vincent-Lancrin, S. (2002) 'International trade in educational services: good or bad?', *Higher Education Management and Policy*, Vol. 14, No. 3, 9–45.

Leithwood K.A., Russell H.H., Clipsham J.S. and Robinson F.G. (1974) 'School change: stages, constructs and research methodology', *Interchange*, Vol. 5, No. 1, 33–48.

Lombardi, J. (2001) 'Quality engines: the strategic principles for competitive universities in the twenty-first century' *The Center Reports* (March). Available at <http://thecen-ter.ufl.edu> (accessed 12 December 2005).

McManus-Czubińska, C. (2005) 'Mass higher education in Poland. Coping with the "Spanish collar"', in T. Tapper and D. Palfreyman (eds.) *Understanding Mass Higher Education: Comparative Perspectives on Access*, London: RoutledgeFalmer, 139–59.

Michelotti, S. (2005) 'The value of higher education is a mass system. The Italian debate', in T. Tapper and D. Palfreyman (eds.) *Understanding Mass Higher Education: Comparative Perspectives on Access*, London: RoutledgeFalmer: 76–91.

Moodie, G. (2004) 'The neglected role of a neglected body: academic boards' role in assur-ing "equivalent" standards', *Australian Universities Review*, Vol. 47, No. 3, 35–41.

National Committee of Inquiry into Higher Education (1997) 'Higher education in the learning society', report of the National Committee of Inquiry into Higher Education (Dearing, Ron, Chair). Available at <http://www.leeds.ac.uk/educol/ncihe/> (accessed 12 December 2005).

Neave, G. (1998) 'Growing pains: the Dearing report from a European perspective', *Higher Education Quarterly,* Vol. 52, No. 1, 118–36.

Neave, G. (2002) 'Anything goes: or, how the accommodation of Europe's universities to European integration integrates an inspiring number of contradictions', *Tertiary Education and Management,* Vol. 8, 181–97.

Nelson, B. (2004) Transcript of the launch of the Carrick Institute for Teaching and Learning in Higher Education, Parliament House, 11 August, Australia: Media Centre. Available at <http://www.dest.gov.au/Ministers/Media/Nelson/2004/08/n853110804. asp> (accessed 12 December 2005).

Ostermann, H. (2005) *'Bildung or Ausbildung?* Reorienting German higher education', in T. Tapper and D. Palfreyman (eds.) *Understanding Mass Higher Education: Comparative Perspectives on Access,* London: RoutledgeFalmer: 51–75.

Reichert, S. (2005a) 'Quality enhancement and quality assurance' in K. Geddie and D. Crozier (eds.) *Trends IV: European Universities Implementing Bologna,* Brussels: European University Association, 27–32. Available at http://www.eua.be/eua/jsp/ en/upload/TrendsIV_final.1114509452430.pdf > (accessed 12 December 2005).

Reichert, S. (2005b) 'Implementing Bologna at higher education institutions: success factors and systemic challenges', in K. Geddie and D. Crozier (eds.) *Trends IV: European Universities Implementing Bologna,* Brussels: European University Association: 40–9. Available at <http://www.eua.be/eua/jsp/en/upload/ TrendsIV_final.1114509452430.pdf >(accessed 12 December 2005).

Reichert, S. and Tauch, C. (2003) 'Bologna four years after: steps toward sustainable reform of higher education in Europe', *Trends 2003: Progress Towards the European Higher Education Area,* No. 1, July 2003, *(AKA: Trends III),* a report prepared for the European University Association, Geneva. Available at <http://www.eua.be/ eua/en/publications.jspx> (accessed 12 December 2005).

Reichert, S. and Tauch, C. (2005) 'Introduction', in K. Geddie and D. Crozier (eds.) *Trends IV: European Universities Implementing Bologna,* Brussels: European University Association: 12–13. Available at <http://www.eua.be/eua/jsp/en/upload/ TrendsIV_final.1114509452430.pdf> (accessed 12 December 2005).

Saunders, M. (1986) 'Developing a large scale "local" evaluation of TVEI: aspects of the Lancaster experience', in D. Hopkins (ed.) *Evaluating TVEI: Some Methodological Issues,* Cambridge: Cambridge Institute of Education.

Schofield, A. (2003) 'A Report on the consultation meetings on the Institute for Learning and Teaching in Higher Education'. Available at <http://www.dest.gov.au/ sectors/higher_education/policy_issues_reviews/key_issues/learning_teaching/report_ consult.htm> (accessed 12 December 2005).

Shattock, M. (1999) 'The impact of the Dearing report on UK higher education', *Higher Education Management,* Vol. 11, No. 1, 7–17.

Tauch, C. (2005) 'Two cycle degree structure', in S. Reichert and C. Tauch (eds.) *Trends IV: European Universities Implementing Bologna,* Brussels: European University Association: 10–19. Available at <http://www.eua.be/eua/jsp/en/upload/ TrendsIV_final.1114509452430.pdf> (accessed 12 December 2005).

Trow, M. (1998) 'The Dearing Report: a transatlantic view', *Higher Education Quarterly*, Vol. 52, No. 1, 93–117.

UK Government (1998) 'Higher education for the 21st Century: Response to the Dearing Report'. Available at <http://www.lifelonglearning.co.uk/dearing/index.htm> (accessed 12 December 2005).

Chapter 3

National initiatives to enhance learning and teaching in higher education

A case study of the planning of the Carrick Institute in Australia

Lesley H. Parker

Introduction

In many parts of the world, governments are directing resources to the advancement of learning and teaching in higher education, although the extent of government support and the associated pace of change are uneven. As Schofield (2003) indicated in his review of major national schemes, the United Kingdom, Sweden, the United States of America and Hong Kong have schemes that have evolved over at least the past two decades. There is also evidence that such schemes are continuing to evolve and spread. In New Zealand and Malaysia activities are beginning, and recently the American Fulbright programme initiated a new international group to advise UNESCO on innovative ways for governments (including those of Ethiopia and Pakistan) to support higher education and to assure its quality (Jaschik 2005).

Over the past 14 years, the Australian government has funded a number of national initiatives focused on university teaching, including the most recent of these, the Carrick Institute for Learning and Teaching in Higher Education, established in August 2004. This chapter begins with a brief description of the context for the establishment of the new institute, the impetus for change, and the new vision for learning and teaching in higher education. It then provides an overview of the planning undertaken to make that vision a reality, and follows with an analysis of the model for change in terms of facilitating factors and barriers. The chapter concludes by suggesting what can be learned from the planning and establishment of the Carrick Institute.

The context and impetus for change

The international context

Internationally, there is wide variation in the nature of the support provided for learning and teaching in higher education – variation in the scale, the structure, the focus, the source of funding, the rationale and the desired outcomes. Yet common themes have emerged (see also Parker 2005). One of these encompasses the dissemination of information about innovations in teaching and successful practice. As McKenzie *et al.* (2005) noted, even defining 'dissemination', 'innovation' and 'success' is a challenge. In brief, there is a need for better understanding of the meaning of 'dissemination' and its relationship to the diffusion, adoption and embedding of good practice.

It has also become clear that there are impediments to what individuals can achieve in improvements in learning and teaching that go beyond their own classrooms, particularly if they are working in relative isolation, without the support of their institution and/or without the support of a network of like-minded colleagues. This has led to a re-thinking of the way in which institutional leadership operates to enhance learning and teaching, and to an increased focus on change management strategies and on collaboration.

An additional theme relates to defining 'excellence' in university teaching. It is now recognised that education is not only about what teachers teach: more importantly, it is about what their students learn in terms of knowledge, skills, attitudes and values. Judgements about excellence in teaching need, therefore, to be based on firm evidence of student learning. Some have even proposed (Tagg 2003) that the 'new mission' for universities is 'to produce learning, not to simply to provide instruction'.

A final theme concerns the extent to which teaching is actually a valued activity in universities. Most modern universities, in their strategic statements, define teaching and research as the joint, core business of the institution. Despite this, however, there is a global perception that research has come to assume higher status and that, for the purposes of internal allocation of funding and the career progression of academics, research outcomes rather than teaching outcomes are of paramount importance. It was in the context of these issues that the Australian government funded the Carrick Institute for Learning and Teaching.

The Australian context 1992–2004: the emergence of a new vision for learning and teaching in Australian higher education

During the years 1992–2004 Australian schemes specifically providing support for university teaching and learning were overseen and administered through major national committees. Academics were able to compete for grants provided under the auspices of the Committee for the Advancement of University Teaching (CAUT, 1992–5), the Committee for University Teaching Staff Development (CUTSD, 1996–9) and the Australian Universities Teaching Committee (AUTC, 2000–4). The support provided by these committees began initially with relatively small grants, mainly to individual academics, for projects aimed at improving the quality of teaching. There was also support for dissemination, through the establishment of five subject-based national clearing houses. Schemes were extended to include staff development initiatives, visits by international scholars and, in 1997, a system of national awards for university teaching. The committees undertook ongoing, informal reviews of these initiatives in terms of their effectiveness in bringing about change, and over the years they implemented modifications aimed at enhancing the success of the various approaches.

A formal review of the CAUT and CUTSD schemes (Schofield and Olsen, 2000) revealed that widespread reform and improvement had been constrained by a number of factors. These were associated with resource levels (most grants were quite small), scope (most projects were short-term, one-off initiatives), reach (there were limited possibilities for widespread impact) and lack of sustainability over time, given that there was no dedicated executive support for the work of the committees and no continuing focal point for accumulating and accessing outcomes of the projects. Of the many projects funded by CAUT, CUTSD and AUTC, few appeared to have had a sustained effect. The exceptions included one of the CAUT clearing houses (the only one of the initial five that had survived) and the awards for excellence in university teaching, which had received dedicated funding since their inception in 1997.

The opportunity for addressing some of these shortcomings came in 2002, when the Australian government launched a major review of the whole higher education sector, framed around a series of discussion papers. Amongst these papers, those of particular interest to learning and teaching were the overview, *Higher Education at the Crossroads* (Commonwealth of Australia Department of Education, Science and Training 2002) and the paper entitled *Striving for Scholarship: Learning, Teaching and Scholarship* (Commonwealth of Australia Department of Education, Science and Training 2002).

The Australian higher education sector and its key stakeholders from business and industry participated actively in responding to these papers, putting forward a variety of perspectives on the changes required to bring about promotion and enhancement of teaching and learning in higher education. Common to many responses were a number of issues. Some of these, focusing on dissemination, leadership, networks and definitions of excellence, reflected international consensus on barriers to change, and provided clear evidence of the growing pressure for demonstrably high quality in university teaching, particularly in terms of a focus on student learning.

Other arguments for change appeared explicitly for the first time. For example, given issues of sustainability raised by the Schofield and Olsen review (2000), it was argued that in Australia the level of support for learning and teaching in higher education was very low. Evidence was cited from the long-standing Carnegie initiatives in the USA and the activities of the Institute for Learning and Teaching in the UK, demonstrating that so much more, of system-wide significance, could be accomplished with more resources. In addition, respondents reiterated the prevailing perceptions that teaching and research were not equally valued in universities and that the undervaluing of teaching was a continuing barrier to resource allocation and career progression.

In its submission to the Higher Education Review, the AUTC emphasised the need for a high-level committee to identify and support national priorities in teaching and learning, and to establish appropriate benchmarks and leverage the outcomes of individual and institutional initiatives for the benefit of the whole sector. In short, it recommended the establishment of a dedicated support structure, staffed by professionals.

The government's review culminated in major reforms for the sector as a whole. These were spelled out in *Our Universities: Backing Australia's Future* (Commonwealth of Australia Department of Education, Science and Training 2003) and included a focus on 'promoting excellence in learning and teaching' (p. 28). The report acknowledged the concerns raised and, in response, proposed a suite of initiatives to begin in 2006, including the establishment of a national institute for learning and teaching in higher education with an annual budget of nearly A\$22 million.

The government's vision for the institute was explicit in its specification of the new organisation's responsibilities (Commonwealth of Australia Department of Education, Science and Training, May 2003: 28):

- management of a major competitive grants scheme for innovation in learning and teaching
- liaison with the sector about options for articulating and monitoring academic standards
- improvement of assessment practices throughout the sector, including investigation of the feasibility of a national portfolio assessment scheme
- facilitation of benchmarking of effective learning and teaching processes at national and international levels
- development of mechanisms for the dissemination of good practice in learning and teaching
- management of a programme for international experts in learning and teaching to visit Australian institutions and the development of reciprocal relationships with international jurisdictions
- coordination of the new Australian Awards for University Teaching, including the Awards presentation event.

Some aspects of this remit, together with the vastly increased budget proposed to support learning and teaching, were greeted with considerable enthusiasm by the Australian higher education sector. At the same time, however, there was some scepticism regarding how a system of 251 annual awards for university teaching might be managed effectively. There was also apprehension regarding the government's requirement for more explicit standards and benchmarking.

As a general point, in the establishment of the new institute, it was clear that there was a need to reconcile competing priorities, between, on the one hand, government imperatives and, on the other hand, the needs of the system as perceived by a range of stakeholders. Perhaps, then, one of the 'realities of change', especially government-funded change, is that 'visions', particularly for national initiatives, inevitably involve compromise.

An additional 'reality of change', particularly obvious in the case of the evolution and establishment of the Carrick Institute, is that all change needs a driver. In this case, a key feature in the success of the various national initiatives in Australia over the years has been the continuity in leadership and strength of vision provided by Professor John Hay, as chairman of CUTSD and the AUTC, as the inaugural chair of the Board of the Carrick Institute, and as a member of the committee advising the Minister on the Review of Higher Education during the critical 2002–4 period.

Planning to make the vision real

Framing the Institute

The initial framing of the proposed Institute was overseen by the outgoing Australian Universities Teaching Committee during the period May–August, 2004. In many ways, the approach taken set the scene for the Institute's subsequent operations, in that it was highly consultative, involved discussion papers and forums, and conveyed a genuine attempt to listen to the sector.

This consultative process resulted in advice to the Minister, which set out, amongst other things, the Institute's mission, objectives and values. The succinct mission statement was 'to promote and advance learning and teaching in Australian higher education'. Six objectives were articulated to achieve this mission, covering key tasks in terms of strategic change, profile raising, fostering and acknowledging excellence in teaching, effective dissemination of good practice, and international links. A unique feature of the initial framing was the statement of five 'Values and Principles for Action'. These made public the commitment of the Institute to ways of operating that would be inclusive and collaborative and would recognise diversity and promote excellence, whilst being oriented to long-term, system-wide change. This statement of values proved to be of fundamental importance to the planning process.

Allowing for a planning phase

The then Minister for Education, Science and Training, Dr Brendan Nelson, essentially accepted the advice of the AUTC, which included the formal statement of mission, objective and values. He launched the national institute on 11 August 2004, naming it the Carrick Institute for Learning and Teaching in Higher Education after Sir John Carrick, a former Australian Minister for Education. The Carrick Institute was established as a wholly owned government company, limited by guarantee, with a board appointed by the Minister.

From the outset, the government recognised that a considerable resource would need to be dedicated to planning the Institute and a realistic budget was identified to enable planning to proceed. I was appointed Planning Director in September, 2004 and Dr Elizabeth McDonald, who had played a key role in the consultations leading to the establishment of the Institute, was appointed Company Secretary. With the support of a very small staff, as well as from the Institute's Board, the government, and people and organisations across the higher education sector, we set about the task of putting in place effective systems that would fulfil the Institute's remit from government and achieve its mission and objectives. It was a great benefit that the planning phase could begin with an agreed statement of the Institute's intended outcomes and, furthermore, that this statement was based on a high level of consultation underpinning its development. This gave rise to a strong sense of ownership across the sector. At the time of writing, the Institute is on target, as planned, to be operational in January 2006.

Analysing the planning phase: factors facilitating change

In a higher education sector reeling under the impact of numerous changes associated with reforms, the establishment of the Institute has achieved a high profile as an initiative that the sector actually wanted, and one from which it could see itself deriving tangible benefits. At the outset of the planning phase, there was a distinct sense of excitement. Expectations were high and quite wide-ranging, and in the early months, it became important to pinpoint very clearly, through documents and extensive face-to-face contact, what the Institute would (and would not) be doing. This process was facilitated by four related factors: first, the trust built up and sustained through adherence to the consultative model for change; second, the anchoring of the planning in well-documented evidence (in some cases from specially commissioned reports) about what was actually happening across the sector; third, the articulation of future directions for the Institute that resonated well with the sector; and fourth, the initiation of actions that went beyond planning as such and moved into the provision of grants for projects in two key areas. Each of these four factors is now discussed.

The model for change and the change agents

In terms of the models of change conceptualised by Feeny and Ruddle (1997), the model framing the planning of the Carrick Institute has been a mixture of incremental-organic (involving wide consultation across the Australian higher education sector) and step-organic (central initiatives aimed at transformational change and the development of new ways of teaching, sector-wide). Because the Institute's values, especially those related to collaboration and inclusiveness, underpinned all aspects of the planning, there was a strong sense of collective commitment associated with these early stages. The Framework for Interaction with Key Stakeholder Groups (www.carrickinstitute.edu.au) produced early in the planning phase, reinforced this collective commitment, emphasising that Australia's higher education providers are both direct beneficiaries *and* active, essential partners in the Institute's activities. In this sense, there are effectively multiple change agents, each with a specific place in the total web of agents fundamental to successful change.

Evidence-based planning

The Carrick Institute was in the particularly fortunate position of being able to learn from the reports of a large number of discipline-specific and generic projects funded or initiated by the Australian Universities Teaching Committee during the period 2000–4. These were truly impressive in their scope, covering curriculum and learning outcomes in many of the major discipline areas taught in Australian universities, as well as a number of key issues such as assessment, clinical education, sessional staff and teaching large classes. Both individually and collectively, these reports provided the Carrick Institute's planning team with valuable material on which to build the future.

The review of the projects carried out by Hicks (2004) also provided a wealth of information on issues that needed to be addressed to maximise the likelihood of a project's success. Two of the most wide-ranging and informative projects concerned the issue of dissemination of good practice (McKenzie *et al.* 2005; Southwell *et al.* 2005). These reports provided an insightful and thorough analysis that informed much of the Carrick Institute's action during the planning phase.

A further invaluable guide to planning and practice for excellence in learning and teaching in Australian higher education draws on activities conducted under the auspices of the Australian Universities Quality Agency (AUQA). In a report commissioned by the Carrick Institute, Stevens (2005) provides an analysis of materials associated with the first 25 of the university audits conducted by AUQA, distilling from this material eleven key strategies for the promotion of teaching and learning (www.carrickinstitute.edu.au).

The choice of the Institute's strategic priorities

The Carrick Institute's Strategic Priority Areas for 2006–8 were developed collaboratively with stakeholders over several months and have been received positively by the sector. The five agreed Strategic Priority Areas are conceptualised as major 'schemes': a Grants scheme (encompassing three large programmes); a scheme for Discipline-based Activities; a scheme to establish and maintain a Resource Identification Network; the Carrick Fellowship scheme; and the Carrick Awards for Australian University Teaching. Details of these may be found on the Carrick Institute website (www.carrickinstitute.edu.au).

For the purposes of this chapter, the important point is that certain basic tenets were followed in the development of all the schemes and programmes. First, care was taken to ensure that there is an understanding of the links of the five areas to the Institute's mission, objectives, values and budget allocation. This included generating an understanding of the strong linkages amongst the areas themselves, and of the ways in which projects in one area would be able to inform possibilities in others. Second, it was critical to demonstrate to the sector that the Institute values and is building on existing excellence and past good practice, and is not redefining excellence in some new and inaccessible way. Third, the importance of communication in delineating and achieving the priorities was also emphasized, with international liaison and a range of communication strategies, including seminars, conferences and workshops, integral to activities in all areas. Finally, the actual scoping of the detail of the schemes and programmes was, like all Carrick Institute planning activities, undertaken in a consistently consultative way, with opportunities for the sector to comment on and discuss draft papers, either in writing or in face-to-face settings.

Actions to initiate projects in key areas

Recognition of the need for action

The Australian university sector, like its counterparts elsewhere in the world, is always suspicious of anything that looks like 'too much planning and too little action'. To forestall this perception, the Carrick Institute's Board took a decision to initiate some projects during the planning phase, rather than await receipt of the Institute's full budget in 2006. Two high priority areas were identified. Specifically these were: assessment, for which four projects were funded, focused on specific disciplines and building on the strong basis provided by a previous AUTC-funded project (James *et al.* 2002); and leadership, which is discussed in more detail in the next section because of its particular interest to this chapter, given its close relationship to change management.

Leadership and change management

In the course of its strategic planning, and supported in particular by the findings of the projects reported by McKenzie *et al.* (2005) and Southwell *et al.* (2005), the Carrick Institute identified the need for systematic, structured support for academic leadership as a major focus of its activities in 2006–8. Accordingly, it developed a programme focused on Effective Leadership for Excellence in Learning and Teaching. The anticipated budget for this programme over 2006–8 is in the order of A$8 million, which will be used to support projects that build leadership capacity in new and stimulating ways.

Fundamental to the programme is the Institute's perspective that leadership for excellence in learning and teaching in contemporary universities needs to be distributed and multi-level. In what is essentially a dynamic, sometimes uncertain and ambiguous context, the capacity of systems, institutions and individuals to respond appropriately to change and to facilitate further change requires forms of leadership that go beyond conventional models. The Carrick Institute is therefore developing a rich and open view of leadership that allows for multiple interpretations. It sees a need to recognise that leadership in learning and teaching may take many forms. For example, the positions of Pro-Vice-Chancellor (Academic) and Head of School or Department have formally defined leadership responsibilities encapsulated in the position titles and descriptions. Other people, however, also have roles (such as policy developer, curriculum developer or classroom innovator) that are critical to quality learning and teaching. In these cases, leadership is more context-dependent and may not be formally defined. The Institute also sees a need to recognise that, within this multi-level concept, there must be cross-level team-work and integration of the levels in order to ensure consistency and maximise institution-wide benefit. Such models of leadership demand whole-of-organisational commitment.

Early signs are that the sector is keen to come to grips with this approach to leadership. Many promising project proposals were received in response to a call for expressions of interest. Two projects have been funded to date, and a further call for proposals for 2006–8 has been initiated. It is anticipated that much will be learned from these projects in terms of change management.

Some possible barriers to change

None of us lives in a perfect world. There are always risks in the implementation of change and the Carrick Institute's plans are no exception. Some of these risks are within the control of the Institute; for example, poor communication is the enemy of effective reform therefore maintaining the quality of communication has been important during the planning phase and will remain important well into the future. Other risks are not so easily controlled by the Institute itself: rather, they are issues that need to be taken into consideration in all of its activities. For example, there is widespread change across the whole sector at present and, while the Institute is part of the reform process, there is a need for sensitivity to the cynicism generated through some of the not-so-welcome reforms and to the considerable imposition that many of these place on staff workloads. There is also, across the sector, some confusion because of contradictory messages associated with the reforms. At the same time that one policy initiative, namely, the establishment of the Institute, is seen to support excellence in learning and teaching, others, namely the still developing Research Quality Framework (www.dest.gov.au) and the Learning and Teaching Performance Fund (Commonwealth of Australia Department of Education, Science and Training 2003) are seen to be inimical to the achievement of the Institute's objectives.

Lessons from the case study of the establishment of the Carrick Institute

In some senses, given the embryonic nature of the Carrick Institute at the time of writing, it is presumptuous to speculate about what has worked and what has not worked during the planning phase. What is known is that, despite strains associated with the whole enterprise of higher education in the current environment, the sector remains positive about Carrick and its initiatives. The perception of the planning team is that some fundamental features of the planning phase and basic tenets followed during the planning have been important to its success.

The mixed incremental-organic and step-organic model for change appears to have been critical, underpinned as it is by the early work of antecedent organisations, the commitment of the Carrick Institute to collaboration and inclusiveness, and the respect shown to stakeholders. Further, the attention given to evidence documenting what was actually happening in the sector and the development of plans on the basis of this evidence ensured a certain robustness in the planning. This was perhaps most evident in the warm and enthusiastic reception given to the Institute's choice of its strategic priority areas. Finally, the Institute's sensitivity to the sector's need for action to be a reality rather than a blueprint appears to have been appreciated. The projects funded during the planning phase appear to have provided sufficient portent for the sector to remain positive. However, context is important, and the challenge for the future is to sustain momentum in the face of tensions arising from the direction and pace of change in the higher education sector more generally.

Bibliography

Commonwealth of Australia Department of Education, Science and Training (2002) *Higher Education at the Crossroads*, Ministerial Discussion Paper, Canberra: DEST.

Commonwealth of Australia Department of Education, Science and Training (2002) *Striving for Quality: Learning, Teaching and Scholarship*, Ministerial Discussion Paper, Canberra: DEST.

Commonwealth of Australia Department of Education, Science and Training (2003) *Our Universities: Backing Australia's Future*, Canberra: DEST Higher Education Consultancy Group.

Feeny, D. and Ruddle, K. (1997) *Transforming the Organization: New Approaches to Management, Measurement and Leadership*, Oxford: Templeton College.

Hicks, O. (2004) *Composite Report on Projects Funded through the Australian Universities Teaching Committee 2000–2003*, report commissioned by the AUTC, Canberra: DEST.

James, R., McInnes, C. and Devlin, M. (2002) *Assessing Learning in Australian Universities*, Melbourne: Centre for the Study of Higher Education.

Jaschik, S. (2005) 'Reforming higher education – worldwide', *Inside Higher Education*, October 2005. Available at <http://insidehighered.com/news/2005/10/03/fulbright> (accessed 12 December 2005).

McKenzie, J., Alexander, S., Harper, C. & Anderson, S. (2005) *Dissemination, Adoption and Adaptation of Project Innovations in Higher Education*, report commissioned by AUTC/Carrick Institute, July 2005. Available at <http://www.carrickinstitute.edu.au/carrick/go/pid/1> (accessed 12 December 2005).

Parker, L.H. (2005) 'Learning and teaching in universities: Building on strong foundations', *HERDSA News*, Vol. 26, No. 3, 1–3.

Schofield, A. (2003) *A Note on Major Developments in Relation to Teaching and Learning Initiatives*, Canberra: DEST Higher Education Consultancy Group.

Schofield, A. and Olsen, A. (2000) *A report for AUTC on: An evaluation of the CUTSD initiative*, Canberra: DEST Higher Education Consultancy Group.

Southwell, D., Gannaway, D., Orrell, J., Chalmers, D. and Abraham, C. (2005) *Strategies for Effective Dissemination of Project Outcomes*, report commissioned by AUTC/Carrick Institute. Available at <http://www.carrickinstitute.edu.au/carrick/go/pid/1> (accessed 12 December 2005).

Stevens, K. (2005) *Promoting and Advancing Learning and Teaching in Higher Education: The Messages from the AUQA Reports*, Carrick Institute for Learning and Teaching in Higher Education. Available at <http://www.carrickinstitute.edu.au/carrick/go/pid/1> (accessed 12 December 2005).

Tagg, J. (2003) *The Learning Paradigm College*, Boston: Anker Publishing.

Chapter 4

Assessment and change in higher education

Craig McInnis

Introduction

The subject of assessing student learning is frequently ignored or, at best, marginalised in many studies of learning and teaching in higher education. Worse, assessment is intimately associated in the minds of many academics with the relentless drudgery of marking assignments and examinations of increasingly large classes. More often than not, it is an add-on component in the curriculum design process that starts with decisions about what course content should be selected, and then how the teaching might be organised. For students, assessment is usually associated with a high anxiety test of their capacity to operate under pressure in an examination room. It is often the primary driver of their highly pragmatic and strategic approach to learning, and their understanding of what a programme of study is about.

This chapter provides a case study of a nation-wide project to reposition student assessment as a strategic tool for enhancing teaching and learning. The Assessing Learning Project (James *et al.* 2002) was commissioned, along with a number of other national projects, by the Australian Universities Teaching Committee (AUTC) in 2000. The AUTC was replaced by the Carrick Institute for Learning and Teaching in 2004.

Over almost three years, the Assessing Learning Project challenged universities in Australia to take a closer look at the place of assessment in their teaching management plans, stimulated individual academics to rethink their teaching habits and assumptions, and persuaded policy-makers to fund ongoing projects to sustain innovations in approaches to assessment. An independent evaluation of the project (Hicks 2004) described it as one of the most widely known and used of all intervention projects at that time nationally, and concluded that 'the usefulness to the sector of this project is immense'.

In its proposal to the AUTC in 2000, the project team argued that, in the rapidly changing context in which students learn, approaches to assessment were largely underestimated and generally poorly understood. There was, at that time, a surprising lack of theoretical and empirical work to inform the contemporary issues identified in the AUTC project brief. Indeed, it was observed that, despite the plethora of innovative projects funded by government and universities over the previous six or seven years, few had directly targeted student assessment.

This was a curious gap given that the assessment of student learning outcomes is pivotal to the success of most teaching innovations in higher education. It says a lot about the taken-for-grantedness of assessment policy and practice. Assessment is such a powerful driver of student learning behaviour that it has the potential to make or break the efforts of academics to redesign their programmes to encourage more effective learning.

The context

The acknowledged impact of the Assessing Learning Project cannot be understood without an account of the broader context in higher education at the time it was commissioned. Indeed, it can be argued that the failure of intervention projects can often be attributed to the failure to appreciate and utilise the changing national policy context. The first of these 'imperatives to renew assessment practices' was the pressure Australian universities were under to assure the government, and the community, that they were preparing students for the workplace with the development of generic skills beyond subject knowledge and technical competencies, such as communication and teamwork skills. The government required all universities to develop clear statements of the generic attributes of their graduates. Little thought had been given as to how these skills might be assessed in programmes of study.

At that time, there was also a major public debate about the perceived growth in plagiarism, particularly amongst international students, and also with the ease of copying from online sources. Fear of this apparent threat to academic standards was heightened during the project by a press campaign against particular universities over supposed 'soft-marking' of fee-paying students. Related to this, was the new national quality assurance process just underway, with some uncertainty as to how far the newly established Australian Quality Assurance Agency (AUQA) would be concerned with the assessment of student work and the setting of standards.

The changing context of learning and teaching also created an environment in which assessment required rethinking. Larger class sizes was the most obvious issue affecting the quality of assessment. Deteriorating staff:student ratios were placing pressure on academic staff to reduce assessment demands on their time to cope with the task of grading. Innovative approaches to learning and teaching were rapidly being adopted, such as the use of online assessment and group activities in the classroom, that were beginning to raise questions about conventional forms of assessment.

There were also major shifts in the nature of student involvement with the university (McInnis 2002). National reports showed that more full-time students were working part-time, and those who were working were working more hours (McInnis et al. 2000). For academics, that meant stronger demands from students for flexibility in the setting of assessment tasks and deadlines. Many felt they were placed in the position of compromising standards by extending deadlines and reducing the length of assignments.

Finally, soon after the project commenced, a national debate over academic standards threw the issue of student assessment into sharp relief with concerns about grading inconsistencies and community confidence in standards. The importance of Australia's credibility with international fee-paying students was at the forefront of media attention. This prompted the AUTC to approach the project directors to extend the brief.

Australia was not alone in the lack of attention to assessment in universities. A report from the Quality Assurance Agency for Higher Education (2003: 27) in the United Kingdom summarised 2,904 reviews of individual academic subjects conducted between 1993 and 2001 across 62 subject areas in UK universities. The report concluded that 'the single intervention by universities and colleges that would improve the quality of the student experience would be the improvement of assessment practices'. During the initial rounds of visits, the UK reviewers 'commented frequently on the narrow range of assessment methods employed, suggesting that an over-reliance on examinations did not allow students to demonstrate their achievement of all learning outcomes'.

The project brief

The broad aim of the AUTC was to promote quality and excellence in teaching in Australian universities. In 2000, the AUTC commissioned the Assessing Learning Project to:

- examine and report on new and emerging issues in assessment but, importantly, to 'avoid going over old ground'
- strategically disseminate practical resources to assist academic staff with contemporary assessment issues
- prepare advice to the AUTC on the relationship between assessment and the demonstration of standards.

A key expectation of the project was that it would provide a national forum for the discussion and dissemination of ideas related to assessment. The specific tasks of the project reflected the context. The project was to investigate and report on:

- the scale of the problem of plagiarism
- issues and best practice in online assessment of student work
- issues and best practice in group assessment
- the impact of class size on forms of assessment
- the impact of the changing nature of student expectations and engagement on forms of assessment and standards
- advice for students unfamiliar with methods of assessment in Australia

- advice to academics on ways of improving assessment in the context of large classes and changing student expectations.

It is perhaps indicative of the approach of the project team that it suggested an additional task to the AUTC – to analyse the changing context in which academics were working and their orientations towards assessment practices. It was felt that this was essential to underpinning an effective dissemination process.

As noted above, the brief was extended by the AUTC to 'investigate and report on issues and practice in the grading of student achievement and the assurance of standards'. For this additional task, the project was asked to examine: the processes by which assessment systems and methods were designed, including moderation; processes for determining levels of student achievement; methods for reporting student achievement, including grading scales; and the institutional policies and systems that directly and indirectly influence assessment and grading practices, including systemic obstacles to change.

The project method

It is more usual for evaluation and innovations projects to be conducted independently, the first hopefully informing the second. While not unique, the Assessing Learning Project had these two activities running simultaneously – an investigation to gather evidence, and a project to promote change.

There were four major elements to the project:

1   The development of a series of case studies of assessment issues in universities. The case studies involved visits to a carefully selected cross-section of departments in eight universities across four states of Australia. They included interviews with academics and students.
2   A collection of examples of good practice in assessment. These were gathered from responses to a national press advertisement, as well as from the case studies.
3   High-profile discussion forums conducted in each capital city. These were preceded by a widely disseminated discussion paper prepared by the project directors. As many as seventy university-nominated leaders and experts attended in each state.
4   A highly strategic dissemination programme primarily based on a publication that included ideas, strategies and resources, complemented by a project website with additional materials.

A key element of the investigation of the issues of academic standards was an invitational forum held with fourteen experts and leaders in higher education policy and research to consider national options. Again, a discussion paper was prepared by the project directors to guide and stimulate discussion at this forum (McInnis and James 2002).

The project was co-directed by two senior academics (James and McInnis) attesting to its ambitious national reach and complexity. Two other staff supported the activities on a part-time basis, delegated with specific responsibilities such as fieldwork coordination, and one member of staff (Devlin) was given the task of preparing guides on five assessment issues for publication. Particularly important in the Australian geopolitical context was the recognition that other universities should have the opportunity to play a role, and the University of Western Australia was invited to assist with research and the forum organisation in that state. Likewise, telephone interviews were conducted with universities unable to send delegates to the capital city forums.

A steering committee was formed as part of the AUTC contract to give direction to the project, and to meet accountability requirements. An international expert, Mantz Yorke, was engaged to provide an independent and critical eye on the project and participate in the state forums.

Challenges for the management of the project

The many challenges presented by this project were initially daunting, not least of which was the charge noted above to 'avoid going over old ground'. Some colleagues expressed disappointment that they had the least sexy of the projects being funded by the AUTC. One of the other projects commissioned by AUTC concerned the issues of teaching large classes – an obvious everyday cause of stress for academics eagerly seeking answers. As it turned out, the assessment project raised the profile of the issues and generated change well beyond everyone's expectations, including those of the AUTC.

The main elements in this successful intervention were shaped by the belief that old assessment issues had to be set in a new context. Unlike the introduction of new technologies or major shifts in pedagogies, the project was essentially a national effort to start a new cycle of review and renewal. The inherent systemic conservatism of academics and students was acknowledged as a basic challenge. We predicted, and our investigations confirmed, that many students do not feel they have been properly assessed unless they have a formal examination.

Among other challenges was the competition for the attention of the academic community in the face of increasing workloads, and the multiple demands of large classes and new technologies was high on the agenda. A national study of academics in Australia (McInnis 2000) also pointed to the need to review approaches to assessment. This included the reduced time academics have to devote to monitoring student progress and providing more informative feedback on academic tasks. The results of the survey revealed considerable discrepancies in the aspects of student performance academics currently assess, and those they think should be assessed. The results indicated that academics felt that depth of knowledge was the most frequently assessed aspect of learning in their area, followed closely by the ability to think critically, written communication skills and problem-solving skills. More than half said they assessed verbal communication skills, and a significant minority (38 per cent) assessed the ability to memorise and fewer (31 per cent) used assessment for diagnostic purposes. However, only 18 per cent believed that the ability of students to memorise ought to be assessed, while 63 per cent believe that assessment should involve the diagnosis of students' strengths and weaknesses.

As a national project, it was a challenge to deal with a diverse range of 38 universities, with various combinations of disciplines and fields of study, as well as significant differences in student profiles. It was inevitable that a level of generality of advice was needed that would not meet the needs of all interest groups. The primary goal was to influence the everyday practice of mainstream academics. The strategy from the outset was to present the issues and findings in a succinct and accessible form to the widest possible audience. The trade-off was that those already familiar with the issues would not find the level of sophistication they needed in the discussion and resources.

There was also a challenge in reaching the locus of change in the universities. Innovations go nowhere if they become the responsibility of marginalised organisational units or individuals. In some cases we had to take the risk of offending people who felt they were the natural homes for the assessment project, since we discovered they had little influence in their universities. Related was the challenge of recognising the limitations of the project. Capturing the attention of the academic community with a new set of resources is one thing: knowing how much scope there is for change is another. Taking a long-term perspective to set the foundations for sustainable change was uppermost in the project design. The project team was highly conscious of the fact that so many initiatives of this kind create a lot of noise but sink without trace.

Making the intervention work: the main elements of success

The project method outlined above is really just the basic formula and would not surprise anyone involved in similar national interventions. It does not give much sense of the strategic thinking behind the method that made it one of the most high profile and successful of its kind. Some of the elements emerged as the project evolved, for example, a constant appraisal of progress and responses to issues raised in the capital city forums generated new ideas.

A planned approach

Starting with the end in mind is the key to effective planning. Ultimately, sustainability is the only worthwhile measure of a successful innovation project. Russell Edgerton (2003) from the Pew Foundation observed that 'the most effective interventions are those that generate a chain reaction of other constructive changes'. He makes the further point that, of the many obstacles to reform ('it goes in fits and starts'), wishful thinking has a blocking effect. The Assessing Learning

Project had a variety of reality checks built into its process, including: the carefully chosen advisory committee; the call for submissions; public forums; and testing ideas with academics in their workplace.

The guidelines for institutional change provided in the assessing learning resource book are basically the same steps applied at the national level (Borland 2002; McInnis 2004). On the face of it, this seemed likely to be stating the obvious. It turned out, however, that we had underestimated the need to provide skills for strategic thinking in universities for academics with ideas for change. Implementation advice is generally missing from innovations projects of this kind. The key steps in the process include:

- making the need for change explicit
- demonstrating the tangible benefits that flow from change
- recognising the everyday reality of obstacles to change
- raising awareness of the issues and generating consensus about the need for improvement
- promoting change on multiple fronts
- providing expertise and support
- connecting change to the national and institutional accountability and reward systems.

Some of the more central of these intervention steps are discussed further in the notes that follow.

Dissemination

The dissemination process drove much of the thinking about the project. We took the view that dissemination is not something that happens after the data is gathered. Some of the most successful policy change agents argue that for every dollar spent on research, another is spent on dissemination. The success of this and similar projects depended very heavily on gaining sector-wide recognition and support. Projects of this kind sometimes seem to disappear from public view while the project team goes about its business. When the report is finished, it then requires a substantial effort to revive interest. Keeping the Assessing Learning Project alive in the minds of the target groups was especially important. At the same time, maintaining the momentum of the dissemination process without saturating the sector is not an easy task.

Dissemination is not just a matter of gaining profile and support; there are significant advantages in contributing to the national policy discussions as they arise, for example, the Australian Senate enquiry. Ongoing dissemination through the life of the project also provides a focal point for stakeholders wanting to provide more evidence or advice, or examples of good practice, which they will do if they see the intervention process as an open and highly visible enterprise.

The substantial 'high production values' booklet produced as the final product was distributed to all universities, with somewhere between 50 to 200 copies for each. Hicks (2004: 30) provides an independent evaluation of the booklet:

> The hard copy publication was designed specifically to engage with its target audiences in the academic community. It is short and almost atomistic in structure, in that it contains very brief 'grabs' of ideas and actions. It covers a wide spectrum of issues, some with appeal to individual academics and some to heads of organizational units within institutions. The hard copy document has strong links to the website. The address appears prominently on the front page and again approximately ten more times within the document. Readers are encouraged to visit the site.

Multiple copies of the handbook were sent to all vice-chancellors, and individual copies sent to key people who might perhaps have been significant change agents, that is, deputy vice-chancellors (teaching and learning), directors of academic development units, and designated contact people for the AUTC. The core elements of the website accurately reflect the scope and intent of the project. The booklet and website provide: an argument for rethinking assessment; reminders of basic pedagogical principles for effective assessment; case studies of good practice; and advice on leading organisational change. All the key material was made available in downloadable portable document format (pdf) files allowing easy printing and reproduction for change agents in universities and departments. PowerPoint templates were provided to enable these people to tailor the presentations to the local context.

Hicks (2004: 29) also identified a number of aspects of the project that fell short of the expectations of both the project team and the sector. While the website was highly successful in many respects, it probably did not realise its potential. The AUTC was not able to fund a site that would require ongoing maintenance. This meant that it did not provide possibilities for conversations and links elsewhere 'for those seeking a more detailed and sophisticated approach to assessment' (Hicks 2004: 29). It also meant that only a limited number of disciplines could be represented in the case study section and opportunities may have been lost for the development of networks around the system.

Understanding the target groups and how to engage them

Engaging with the target groups actually started with the formation of a steering committee. The profile of the committee is a good test of the understanding of the groups the project aims to influence. The government and university groups represented on the committee need to be thought of as influential change agents in their own right. It is a major error of project management to allow such committees or panels to fall into the narrow role of watchdog. The co-directors had conducted twenty or so national projects between them at the time, and had seen how advisory or steering committees can add significant value to a project; typically, the ministry representatives and academics from other universities were of enormous assistance. The project directors spent considerable time constructing a steering committee that would give it as much flexibility as possible (since it was embarking on new territory in some respects) but, more importantly, creating a group of stakeholders who would actively support the project and give it sector-wide credibility. The project team kept the steering committee regularly informed and sought their views either face-to-face or by teleconference.

As indicated in the list of challenges, the project team had to identify and reach the locus point of change in each university. Obviously this could not address the organisational and cultural idiosyncrasies of each of the 38 universities. Instead, we worked on the assumption that there was no single best way of tapping into the organisational dynamics for change, and that diverse approaches to gathering information, securing support and disseminating ideas for change was key: put simply, what works in some institutions does not work for others, and a formulaic approach to change management is generally constraining.

While the mainstream academic was the primary focus of attention for every-day resources, the academic leaders were singled out with a separate set of activities to ensure that they would make an investment in the project from the outset. The independent evaluation of the project (Hicks 2004) concluded that there was a high level of awareness amongst senior staff across the system of the project and its resources.

The motives and interests of academic leaders relative to their positions had to be appreciated. In a sense, the most fundamental of good teaching principles were followed: start with where the learner/change agent is. Each target group has its own needs, all have busy lives, and getting them to pay attention to requires a creative approach – and persistence. Understanding the daily reality of academic workload and competing pressures on priorities was crucial to the design and implementation of the dissemination programme. It is a fatal error of change agents to assume that the importance of an initiative is self-evident. In developing the dissemination strategy outlined above, the project directors considered factors such as:

- the wide range and different types of need and levels of influence, for example, casual teaching staff, department heads and academic developers
- the merit in short, sharp, easily accessible advice on assessment issue and implementing good practice
- the practical value of ready-to-use resources and checklists.

Making a case for change

The project team worked hard at giving a significant edge to the conventional issues surrounding assessment. The context was characterised as a 'new era for assessment in higher education' and was explicitly addressed as such from start to finish. Restating the fundamentals of assessment in ways that capture attention and convince the most cynical of academics that there is a genuine problem was vital. The notion that the assessment of student learning outcomes is pivotal to the success of the many teaching innovations funded in higher education was a key factor in attracting the interest of the opinion leaders and change agents in universities.

The case for change needs to be supported with a foundation of strong but not esoteric theory, spelling out first principles in plain language, and providing meaningful empirical evidence. University leaders are best equipped to lead change if they are well-informed about the issues and if they are able to draw on sound pedagogical principles. They are particularly keen to use empirical evidence so long as it is presented in a readily accessible form. Likewise, academics are far more inclined to respond positively to strong, evidence-based material, but they will also vehemently dismiss a project if it is packaged as a 'corporate fashion statement' or is jargon-ridden. They particularly object to the use of levers for change such as the implied threats from external bodies, and their resistance to this kind of pressure is well known.

The project team had a high level of credibility across the sector from its own national research, and a good deal of empirical evidence about the attitudes and preferences of academics and students on assessment policies and practices. However, it was strategic and essential to get fresh evidence, particularly since we had argued that the context was undergoing rapid change. Academics were interviewed across a range of disciplines. It was useful in forums to place before them exactly what students were saying they valued in assessment. These were distilled in the project book to just a few key points: for example, we concluded that students value clear and unambiguous expectations; they want assessment tasks to be authentic, that is, 'real'; and they value some choice and flexibility. The student preference for 'negotiated assessment' became a widely contested issue.

Conclusions

The unifying question throughout the project, the policy and implementation advice, and the development of the resources was 'how can assessment be designed so as to improve student learning?'. The ongoing trends uncovered or stimulated by the various activities included an increase in policy activity by universities as the project developed, but there was clearly more scope for stronger alignment of assessment policies and assessment practices. Most universities initiated investigations into plagiarism and developed academic honesty policies and counter-measures. A culture of testing by examination remained strong but there appeared to be greater acceptance of the need for low-stakes, early assessment of students for the purposes of feedback, despite the demands on academic time. Group work and group assessment was increasing but the project provided strong evidence that this needed careful handling given the clear message that students were not happy with the management of group work, and particularly the forms of assessment commonly used.

At the time the project commenced, the potential of online assessment was far from transforming the process of learning and teaching; the project identified significant gaps in the pedagogy underpinning the use of new technologies. Finally, it was clear from the investigations that there were many implicit, informal collegial mechanisms for assuring academic standards, but that this was not sufficient to gain the confidence of the community. Most universities have since embarked on developing more explicit processes for setting and maintaining standards, although there is still much to be done at the level of disciplines.

Boud (2004: 41) makes the critical observation that 'There are still many universities with entrenched policy ideas that undermine learning outcomes. This is particularly so with regard to assessment.' The entrenched policy ideas to which he refers are very much the product of a lack of analysis of existing practices. Nevertheless, while the long-term evidence of the impact of the Assessing Learning Project is yet to come, the indications are positive. Many universities have since embarked on institution-wide reviews of assessment policy, academic developers and classroom practitioners have been accessing the online resources from the project in remarkable numbers, and student responses to national surveys on the student experience suggest increasing numbers are satisfied with the quality of feedback on their progress they receive.

The independent evaluation of the project (Hicks 2004), noted that almost two-thirds of directors of academic development units in Australia were using resources from the project in a variety of ways, including induction programmes for new staff, presentations to university and faculty policy committees, curriculum design work, and for university or faculty reviews of assessment codes and practices. Indeed, Hicks suggested that 'the impact of the project is likely to be greater than reported'. Of course, the long-term test of the project will be the extent to which academics reposition the role of assessment in the design and delivery of subjects, and the impact that has on the ways students go about learning.

Bibliography

Borland, K. (2002) 'Towards a culture of assessment', in P. Schwartz and G. Webb (eds.) *Assessment: Case Studies, Experience and Practice from Higher Education,* London: Kogan Page.

Boud, D. (2004) 'Creating assessment for learning throughout life', in V. Gil, I. Alarcao and H. Hooghoff (eds.) *Challenges in Teaching and Learning in Higher Education,* Portugal: University of Aveiro.

Edgerton, R. (2003) *Getting from Here to There or the Strategy for Change,* paper presented at the conference Teaching and Learning in Higher Education: New Trends and Innovations, University of Aveiro, Portugal 13–17 April 2003.

Hicks, O. (2004) *Composite Report on Projects Funded through the Australian Universities Teaching Committee 2000–2003.* Available at <http://www.carrickinstitute.edu.au/carrick/go/pid/44> (accessed 12 December 2005).

James, R., McInnis, C. and Devlin, M. (2002) *Assessing Learning in Australian Universities,* Canberra: Australian Universities Teaching Committee.

McInnis, C. (2000) 'Changing perspectives and work practices of academics in Australian universities', in M. Tight (ed.) *International Perspectives on Higher Education Research Vol 1 Academic Work and Life: What it is to be an Academic and How this is Changing,* New York: JAI Elsevier, 117–45.

McInnis, C. (2002) 'Signs of disengagement: responding to the changing work patterns of full-time undergraduates in Australian universities', in J. Enders and O. Fulton (eds.) *Higher Education in the 21ˢᵗ Century,* London: Elsevier.

McInnis, C. (2004) *Connecting Institutional Policies with Practice: Implementing a Learning and Teaching Reform Agenda,* keynote address to the Higher Education Research and Development Society of Australia (HERDSA) Annual Conference Miri Malaysia. July 2004. Available at <http://www.herdsa.org.au/conference2004/> (accessed 12 December 2005).

McInnis, C. and James R. (2002) *Assessment Practices and Academic Standards in Australian Universities,* paper prepared for the invitational symposium on academic standards, the Australian Universities Teaching Committee, University of Melbourne 2002.

McInnis, C., James R. and Hartley, R. (2000) *Trends in the First Year Experience in Australia,* Canberra: Australian Government Publishing Service.

Quality Assurance Agency for Higher Education (2003) *Learning from Subject Review.* Available at <www.qaa.ac.uk> (accessed 12 December 2005).

Chapter 5

Quality assurance and change in higher education

Alison Thair, Patrick Garnett and Susan King

Introduction

This case study examines whole-of-university changes to promote learning and teaching that arise from quality assurance processes. The setting is Edith Cowan University (ECU), Perth, Western Australia, where changes have been driven by external and internal forces. Externally, increasing accountability requirements of the federal government and competitive changes in the higher education environment have influenced change. The University has been responsive to this changing environment, which has occurred concurrently with a greater internal focus on strategic planning and enhanced quality assurance processes.

In Australia, a key government strategy has been the introduction of the Australian Universities Quality Agency (AUQA), which is similar to the British Quality Assurance Agency (QAA). Both are designed to establish accountability for government spending on higher education. In Australia, AUQA provides independent review of university activities, including teaching and learning, every five years. However, its influence extends well beyond the time of review because the preparation of each university's portfolio requires reflection and drives change. Further, the response to the Audit Report requires universities to improve quality assurance processes and outcomes and to provide evidence of action taken in response to the report. This chapter describes how the AUQA review process at ECU became a driving force for change in teaching and learning.

National drivers of change

National policy initiatives that provided the impetus for institutional changes in quality assurance came to prominence in Australia in the early 1990s through the establishment of the Committee for Quality Assurance in Higher Education (CQAHE). The Committee held three rounds of assessments (in 1993, 1994 and 1995) that focused on quality assurance systems in universities. In each of its three years of operation, the CQAHE reported its assessment of institutions in a number of hierarchical bands and published the performance of every Australian university. The reports were widely criticised, but they did identify major areas of weakness and encouraged universities to focus more clearly on the need for continuous improvement and the importance of stakeholders, particularly students. Subsequently, in 1998 the Australian Federal Government requested that universities provide Quality Assurance and Improvement Plans (QAIPs) as part of required educational profile submissions, which were published by the then Department of Education, Training and Youth Affairs (DETYA) (1999). QAIPs were expected to reflect an institution's commitment to the delivery of quality services in a number of core areas including learning and teaching, and to include data from two annual national surveys of students: the Course Experience Questionnaire (CEQ) and the Graduate Destination Survey (GDS). Both surveys are coordinated by Graduate Careers Australia.

The CEQ is a survey of graduates of Australian universities that seeks information about the graduates' attitudes towards their courses and the skills they acquired at university. Specifically, graduates provide information about their satisfaction with the course, the quality of teaching experienced within the course and generic skills developed as part of the course. The GDS is an annual review of graduates' employment status, type of work gained and further study undertaken. It identifies the graduates' success in obtaining employment or further study opportunities.

The CEQ and GDS outcomes have become important drivers for change because they are used extensively in privately produced prospective university student guides. Importantly, they are now used by government to distribute significant amounts of funding based on learning and teaching performance. The Learning and Teaching Performance Fund is designed to reward institutions demonstrating excellence in learning and teaching. Funding is based largely on a quantitative assessment of performance in three areas: student satisfaction (CEQ data), outcomes (GDS data) and success (first year retention and student progress rates).

In 2000 the federal government established AUQA with a mandate to conduct regular audits of self-accrediting higher education institutions covering all institutional activities including learning and teaching (Department of Education, Training and Youth Affairs 2000). Public audit reports provide information on the processes and practices of universities and include commendations, affirmations and recommendations. Universities are expected to implement strategies to improve quality assurance processes and to provide publicly accessible progress reports 18 months after the publication of their audit report. This national focus on quality was a significant influence on higher education in Australia, and the prospect of an AUQA audit focused the attention of universities on what they were doing to address quality in core areas of their work, including teaching and learning.

Institutional drivers of change: ECU case study

Teaching and learning have always been central to the mission of Edith Cowan University. However, there is no doubt that the external quality agenda has facilitated a university-wide commitment to systematic strategic planning, and the development of the Quality@ECU framework (www.ecu.edu.au/Quality@ECU/) has focused institutional attention on developing a holistic University approach to enhancing the quality of learning and teaching. At the start of the process that culminated in the AUQA review, and consistent with change management literature (Kotter 1995; Beer *et al.* 1990; Whittles and Lovell 1994), ECU leadership identified a range of factors identified as critical in driving institutional change. These included:

- establishing a sense of urgency
- creating a strategic vision or plan
- communicating the vision and empowering others to execute the plan
- aligning organisational structures, systems and processes
- evaluation and review.

This brief case study elucidates how each of these factors was addressed and identifies how the development of a quality framework served to enhance learning and teaching at ECU.

Establishing a sense of urgency

The introductory phase of the change process at ECU involved intense periods of staff consultation, including staff residential workshops, seminars and planning meetings, with considerable opportunity for staff input into the process. Kotter (1995) describes 'a sense of urgency', which he identifies as an important first step required for organisational transformation. These staff meetings and discussions focused on ECU's positioning in the higher education marketplace; the need to develop a distinctive educational 'brand' and build significant course strengths; and the importance of adopting a student service culture throughout the institution. These activities helped to develop that 'sense of urgency'.

Creating a strategic vision or plan

ECU developed its first strategic plan in 1998 and shortly afterwards adopted a university-wide approach to quality. These dual initiatives fostered a culture of continuous quality improvement. Both the first ECU Strategic Plan 1998–2002 and the subsequent ECU Strategic Plan 2003–7: A Stronger ECU (www.ecu.edu.au/GPPS/ecuonly/StratPlan2003_2007.pdf) placed significant emphasis on enhancing the quality of learning and teaching and aligning ECU's learning environment with its mission and vision to become a national leader in education for the knowledge-based service professions. These plans focused particularly on the following:

- the development of significant course strengths
- enhancing flexibility in student choice
- the provision of relevant knowledge, skills and attributes (i.e. authentic curriculum and assessment practices)
- stronger links with industry and the professions
- the innovative application of new information technologies.

Beer *et al.*(1990) suggest that alignment of plans (together with structures, systems and processes, see below) is critical to achieving transformational change. At ECU considerable effort was expended in aligning planning at various levels within the University with the University's Strategic Plan. The Planning at ECU Framework supports a single strategic plan for the University, with several second-level functional plans addressing core activities of the University. One of these plans, the ECU Teaching and Learning Functional Plan (www.ecu.edu.au/LDS/directorate/about/TLFP.pdf), guides and leads change in the University's teaching and learning. The ECU Teaching and Learning Functional Plan then informs the teaching and learning components of individual faculty and school operational plans.

Communicating the vision and empowering others to execute the plan

Several leading theorists (Kotter 1995; Southwell *et al.* 2005) suggest that one important component of leading transformational change is that the vision is widely communicated. Following University Council's approval of the strategic plan, staff forums on each campus, faculty and school meetings and planning days were used to ensure that the contents of the plan were widely communicated throughout the institution.

At University level, a Learning and Development Services Office was created. This was initially under the leadership of the Deputy Vice-Chancellor (Academic) and subsequently the Pro Vice-Chancellor (Teaching and Learning). Within each faculty an Associate Dean (Teaching and Learning) was created, together with a Teaching and Learning Office, to give effect to the University plan.

Alignment of organisational structures, systems and processes

Organisational alignment, including structures, systems and processes, is seen as critical to transformational change (see, for example, Beer *et al.* 1990). The alignment of University Plans for teaching and learning across the University has been described previously. This section will outline how other University structures and processes were aligned to ensure that change was effected throughout the University.

Organisational structures

A significant outcome of the 1998–2002 strategic plan and concomitant (1998) faculty reconfiguration was the establishment of a Teaching and Learning Office within each faculty headed by an Associate Dean and an integrated committee structure that supported and implemented the University's teaching and learning objectives. This alignment of organisational structures was an important element in embedding the change agenda and focusing on quality throughout the University. Associate Deans of Teaching and Learning acted as agents of change and champions of teaching and learning throughout the institution. Together with their Executive Deans, they are empowered to implement change and focus on enhanced quality in teaching and learning in their own faculties.

Committee structures are an important feature of organisational alignment. Like most universities, at ECU the Academic Board plays a pivotal role in academic quality and it is the Academic Board's responsibility to ensure that the University has a clear, rational, and accessible set of policies and practices underpinning the provision of teaching and learning. The Academic Board has, as one of three subsidiary committees, the Curriculum, Teaching and Learning Committee (CTLC). The Curriculum, Teaching and Learning Committee is responsible for the ECU Teaching and Learning Functional Plan and ensuring the quality of University courses and units. It establishes the University's objectives in teaching and learning and has formulated a range of policies and procedures aimed at achieving high standards and quality outcomes in teaching and learning. Whittles and Lovell (1994) suggest that the establishment of clear objectives is seen as an essential component in managing planned change.

Quality processes

ECU's approach to the promotion of learning and teaching accords with its quality assurance framework which adopts a Plan-Do-Review-Improve (PDRI) model (Figure 5.1).

The Quality@ECU Framework is articulated through seven quality principles adapted from the Australian Business Excellence Framework (ABEF) (see http://www.businessexcellenceaustralia.com.au/GROUPS/ABEF/) and relates to:

- improving core activities (e.g. teaching and learning, research and creativity, professional and community engagement, and university service)
- aligning activities, budgets and resources with the strategic plan
- demonstrating leadership, innovation and enterprise in all activities
- knowing the needs of students, other customers, stakeholders and markets
- valuing and investing in staff
- using data, information and knowledge to inform decision making
- improving outcomes.

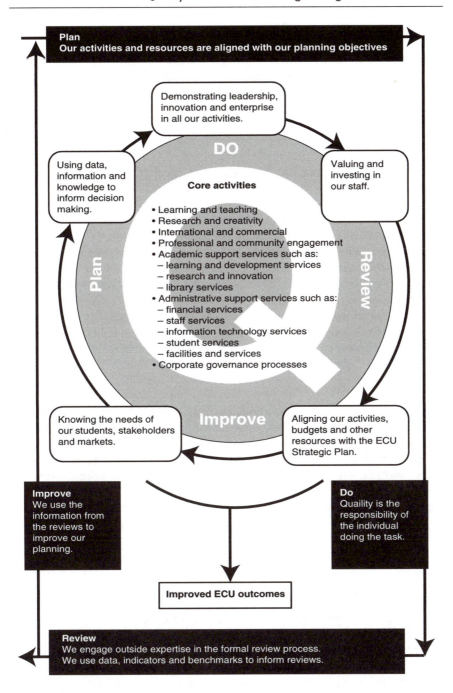

Figure 5.1 Edith Cowan University's Quality@ECU Framework: relationship of the seven principles

ECU's quality model is embedded into the core activities of the University, particularly within its planning and review frameworks and all staff are encouraged to be responsible for quality and to improve processes, services and outcomes. The adoption of the Quality@ECU Framework has led to a culture of continuous quality improvement, which has been an important element in facilitating the University's change agenda.

Policies

Following the development of University and Faculty Teaching and Learning Plans, new teaching and learning policies have emerged. These include:

- the approval and review of courses and units
- a comprehensive unit and teaching evaluation policy
- policies relating to the selection, probation and promotion of academic staff
- the establishment of a teaching and learning performance fund
- the provision of grants to undertake teaching and learning innovations and developments
- the enhancement of the teaching and learning environment through the innovative use of technology
- a range of processes for recognising teaching excellence.

Course and unit approvals

A specific example of how such policies may be used to promote learning and teaching may be seen in the Course and Unit Approval and Review Policy that is designed to ensure that courses and units offered by the University are of high quality. Within this policy, clarity is provided regarding levels of delegation of course and unit approval and the process is managed through the University's home-grown electronic Course Management System (CMS). This system requires course and unit developers to complete a range of requirements, including identifying the purpose of the course, the need and probable demand for the course, the principles underlying the course, and the alignment of the course with University and Faculty Plans.

Unit and teaching evaluation

The University's Unit and Teaching Evaluation Instrument (UTEI) Policy mandates that the UTEI be administered in every unit on each occasion that the unit is offered. The purpose of applying the UTEI is to obtain feedback from students about their perceptions of the unit, the learning environment and the quality of teaching provided by lecturers and, where appropriate, supporting tutors. The data obtained from the administration of the UTEI is used to improve the quality of units, including the quality of teaching, to improve the performance of individual staff in relation to their teaching, and to inform the assessment of academic staff in processes including Management for Performance, Probation, and Academic Promotions.

Staffing policies

At Edith Cowan University all academic staff are required, following appointment, to participate in the University's 'Professional Development for Tertiary Teachers' programme. For experienced tertiary teachers new to ECU, this programme is designed to allow teachers to come quickly to grips with the ethos, facilities, services, policies and procedures associated with teaching and learning at ECU. A more structured programme for academic staff new to tertiary teaching is offered across a semester and is equivalent to a full 15 credit point unit at the University and can be used for credit within the Graduate Certificate in Education (Tertiary Teaching).

The University also provides a wide range of teaching-related professional development activities, including training for Course and Unit Coordinators, training in specific teaching and learning strategies, and faculty- and university-based teaching and learning forums. ECU's Academic Staff Probation Policy also reinforces the University's commitment to excellence in teaching and learning. To obtain 'ongoing' status, staff are required to highlight their performance on four key components of academic work, with specific attention to teaching and learning.

Another important driver in emphasising the importance of teaching and learning at ECU is the University's Academic Staff Promotion Policy. Consistent with this Policy, staff are generally rated on four criteria: teaching and learning; research and creativity; professional and community engagement; and service to the University (including enterprise on behalf of the University). Performance on these four elements is differentially weighted within certain allowed ranges. Performance on the teaching and learning criterion can be weighted up to 70 per cent for staff seeking promotion to level B and up to 60 per cent for level C (Senior Lecturer) and level D (Associate Professor). Thus performance on teaching and learning can be a major contribution to an applicant's chances of being promoted.

Teaching and learning performance fund

A performance fund based on teaching and learning outcomes also serves to focus the attention of school and faculty leadership on work practices that influence the quality of teaching and learning. As part of its budget allocation process, ECU now allocates approximately 5 per cent of faculty budgets on the basis of a 'teaching and learning performance index' that incorporates elements from CEQ data (good teaching and overall satisfaction), student retention, and performance on the ECU UTEI.

Teaching and learning grants

Each year ECU provides staff opportunities to apply for teaching and learning grants to help finance initiatives that will benefit teaching and learning. These small grants are intended to help academics foster some aspect of their teaching with the express purpose of improving learning outcomes for students. Each year Learning and Development Services, with input from Associate Deans of Teaching & Learning, establishes a list of priority target areas for these grants. These grants are often supplemented by individual faculties and schools.

Commitment to enhancing the teaching and learning environment through the innovative use of technology

As part of its new policy environment, ECU has developed a Flexible Learning Policy. One aspect of flexible learning has been the creation of online learning opportunities in significant numbers of units, which provide students with additional flexibility and support. These can range from the provision of online learning resources (e.g. unit descriptions and study guides, examination information, assessment information and reading lists) through to units in which all interactions between staff and students, education content, learning activities, assessment and support services are integrated and delivered online.

As part of this commitment, the University has created MyECU, an institution-wide online learning environment using the Blackboard Learning Management System. Since its installation, Blackboard has proved to be a stable and popular tool for building, managing and delivering online units and the University is looking at ways to customise this technology further. Staff and student use of this resource is increasing at a rapid rate.

ECU has continued its commitment to the innovative use of IT to enhance teaching and learning through its association with IBM and the ECU Advantage project. This project is designed to provide for the integration of new technologies into mainstream teaching and learning practices by giving students affordable access to high specification laptop computers and by providing wireless connectivity through a campus-wide wireless network environment. An evaluation of the pilot phase of this project showed strong support from students, making real differences to students' perceptions of their own learning, their ability to develop as independent learners and their organisational skills.

Teaching and learning awards

The Vice-Chancellor's Awards for Excellence in Teaching were developed specifically to encourage and recognise excellence in teaching. These awards are highly sought after with several winners subsequently applying for Australian Awards for University Teaching (AAUT), with some success. An important element of these awards is the possibility of applying on an individual or team basis. Faculties have also developed strategies for recognising and rewarding innovation and excellence in teaching, such as Teaching Activity Indices and various faculty awards.

Evaluation and review

Evaluation and review is a critical component of assessing and reinforcing the change process (Whittles and Lovell 1994). ECU has a comprehensive review process. Annual Reviews (www.ecu.edu.au/Quality@ECU/annual_review.html) of every faculty and centre are undertaken, which include preparation by the faculty/centre of a self-appraisal report that is submitted to the Vice Chancellery Team and is then the subject of discussion between that team and senior staff of the faculty/centre. The self-appraisal report includes reference to several achievements, particularly in core activities including learning and teaching, progress in the closing of previously identified and agreed gaps, and consideration of future priorities, setting these in the context of the Strategic Plan.

Area of Scholarship (School) Reviews (www.ecu.edu.au/Quality @ECU/aosr.html) take place on a five-yearly cycle. They consider all aspects of a school's activities including teaching and learning. Area of Scholarship Reviews comprise:

- a self-assessment report
- assessment of that report and a validation visit by an external panel of experts
- a Panel Report
- preparation by the school of an action plan to address recommendations within the Panel Report
- approval of the action plan by the Academic Board
- a 12-month anniversary report to the Academic Board on progress against the action plan.

Self-assessment encourages ownership and responsibility for the school's performance, which Jary and Parker (1998) consider to be critical to successful implementation of change management.

Formal course reviews are required, at a minimum of every five years, normally prior to an Area of Scholarship (School) Review. These course reviews must assess the health of the course, including enrolment numbers and retention rates, performance indicators including data from the Graduate Careers Australia Course Experience Questionnaire (good teaching, generic skills, overall satisfaction) and Graduate Destination Survey results (employment and further study rates), information from Course Coordinator Reports, results of professional accreditation, and any relevant Triennial Offshore Program Reviews. An outcome of these Course Reviews is a set of recommendations that are considered by the relevant Faculty Board.

Have the changes worked?

The quality framework and approach described in this case study has contributed in a major way to building a culture of continuous improvement with regard to teaching and learning at Edith Cowan University. The change process was driven by a concurrence of forces, including a federal government reform agenda, an increasingly competitive higher education environment and University leadership committed to enhanced strategic planning and quality assurance. The process has been highly successful, with ECU now enjoying a differentiated institutional profile, an improved local and national reputation, some significant course strengths, enhanced teaching and learning outcomes and a greater focus on the importance of teaching and learning throughout the University. While the beginning phases of the change process – 'establishing a sense of urgency' – resulted in considerable anxiety in many parts of the University, the changes are now widely accepted and well embedded throughout the institution.

In March 2004 the University was externally audited by AUQA, with the Audit Panel meeting with more than 250 staff, students and other stakeholders. The ensuing AUQA Audit Report contained 23 commendations recognising the University's strategic approach, particularly its diverse and differentiated programmes and its focus on the service professions, and crediting it with good practices in its core and enabling processes. The AUQA Audit Report endorsed ECU's commitment to teaching (AUQA 2004: 3), emphasising that:

> The history of ECU is one of strong commitment to teaching and to students. This commitment is clearly evident today, is appreciated by students, and is well supported with resources such as the valuable Teaching@ECU booklet, designed to mainstream best practices; and also is evident through support provided by the Learning Development Services.

Edith Cowan University has made considerable progress in its journey to develop a reputation for excellence in teaching and learning, build a culture of continuous improvement with a vision of becoming 'a national leader in the education of learners for the knowledge-based service professions' (Strategic Plan 2003–7). This has been achieved through the application of successful change management strategies, including:

- establishing a sense of urgency
- creating a strategic vision or plan
- communicating the vision and empowering others to execute the plan
- aligning organisational structures, systems and processes
- evaluation and review.

While much has been achieved, the journey has only just begun and the University remains committed to the realisation of its vision.

Bibliography

AUQA (2004) *Report of an Audit of Edith Cowan University,* AUQA Audit Report Number 26, Melbourne: Australian Universities Quality Agency.

Beer, M., Eisenstat, R. and Spector, B (1990) *The Critical Path to Corporate Renewal,* Boston: Harvard Business School Press.

Department of Education, Training and Youth Affairs (1999) *The Quality of Higher Education.* Available at <http://www.dest.gov.au/archive/highered/pubs/quality/contents.htm> (accessed 27 September 2005).

Department of Education, Training and Youth Affairs (2000) *The Australian Higher Education Quality Assurance Framework.* Available at <http://www.dest. gov.au/archive/highered/occpaper/00g/00g.pdf> (accessed 27 September 2005).

Jary, D. and Parker, M. (1998) *The New Higher Education: Issues and Directions for the Post-Dearing University,* Stoke-on-Trent: Staffordshire University Press.

Kotter, J.P. (1995) 'Leading change: why transformation efforts fail', *Harvard Business Review,* March/April 1995, Product no. 95204.

Southwell, D., Gannaway, D., Orrell, J., Chalmers, D. and Abraham, C. (2005) *Strategies for Effective Dissemination of Project Outcomes,* A report for the Carrick Institute for Learning and Teaching in Higher Education, Sydney, NSW: Carrick Institute.

Whittles, T. and Lovell, R. (1994) 'Managing the project', in R. Lovell (ed.) *Managing Change in the Public Sector,* Harlow: Longman.

Chapter 6

A community development model of change

The role of teaching and learning centres

Lynne Hunt

Introduction

This case study shows how a community development model of change management may be applied to the promotion of teaching and learning in universities. In so doing, it addresses the change-agency role of university teaching and learning development centres. The description of steps in the change management process provides rich detail of what actually happened in a new teaching centre. A key point is that the promotion of teaching and learning in universities requires organisational reorientation through a process that engages the hearts and minds of staff. In short, process is as important as product. This exploration of an empowering model of change management raises analytical points about dichotomised perceptions of change, and suggests that a multi-level approach, which includes 'middle-out' change, may be a useful conceptualisation of educational leadership to effect change in teaching and learning in universities.

The setting

Australia's Charles Darwin University emerged in 2003, from the amalgamation of the former Northern Territory University and Centralian College. The Teaching and Learning Development Group (TLDG) evolved in the restructuring of the new university. Formerly, it had been a flexible delivery centre focused largely on the production of resources for students studying off-campus. Its reorientation to the promotion of learning and teaching across the whole institution required significant change: a professor (Leader of Teaching and Learning) was appointed in April 2005, to set the pace and direction of that change. The finite time in which change has happened – less than a year – sets clear parameters to the case study and provides the opportunity to document the vision, plans, resources and strategies used to bring about change. Consultation about organisational processes for the new university had been ongoing since its inception. This case study of change management to promote teaching is, therefore, contextualised by wider organisational change at the university.

Managing change through teaching and learning centres

Teaching and learning centres are a feature of many Western universities. However, their operation varies in ways that reflect contrasting philosophies of change management and, in particular, the debate about separatist or mainstreamed approaches to change. For example, should change to promote learning and teaching be centralised in a group dedicated to the task, or, alternatively, devolved to faculties, schools and departments, where teaching actually happens? This debate is part of wider discussion of mainstreamed or separate organisational structures, to which Southwell *et al.* (2005:1) alluded:

> The successful organisation of the promotion and development of teaching and learning may be centralised in teaching and learning centres or devolved to more mainstreamed, faculty roles or a combination of both. There are advantages and drawbacks in each approach. Centralised teaching and learning centres risk marginalisation from faculties and schools. Mainstreamed roles, such as Associate Deans (Teaching and Learning) and Course Coordinators, are embedded in faculties but risk isolation from broader international, national and university strategic initiatives to enhance students' learning outcomes. Further, there is emerging evidence that they lack the power to make or manage change effectively. Associate Deans (T&L), for example, have been described as a: 'relatively new class of committed individuals interposed between top level university management structure, on the one hand, and the overcrowded classroom and overburdened teacher, on the other'.
>
> (Kift 2004: 8)

Discussion about change management is often dichotomised: separate-mainstreamed; top-down; or bottom-up. Such dichotomy has a long history. Lewin's (1951) 'force field analysis', for example, used the terms 'driving forces' and 'restraining forces', suggesting the polarisation of change and resistance. However, in practice, the operation of teaching and learning centres blurs the lines of difference by focusing on what may be described as 'middle-out' change (Cummings *et al.* 2005). Such centres typically nestle between senior university management and faculties. They manage upwards as well as downwards in middle-out fashion. As a consequence, they may be both the conduit and champion of change as well as its initiator.

The composition and size of teaching and learning centres varies considerably. Indeed, following the 2005 rankings of Australian universities on teaching outcomes (http://www.dest.gov.au/sectors/higher_education/policy_issues_reviews/key_issues/learning_teaching/ltpf/qa_learning_teaching_performance_fund_outcomes_2006.htm), there were incipient attempts on the email circuits of one professional organisation to argue that size really did matter and that the universities with the biggest teaching and learning centres fared best. This is difficult to prove, especially when functions vary as widely as they do. Charles Darwin University itself is comparatively small. The Teaching and Learning Development Group (TLDG) has 16 staff, a figure that varies, at times, with the employment of temporary staff. Six members of the administrative staff are responsible for processing materials for off-campus students. Traditionally these were print materials, but there is now a strong move towards e-learning and the use of CDRom. There are two web and multimedia staff, and five educational designers. A project manager drives forward TLDG projects and two communities of practice (Cox 2006) designed to enhance the scholarship of teaching and learning, and mentor staff for national teaching awards. The Leader (Teaching and Learning) creates the framework for change. The centre overall is managed by an administrative officer.

The baseline for change

Early in the evolution of the management process, it became clear that educational design staff and resource production staff were not working closely together. This risked teaching materials, in need of quality improvement, being recycled through an administrative process of production and distribution. A key point of intervention for improvement was being missed. Moreover, there was no coherent professional development programme beyond workshops to train staff in online learning techniques. While the university had already developed its strategic directions and plans, these had yet to be translated into an operational teaching and learning plan.

It is now required of Australian universities that they embed graduate attributes in curricula better to prepare students for the workforce. Earlier work on graduate attributes at Charles Darwin University had not been brought to fruition and needed to be resurrected and redesigned to mesh with the new strategic plan. There was no clear pathway for the move to flexible delivery and a considerable amount of work was needed to revisit unit (module) and course accreditation processes. The introduction of a course management system loomed. Further, internal teaching and learning awards had been put aside in the transition to the new university. These needed to be revived and aligned with new, Australia-wide teaching awards (http://www.carrickinstitute.edu.au/carrick/go/aaut). Staff cynicism about the value of teaching and learning achievements in career development was as high as elsewhere in the Australian higher education sector. In brief, there was much to be done. Daunting though this was, it represented an opportunity to see if change management models designed for communities could also be applied in a university setting.

A community development model of change

A first step in any change management process is to chart the way forward. In this case, a community development model of change was chosen because it is empowering and participative rather than imposing. It builds capacity and seeks to involve the hearts and minds of those involved in the change process. It may be characterised as simultaneously 'top-down', 'bottom-up' and 'middle-out'. In a university setting, this means appropriate policy and resources are provided from the top, to foster relevant initiative, while local ownership of change is embedded at faculty and departmental level. The TLDG is the change agent that drives the processes and ensures that things happen.

Community development models have the advantage of being tried and tested. They were developed and honed in the field of public health and in projects in developing countries. It has been shown (Oakley *et al.* 1997) that they:

- result in the efficient use of funding
- establish greater relevance
- build capacity to manage at the local level
- increase the population coverage of initiatives
- lead to better targeting of benefits
- facilitate sustainability.

The nine key steps of the community development model deployed at Charles Darwin University were adapted from community development sources (World Bank Participation Sourcebook 1996):

1   securing financial support
2   establishing a policy framework
3   reorientating services
4   the identification of stakeholders
5   providing incentives to participate
6   participatory planning and decision-making
7   creating a learning mood
8   building community capacity
9   inter-sectoral collaboration.

There is nothing unique about the World Bank model. Similar principles and practices are espoused around the world. For example, the same strategies were recommended in the Ottawa Charter (1986) for the promotion of public health. These include: the creation of supportive environments; policy development; community action; the reorientation of organisations; and the development of personal skills. The originality of the processes described in this chapter is the adaptation of community development strategies to the promotion of learning and teaching in a university. It is an approach that has much in common with learning organisations (Tagg 2003) because it is holistic and recognises the need for structural and cultural reorientation for change to be effective.

Community development models have the advantage of describing what is needed for change to be effective. Essentially, they are resource-based models. The actual processes of change accord with those described by organisational theorists. For example, Burnes' (2004) model of organisational change also included the need to develop: vision; participative strategies; the right culture and conditions of change; and implementation plans. In brief, there is considerable agreement about what needs to be done to manage change.

Benchmarking

A reassuring step in any change management process is to benchmark with what others are doing and to build on current practice. In this case, comparison with Stevens' (2005) analysis of the outcomes of quality reviews of the majority of Australian universities showed that the nine steps of a community development model of change accorded, almost exactly, with what Australian universities are currently doing to promote learning and teaching. For example, most universities have introduced a range of ways of resourcing teaching (Step 1: securing financial support), including performance-based funding that provides bigger budgets to departments that achieve higher outcomes in students' evaluations of teaching. All universities have vision statements, policies and plans detailing what they wish to achieve in regard to learning and teaching (Step 2: establishing a policy framework). Academic leadership of teaching and learning, in its variety of forms, has been established in Australian universities (Step 3: reorientating services). Course and unit (module) review, often associated with professional accreditation and based on student feedback, is now common (Step 4: identification of stakeholders). University-based teaching awards and grants are now common (Step 5: provision of incentives to participate). Participatory planning and decision-making (Step 6:) through various learning and teaching committees is the norm, though Stevens (2005) noted that one barrier to the promotion of learning and teaching is 'lack of awareness by planners as to the benefits of good planning for learning and teaching'. The establishment of a learning mood and capacity-building for teaching (Steps 7 and 8) are managed through a range of professional development strategies including 'introduction to tertiary teaching' programmes and graduate certificate courses in tertiary teaching. Collaboration across different university departments, such as library and information technology services, addresses Step 9, but inter-sectoral collaboration also includes the development of connections with external agencies, of which the partnership between Charles Darwin University and the government of the Northern Territory of Australia is an example (http://www.cdu.edu.au/government/). In brief, the change management processes selected by the TLDG reflected best practice in Australia.

Application of the community development model of change management

This case study of the change management process adopted by the TLDG details specific processes and events designed to promote teaching. It is structured in terms of the steps of the community development model. Yet it implies no chronology because the reality of change is fluid and several dimensions of change may occur contemporaneously. However, some things do need early consideration. For example, in a higher education sector that traditionally has emphasised the preeminence of research over teaching and learning, it is crucial to start with human resource policy and practice. This needs to ensure that staff contributions to learning and teaching are appropriately considered in applications for appointment, tenure, promotion and study leave. In brief, the change management process will be effective when, to use a slang expression, participants see that 'there is a quid [dollar] in it for teachers'. In other words, teaching must have career-building capacity. Collaboration with human resource staff of the University quickly established criteria for the inclusion of teaching and learning criteria in career development processes. Ongoing consultations hinge on the relative merits of using teaching and learning portfolios as evidence in, for example, applications for promotions because the development of portfolios is, of itself, capacity-building.

Step 1: Securing financial support

A fundamental, early step in the community development model is securing financial support. This underpins all other steps, for without resources change is inhibited. The TLDG already had a budget to cover operational costs. This needed to be reviewed to accommodate an increase in staff and the revival of teaching awards and fellowships.

Step 2: Establishing a policy framework

Strategic directions for Charles Darwin University had been set in its strategic plan and an immediate task was to translate this to a teaching and learning operational plan. The Deputy Vice-Chancellor, Professor Charles Webb, worked in collaboration with the TLDG to produce plans (http://www.cdu.edu.au/teachingandlearning/docs/tlopp031105.pdf) that accorded both with the University's strategic plan and with 'drivers of change' to enhance teaching and learning that had been determined by TLDG. These were:

1   learning technologies
2   assessment
3   graduate attributes
4   leadership
5   quality improvement
6   learning support.

The Operational Plan created the context for the development of a functional plan for the Teaching and Learning Development Group. It is entitled 'Project Projects' (http://www.cdu.edu.au/tldg/index.html) because it established projects for each of the six drivers of change listed above. Each project is guided by a reference group with faculty representation. The aim is to encourage dialogue about teaching and to disseminate knowledge to faculties as well as receive feedback about how to enhance teaching and learning. Project Projects also allowed the TLDG to move ahead on a number of fronts at the same time.

Step 3: Reorientating services

Reorienting services is central to change management processes to enhance teaching and learning because it entails embedding teaching interests in core university processes, hopefully with a status equal to that of research. A key strategy was the development of a Course and Unit Quality Improvement Plan (CUQIP). Essentially, this is a service level agreement designed to fit faculty needs to available TLDG working hours. However, it was named to focus attention on the task at hand, which was to improve the quality of teaching materials. Whilst the actual processes of production changed little, CUQIP did focus attention on quality improvement.

CUQIP showed faculty staff the type and extent of services available. Prior to its introduction, educational design staff had simply responded to requests for assistance from staff rather than working in a planned way geared to upgrade teaching materials. Consequently, they often worked with the converted – those staff who were already committed teachers. The CUQIP process reorientated services to course level intervention and a process of reaching out to those unfamiliar with how best to work with an educational designer.

However, raised expectations can lead to increased demand, so it became necessary to delimit the amount and type of available educational design support. As a consequence, a checklist was developed that could be used to shape expectations of what might be expected of educational designers. Alternatively, it could be used by faculty staff to run an independent check on the quality of their units. Examples of the features of unit design that were highlighted in the checklist include:

- Are the learning outcomes/objectives/competencies SMART: Specific, Measurable, Achievable, Realistic, Time-framed? In other words, statements of outcomes must be precise, for vague statements, such as 'students will understand or appreciate', are insufficiently specific to be assessed.
- Is there alignment between the specified learning outcomes, the learning and teaching strategies, assessment, readings/texts and graduate attributes?

Step 4: The identification of stakeholders

The importance of identifying stakeholders and defining ways of working with them may be gleaned from the fact that one of the first tasks of Australia's new Carrick Institute for Learning and Teaching was to develop a stakeholder framework (http://www.carrickinstitute.edu.au/carrick/go/pid/74). In the TLDG, the identification of key stakeholders within the university was an informal process. Each TLDG staff member was interviewed by the incoming Leader (Teaching and Learning) for at least one hour. This gave rise to an incipient list of faculty staff who might be drawn into the orbit of the TLDG.

The structural framework for working with stakeholders was Project Projects. The reference group for each project comprised key stakeholders such as faculty staff, and staff of relevant service centres including the library, student administration and technology support services. It also included staff of the two areas of TLDG: resource production and educational design. These two groups had operated somewhat independently; the reference groups built working relationships and taught staff how to collaborate. This was learning by doing.

At first, TLDG staff were the most important stakeholders because they needed training before they could be expected to become change agents to enhance teaching within the University. This was a significant change for them because previously they had been seen as working only on the production of teaching materials. The reorientation to a focus on quality improvement and working in an advisory capacity with faculty staff represented a significant change.

Beyond social functions associated with team-building, a series of 'retreats' was organised to ensure that staff understood the strategic directions of TLDG and the University. Such retreats often included the Deputy Vice-Chancellor (Teaching and Learning), both to lend authority to non-negotiable elements of strategic directions and to ensure that he was seen to be part of the team. This is an on-going process of managing upwards because the Deputy Vice-Chancellor translates teaching and learning initiatives to other members of the senior management team of the University as well as to high-level university committees.

Teaching and Learning Champions are staff in each school designated to promote learning and teaching. Their engagement as stakeholders in the change process has, so far, been limited to involvement in various teaching and learning committees and events. A small, informal survey has established baseline information about their needs. The plan is to provide specific support by organising a Teaching and Learning Summit at the start of each academic year to disseminate new teaching and learning processes and opportunities for development. Further, in collaboration with two other universities, TLDG has secured external funding for an educational leadership programme focused on Teaching and Learning Champions and Course Coordinators (http://www.carrickinstitute.edu.au/carrick/webdav/site/carricksite/users/siteadmin/public/Leadership%20Program%20Guidelines.doc). The important point is that established academic leaders are important stakeholders in change management to promote teaching.

How stakeholders are engaged is just as important as who is engaged. It is important to value and respect those who are already committed to teaching. One of the first tasks, therefore, was to mentor and support effective teachers in applications for national and professional teaching awards. In just eight months, staff of the University won four major prizes including, the premier award, the Prime Minister's Award for University Teacher of the Year (http://www.carrickinstitute.edu.au/carrick/go/pid/100).

Step 5: Providing incentives to participate

Awards for teaching excellence were in abeyance during the transition to the new Charles Darwin University. These had to be revived and dovetailed to the new format for national teaching awards. Accordingly, a document was prepared for submission to senior university committees. It specified a package of awards, grants and fellowships. At the same time, the document was presented as part of the budget papers, to ensure that the package would be resourced. These future awards will create the building blocks of lecturers' teaching portfolios.

Step 6: Participatory planning and decision-making

Participatory decision-making engages the hearts and minds of those involved in promoting teaching and learning. It creates a sense of ownership and takes advantage of existing expertise and initiatives. This approach:

> ... is built upon the basis of dialogue among the various actors, during which the agenda is jointly set, and local views and indigenous knowledge are deliberately sought and respected. This implies negotiation rather than the dominance of an externally set ... agenda. Thus people become actors instead of beneficiaries.
>
> (OECD 1994 in Oakley et al.1997)

A distinction is usually made between 'participation as a means' and 'participation as an end'. In this case, participation was used as a means to enhance teaching and learning but also as an end in itself, serving to educate staff through involvement and to build faculty and departmental capacity to promote teaching and learning. The project reference groups were designed to encourage participatory decision-making.

Some reorientation of management structures within TLDG was also required to engage staff in decisions. In broad terms, the trend was towards whole-of-TLDG meetings to break down barriers between component parts of the group. In addition, there has been an increase in the formation of functional working groups to facilitate shared decision-making about coal-face matters.

Some participatory, or collegial, structures were already in place, namely the faculty Teaching and Learning Groups. These had been variously successful.

Some operated regularly and effectively to provide quality assurance of new courses and units (modules), as well as to drive forward teaching and learning initiatives. Others met episodically and only for the purposes of course accreditation. The Leader (Teaching and Learning) worked with deans of faculties to revitalise these groups.

Search conferences have been used for troubleshooting and for one-off consultations on particular issues, for example, the development of a flexible delivery plan. 'Search conference' is a fancy title for an event that simply invites key stakeholders to a meeting to achieve an outcome on a specified topic. However, it has the advantage of suggesting that staff are not making a long-term commitment and that their expertise is valued. They have been well attended with, at times, up to forty staff involved. The outcome of this process is that draft plans on flexible delivery were quickly developed in a manner that incorporated the views of key stakeholders.

Step 7: Creating a learning mood

Clearly, the whole process of participative decision-making raises awareness of teaching and learning matters, but more is required to create a learning mood. As a consequence, key initiatives were brought together in an inaugural Teaching and Learning Week that introduced key initiatives in one hit. The agenda for the week included:

- an inaugural 'webinar' on rural and remote learning, which, of itself, engaged remote campus staff in a web-based discussion group
- an inaugural paper-bag lunch (informal seminar) that revisited the pedagogy of online learning
- faculty teaching and learning morning teas
- two inaugural communities of practice on award winning and teaching and learning scholarship
- the inaugural lecture of the incoming professor, Leader (Teaching and Learning).

Step 8: Building community capacity

Stevens (2005: 21) concluded her analysis of what Australian universities are doing to plan the advancement of learning and teaching with the observation that there is 'a need to attend to the three 'Cs' in learning and teaching administration: currency of process, communication of processes and compliance with process'. These are reflected in the process-driven approach taken by the TLDG. Processes have been developed, documented, and disseminated. In the first instance, different processes have been circulated as one-page brochures. Eventually, these will be collated on the new Teaching4Learning@CDU website that is under construction. Indeed, the development of the new TLDG website (http://www.cdu.edu.au/tldg/index.html), which will host the Teaching4Learning@CDU website, has been redeveloped only recently. Of itself, it forms part of the capacity-building strategy.

Because TLDG planning was built on six projects, it became necessary to build the capacity of staff to manage projects. A new project manager position was established and two members of staff undertook a three-day project management course. Their administrative skills now drive forward the projects. The administrative and organisational principles and practice of project management have been an invaluable support to a community development framework of change because it creates a structure for managing numerous initiatives and facilitates short-term and long-term goals, allowing some initiatives to fall into abeyance as they are addressed.

An important feature of capacity-building for teaching and learning is professional development. At Charles Darwin University, this incorporates customary workshops, but also communities of practice and informal events such as lunchtime seminars. As far as possible, the aim is to showcase initiatives of staff of the University. This aim will be extended into a teaching and learning forum to be held, as an annual event, as part of Teaching and Learning Week. A key element of the draft professional development plan is the 'induction to tertiary teaching programme' that is still under review and development. This has been linked to a postgraduate course on tertiary teaching. The University has encouraged participation through the provision of free places for its staff.

Much of this chapter has focused on building the capacity of staff to teach effectively. However, it is also important to build the capacity of students to compete successfully for employment or postgraduate study. Accordingly, TLDG initiated a project to develop a set of graduate attributes for students of the University. This happened comparatively quickly because considerable work had been completed by staff of Charles Darwin University's antecedent institution. The task, now, is to introduce graduate attributes in ways that educate staff and enhance the quality of teaching and learning, so that the process is itself capacity-building. The customary strategy is to customise graduate attributes to courses and/or disciplines, then to map graduate attributes across units that constitute a programme of study, and then to align them to the learning outcomes and assessment (Biggs 2003).

Step 9: Inter-sectoral collaboration

Inter-sectoral collaboration may be both internal and external. Within the University, the Library and Information Service and various student service groups are represented on TLDG's project reference groups. Externally, TLDG supports staff membership of professional groups such as the Australasian Council on Open, Distance and E-Learning (http://www.acode.edu.au/), and the Higher Education Research and Development Society of Australasia (http://www.herdsa.org.au/). A successful application for an educational leadership project was developed in conjunction with Queensland University of

Technology and the University of New South Wales. There is constant encouragement to add value to conference attendance by using the opportunity of travelling to network with other universities. The outcomes of such networking and conference attendance are then disseminated at TLDG Echo Conferences to be held twice a year.

Conclusion

Question: What do you do when it seems that everything should be done at once? Answer: Work within a framework that helps to establish priorities and also engages sufficient people in participatory decision-making to drive forward development on many fronts at the same time. The community development model of change, supported by the organisational principles and practice of project management, does both. Further, because it is empowering and participative, it has affinity with the culture of collegial decision-making long the hallmark of university culture in the Western world. In brief, this model starts from the perspective that a university is a community and that how something is done is as important as what is done.

What might be learned from this case study? It has emphasised the importance of community development strategies. In so doing, it has described processes and strategies, and explored innovations and interventions. Key features of the community development model so described include: policy development; organisational change; capacity building; dissemination of good practice; the development of resources such as Web sites; and the centrality of inter-sectoral collaboration and middle-out development work. Strategies have included search conferences, retreats, summits, new management structures, paper-bag lunches, teaching and learning weeks and forums, and the development of incentive schemes such as teaching and learning awards, grants and fellowships.

The intention of this chapter was to describe a change management process that is empowering and engaging. Did it work? Yes. The outcomes have been significant: teaching and learning processes and guidelines have been developed, websites have been produced and consciousness has been raised. Outcomes in terms of students' learning, the quality of teaching materials and students' assessment of the learning process will emerge slowly. However, it is not the purpose of this chapter to evaluate the outcomes of change. Rather, the point is to show that process, in this case a community development approach, is as important as product. Indeed, evaluation itself may look different in participatory models of change because they will focus on process and outcome. For example, according to Jackson (1997), evaluation of community development models of change might feature:

- evidence of shared decision-making among participants and staff
- signs of commitment among participants to the group's goals and activities
- evidence of shared leadership

- signs of solidarity and cohesion
- capacity for self-reflection and critical analysis
- capacity to take action in relation to problems identified.

A key point in the discussion concerned the extent to which a community development model of change is suited to the collegial or participative decision-making characteristic of universities. There is no space here to engage with larger debates about the corporatisation of human service organisations such as universities (Dominelli and Hoogvelt 1996, Considine 1988), nor with long-standing debates about levels of participation (Arnstein 1969). However, it is possible to note that aspects of the promotion of teaching and learning are process-driven and that this does introduce elements of corporatisation that may be opposed by university staff. For example, the Course and Unit Quality Improvement Plan, course and unit accreditation and review, and standardised documentation and reporting, discussed as strategies in this chapter, do require academic departments to be accountable for the quality of their teaching and learning. This may be seen as an imposition on staff time and an inroad into academic freedom. Indeed, staff of the TLDG have struggled against the notion that they should become the 'quality police' of teaching and learning. Yet there may be a need for intervention to ensure that students get the best possible learning experiences – the ultimate benchmark. The argument in this chapter is that the required outcome is best achieved through the empowering processes of a community development model of change.

A final lesson is that the promotion of teaching and learning requires changes in structure and in culture. These are intertwined because changes in structure, such as the development of project reference groups, retreats and search conferences, gives rise to a culture in which staff come together to share values, attitudes and good practice. Essentially, this chapter has described change management processes that practise what is preached about good teaching and learning, for staff have been engaged in learning by doing. How could it be otherwise? It would be a contradiction in intention to dragoon staff into empowering students.

Bibliography

Arnstein, S. R. (1969) 'A Ladder of Citizen Participation', *Journal of the American Institute of Planners,* Vol. 35, No. 4, 216–24.

Biggs, J.B. (2003) *Teaching for Quality Learning at University,* Buckingham: Open University Press/McGraw Hill Educational.

Burns, B. (2004) *Managing Change,* London: Prentice Hall.

Considine, M. (1988) 'The corporate management framework as administrative science: a critique', *Australian Journal of Public Administration,* Vol. XLVII, No. 1, 4–18.

Cox, M. (2006) 'Anatomy of change: phases in planning the development of higher education communities of practice', in L. Hunt, A. Bromage and B. Tomkinson (eds.) *The Realities of Change: Interventions to Promote Learning and Teaching in Higher Education,* London: Taylor & Francis.

Cummings, R., Phillips, R., Lowe, K. and Tilbrook, R. (2005) 'Middle-out approaches to university reform: champions striding between the top-down and bottom-up approaches', *International Review of Research in Open and Distance Learning*. Available at <http://www.irrodl.or/content/v6.1/cummings.html> (accessed 22 February 2006).

Dominelli, L. and Hoogvelt, A. (1996) 'Globalisation, contract government and the taylorization of intellectual labour in academia', *Studies in Political Economy*, Vol. 49, 71–100.

Jackson, E.T. (1997) *Three Indicators of Change: Results-Based Management and Participatory Evaluation*, IDRC Books. Available at <http://www.idrc.ca/en/ev-88062–201–1-DO_TOPIC.html> (accessed 18 December 2005).

Kift, S. (2004) 'Between a rock and several hard places: where does a faculty learning and teaching sub-dean sit and what is that role?', *HERDSA News*, Vol. 26, No. 3 8–11.

Lewin, K. (1951) *Field Theory in Social Science*, New York: Harper & Row.

Oakley, P. et al. (1997) *UNDP Guidebook on Participation* (draft copy).

Ottawa Charter (1986) Available at <http://www.who.int/healthpromotion/conferences/previous/ottawa/en/> (accessed 18 December 2005).

Southwell, D., Scoufis, M. and Hunt, L. (2005) *Caught between a rock and several hard places: cultivating the roles of the Associate Dean (Teaching and Learning) and the Course Coordinator: overview of a Carrick Institutional Leadership Project*, unpublished manuscript, Queensland University of Technology, Brisbane, Queensland, Australia.

Stevens, K. (2005) *Promoting and Advancing Learning and Teaching in Higher Education: The Messages from the AUQA Reports*, Carrick Institute for Learning and Teaching in Higher Education. Available at <http://www.carrickinstitute.edu.au/carrick/go/pid/1> (accessed 12 December 2005).

Tagg, J. (2003) *The Learning Paradigm College*, Boston: Anker Publishing.

World Bank Participation Sourcebook (1996) Washington: The International Bank for Reconstruction and Development. Available at <http://www.worldbank.org/html/edi/sourcebook/sbhome.html> (accessed 18 December 2005).

Chapter 7

The scholarship of teaching and learning and change in higher education

Craig E. Nelson and Jennifer Meta Robinson

Introduction

Teaching often draws on contextual knowledge and folk wisdom that faculty members develop and gather over time, first as students and then from their experiences working with students (Carr and Kemmis 1968). Individual teachers assemble partially tacit knowledge that includes unexamined assumptions, fundamental misconceptions, lapses in logic, emotional responses, and, yes, many valid observations and successful practices. Teaching has also long been treated as a private matter, grounded in the mentoring relationship between student and 'expert'. How, then, to change an institutional culture so that teaching becomes open to formative examination, and learning becomes a truly common goal available for improvement?

The Indiana University Scholarship of Teaching and Learning (SOTL) Program uses strategies designed for evolutionary and transformative change that build on strengths already present in a research faculty. The programme invites teachers in higher education to formalise their knowledge about teaching and to gather evidence to test it. It assumes that, as the collective knowledge about teaching and learning becomes more grounded in evidence and more available for analysis, as with any complex phenomenon, questions will emerge. The purposeful construction of a community in which scholars can converse about the creation, dissemination and application of research on teaching and learning enhances both student learning and faculty experience with teaching. The resulting 'transformative gestalt' nurtures instructional, organisational, and personal development (Zahorski 2002). Consistent with Bromage (2006), the development of a vigorous Scholarship of Teaching and Learning Program on the Bloomington campus of Indiana University suggests that change can be made through a series of strategies that treat the institution as a 'learning organisation', building on values recognized in the culture of the institution, such as mutual learning, collegiality, and evidence (Trice and Beyer 1992).

Contextual constraints on models of change

Change in teaching and learning in American research-focused institutions, such as Indiana University, Bloomington, is subject to local control. In contrast to the influence of government and policy that may be in effect elsewhere around the world, as cited by Bromage (2006), no centralised national, regional or state body has significant power over teaching and learning at research universities in the United States. Accrediting bodies have some influence over institutions, but their recommendations may have little effect on classroom activities. Similarly, new post-secondary educational initiatives receive relatively little attention, partly because the reward system for faculty focuses on disciplinary and basic research, partly because even funded initiatives have short-lived funding streams, and partly because the financial terms of federal education funding have frequently been much less attractive than those for basic research.

A second, similar hurdle applies within Indiana University and similar institutions in the US. The ways faculty members teach are usually regarded as a matter of academic freedom in direct parallel to their choice of topics for research. Persuasion or coercion to alter teaching is usually applied by departmental chairs only in cases of gross student dissatisfaction, or of grades so low as to endanger the number of majors or of grades so high as to be regarded as obviously inflated. Consequently, most administrative attempts to change teaching at Indiana University (and many similar institutions) have been specially funded initiatives and most have ceased when administrative interest and funding have lapsed.

A successful model of change

These two realities – nearly absolute institutional and faculty autonomy over teaching and learning – constrain the models of change that can successfully be applied to these activities at institutions such as Indiana University. Thus it is that both the faculty and administration perceive the power to choose teaching approaches as lying almost exclusively with the faculty members who decide what changes if any will be made (see also Bromage's discussion of Lovell, 1994). Taking into account this situation, the organisers of the SOTL Program at Indiana University recognised that grassroots engagement aided by central administrative resources would be necessary for organisation-wide change in approaches to teaching and learning. Following a tacit development model similar to Feeny and Ruddles' incremental-organic model (1997), the programme's development was evolutionary, starting small and expanding the view of the central objectives and the means to achieve them as the client base grew. The programme's trajectory grew responsively alongside faculty interests; beginning with informal conversations, it progressed to publicly announced guided conversations, and coalesced as a formal and funded programme with staffing and institutional presence.

The initiative's model of managed organisational change can be transferable to other institutions. Indeed, the reactions of national leaders, their dissemination of Indiana University materials to other campuses, and the campus' leadership in national consortia suggest that the Indiana University SOTL structures already serve as a model for other institutions of a new kind of faculty development – one that aims to improve undergraduate learning by engaging the research talents of the faculty.[1]

The programme fits Elton's 'new collegiality', as summarised by Bromage (2006), employing a complementary mix of top-down and bottom-up support for changes in teaching and learning. This collegial blend of cultivated and managed change emphasises faculty ownership and initiative in what we know about how people learn in the higher education context. It supports faculty members as they build on the existing base of high-quality evidence that justifies changes in teaching to produce increased learning. Individual faculty members are encouraged to focus on issues they would like to know more about relative to their own classes and to apply analytical frameworks that rest on their own disciplinary training. Thus, the opinions of stake-holding academics are not only acknowledged but also their skills, talents, and creativity are leveraged to support and refine further study of teaching and learning. Overall, the process used fits Bromage's (2006) cross-model conclusions almost point by point.

Change and the scholarship of teaching and learning

A change in institutional culture is underway at Indiana University, in part because the initiative has capitalised on a context that already exists: the SOTL program builds on the institution's mission and the faculty's orientation toward learning and research. From that base, the SOTL Program advances institutional change through an organic, contextualised strategy. One key means of cultivating stakeholders and fostering the bottom-up component of a complex change strategy as advocated by Elton (1994), has relied on the faculty's pre-existing commitment to research.

The SOTL Program has invited faculty members to use their creative and research skills – the same habits of mind they use in their disciplinary scholarship – to learn about a new subject: the relationship between teaching and learning in particular contexts. The programme has sought to support individual, highly particularised efforts while also drawing those individuals into an interdisciplinary community centred on teaching and learning. This support system encourages individuals to pursue research questions that they themselves find compelling and relevant to their own disciplines and classroom experiences.

This approach to change, through individual stakeholders who 'own' their involvement in a common agenda (teaching and learning), renews and broadens general faculty participation in the project: as more faculty members address more learning outcomes and explore more alternative learning environments, they use increasingly diverse and sophisticated techniques to examine the effectiveness of their educational strategies, making their work more compelling to more colleagues. On a research campus, such intellectual engagement is crucial in reorienting the conversations that we have about teaching (Bass 1999), in order to spur us to rethink the value accorded to teaching and redefine what we think of as appropriate fields for scholarship.

Grassroots stakeholders 1: Opening doors

In order to build grassroots support for change, as suggested by Elton (1994), by Lovell (1994) and by Feeny and Ruddle (1997), Indiana University joined the Campus Conversations programme of the Carnegie Academy for the Scholarship of Teaching and Learning (CASTL, Carnegie Foundation 2005). Locally, the key activity was a series of small meetings among groups of faculty that focused on Boyer's (1990) idea of a scholarship of teaching and learning that would parallel the scholarships of discovery, application, and integration and asked what educational issues might deserve further study. These meetings, sponsored by the Office of the Dean of the Faculties, allowed a broad-based faculty constituency to explore new ideas.

A few faculty members at Indiana University were already innovators and early adopters with regard to SOTL (Rogers 1995), and they were recognised as a significant early resource. However, ownership and buy-in had to be cultivated among those newer to the field. That meant, in part, offering them guidance in navigating new literature, new methods, and new audiences. Participants in these conversations in 1990 formed the first core of a local SOTL community. It quickly became apparent that faculty had a range of ideas as to what constituted scholarship on teaching and how it should be pursued.

To broaden the base of faculty support and accommodate their diverse approaches, the programme emphasised different genres of SOTL (Nelson 2003). Also, an array of activities simultaneously provided ideas on how to directly improve teaching, how to base teaching on others' pedagogical research (scholarly teaching), and how to begin one's own inquiries into ways of understanding and improving student learning. Such diverse programming allowed individuals to enter the discussion with varying goals and perspectives, thus keeping open the base of potential participants in a community of change (Wenger 1998).

Grassroots stakeholders 2: Supporting individuals

Many SOTL scholars were entering a new area of study, bringing with them questions about methods, ethical considerations, established literature, and readership. The programme fostered new projects and supported ongoing ones in five key ways:

- with consultation on designing, carrying out, and analysing individual projects
- with help in preparing required proposals to the institutional review board for the use of human subjects in research

- with a series of small grants
- with workshops that addressed research skills, strategic planning, and project mentoring
- through small topical learning communities that collaboratively investigated educational questions.

The small peer groups, in particular, show great potential for fostering scholarship because they both provide attention to individuals' concerns and invite them into a community as readers, reviewers, and colleagues. These faculty learning communities of 5–15 members met regularly to consider particular research topics, such as students' naïve theories and integration of critical writing. These small groups provide a generative atmosphere that encourages and supports new studies of student learning. Such 'communities of practice' can 'create, expand, and exchange knowledge and develop individual capabilities' in new ways that formal departments, project teams, and other institutionally mandated gatherings cannot (Wenger *et al.* 2002).

This approach to organisational change capitalises on a part of organisational life that often flies below the radar of those who manage organisations. These communities can develop loyalties, projects and new knowledge in unpredictable but exciting directions (Handy 1993; Lovell 1994), particularly when providing institutional supports for evolutionary and open dialogues within and between disciplinary perspectives and for combining different levels of participation (Wenger *et al.* 2002). 'Jump-start' workshops, although demanding less commitment to a social group, have also provided a forum for faculty members to develop and refine their own SOTL research questions, consider alternative methods of gathering data, use relevant bibliographic tools such as the Education Resources Information Center (ERIC) database, and learn about further sources of research support.

Grassroots stakeholders 3: Fostering public engagement

Indiana University has consistently used centralised resources to develop a community of scholars of teaching and learning that would link individuals and smaller communities of practice. It has sought to provide scholars with opportunities for conversation, on the assumption that, given the chance, their training in disciplinary study will help them to transfer, refine and develop new knowledge about learning and teaching. The programme negotiates both discipline-specific and interdisciplinary goals (Kogan 2000). Disciplines have ways of knowing, analysing, and reporting that are powerful factors among the faculty. These contexts have their own assumptions, priorities, expectations and frameworks. They present various criteria for expressing and evaluating ideas and arguments that faculty members, by virtue of being experts, have long internalised. In multidisciplinary conversations, those assumptions are made available for critique, refinement and application.

This practice of 'going public' appeals to professors from all departments, as they understand that thinking must be made available for review, application and development (Hutchings and Shulman 2004). They know that public work and publications are the currency of our research university context. As a consequence of this emphasis, Indiana University has dozens of new or forthcoming products that make learning and teaching, and the relationship between them, visible including articles, books, book chapters, journal issues, course portfolios and websites.

Projects are also made public through a series of high-profile colloquia that have served as the lynchpin of SOTL activity on campus. As public models, they illustrate ways of doing SOTL in a research university context and emphasise the importance of evidence-based and theory-framed approaches to teaching. Since their initiation in 1999, presenters at these colloquia have primarily been local scholars from a variety of fields. The colloquia provide the presenting scholars with an opportunity for going public with their research before a critical audience (Boyer 1990), thus rewarding and reinforcing grassroots participants. At the same time, the colloquia provide a visible forum for the campus community to discuss ideas that implicate change. Each colloquium has allowed substantial time for networking and for small group discussion of educational issues. The colloquia themselves are a major locus of grassroots participation, seeding the departments and programmes on campus with potential faculty leaders. Such opportunities for public engagement with these ideas reinforce the identification of individuals with a transformative community.

Grassroots stakeholders 4: Linking with allied initiatives

Grassroots support for SOTL broadens as organisers and participants create links with compatible projects and their memberships. The Pew-funded Peer Review of Teaching Course Portfolio Initiative, a five-campus project led by the University of Nebraska-Lincoln (www.courseportfolio.org), was integrated into the SOTL Program in Bloomington, as a complementary inquiry effort. The primary objectives of the Peer Review Project – to facilitate the process of documentation, enhancement and review of teaching – were adapted by several faculty members here to aid them in developing SOTL research questions and inquiry methods. The Freshman Learning Project, originally a Lilly-funded first-year retention effort, is now internally funded to foster scholarly teaching and classroom assessment among campus opinion-leaders. Some course portfolio and Freshman Learning Project fellows go on to publish scholarship of teaching. This kind of partnering helps to cross-pollinate initiatives with those interested in changes in learning and teaching.

Administrative support I: Recognising opportunities

The institutional problem that the SOTL initiative addresses rests in the gap between highly rewarded, world-class research and teaching that tends to be relatively traditional, unexamined and under-rewarded. Seeing the problem this way, the goal of the SOTL Program is to foster teaching that is more reflective and examined in larger contexts. As noted, all real power for changing pedagogy lies in the hands of the faculty. Consequently, a central administration can foster lasting change primarily through actions that allow and enable grassroots buy-in, including recognising opportunities, allocating resources and facilitating collaboration. In 1998, members of the administration recognised that the scholarship of teaching and learning, which was just rising to national prominence, could be a way to bridge the research teaching gap; that is, faculty research skills could be applied in the classroom as a powerful means for improving teaching (Angelo and Cross 1993; Glassick *et al.* 1997; Rice 1996). Because the campus has a long tradition and strong administrative support for faculty development of teaching excellence, the emphasis on SOTL presented a natural extension of prior efforts – an organic model for change.

A few faculty members, teaching centre staff and administrators became key agents of this change. In a chance conversation with a new instructional developer, a faculty member suggested that SOTL was an important new approach. They took that idea to an associate dean, who 'immediately grasped the potential' of SOTL (Thompson 2003). The Associate Dean subsequently noted that administrative leadership in a research university frequently means recognising and supporting good ideas as they emerge from the faculty. The Vice-President for Research then argued that high-quality SOTL should become part of the research mission of all major universities. The administrative support of a new scholarship that would bridge teaching and research and address common teaching concerns through the familiar intellectual lens of research resonated with many faculty members who, as classroom teachers, and as authors of that new scholarship, would be the essential agents for change.

Administrative support 2: Allocating resources to facilitate collaboration

Given our assumption that transformative change would require both central support and grassroots engagement and, of necessity, be incremental, collaborations among administrators and faculty have always been crucial. The Office of the Vice-Chancellor for Academic Affairs and Dean of the Faculties publicly launched the programme in the spring of 2000 by funding a 'Celebration of Teaching' banquet attended by some 200 faculty members. That office also redirected staff to facilitate the local Campus Conversations. These initial efforts led to the formation of steering committees that allow for faculty leadership in collaboration with librarians, staff and administrators. Subsequent partnerships have been facilitated by the programme director through informal nexuses of stakeholders and administrators. Intensive collaboration has taken place at institutes of the Carnegie Academy for the Scholarship of Teaching and Learning (CASTL) and the American Association for Higher Education (AAHE), institutes to which Indiana University sent representatives and teams. Programme managers, drawn from the campus's Instructional Support Services, build coalitions, so that together managers, administrators, and faculty advisers can steer the initiative through emerging contexts, competing priorities, funding conundrums and multiple constituencies. These partnerships assemble various resources, knowledge, skills and authority that together can move the institution toward new and lasting perspectives on higher education (Robinson 2004; Giroux 1999).

Larger contexts: Building national and international SOTL initiatives

In order to validate or 'legitimate' the substantial local momentum for change established at Indiana University, the initiative needed an 'outer context' (Pettigrew 1985). Participation by both local scholars and the campus in national and international programmes has been an important part of establishing SOTL as a credible field of research.

As part of the CASTL Program, Indiana University led a three-year consortium of research campuses from the United States, Australia and Canada that considered the role of scholarship of teaching and learning in that particular context. The exchange of knowledge taking place helped to further situate SOTL in a larger context. Six Indiana University faculty members have been involved in a major initiative of The Carnegie Foundation for the Advancement of Teaching, The Carnegie Academy for the Scholarship of Teaching and Learning (CASTL). The six were designated 'Carnegie Scholars', two of whom were invited back as mentors for subsequent groups of scholars. Their participation in CASTL has enhanced their individual projects, significantly enriched our local conversations, and greatly broadened Indiana University's connections with the national SOTL community. These awards also enhanced the local credibility of CASTL and emphasised the multidisciplinary aspects of SOTL: the CASTL scholars came from Biology, Criminal Justice, Communication and Culture, History, Medical Sciences, and Public and Environmental Affairs.

In an additional response to the need to situate SOTL in a wider environment, the Indiana University programme took the lead in establishing a new professional society for scholars engaged in the study of teaching and learning: the International Society for the Scholarship of Teaching and Learning (ISSOTL). The first meeting of this society was held in Bloomington in 2004 and attracted over 400 participants from 117 institutions in eight countries. Seventy-one Bloomington faculty and graduate students presented posters and papers at the conference. Thus the provision of a larger context expanded and reinforced grassroots participation in the change initiative.

Indications of change: outcomes and obstacles

Outcomes

The most important indication of change resulting from the Indiana University SOTL Program is the increasing attention paid by additional faculty and graduate students to the importance of inquiry into teaching and learning and to evidence-based pedagogical choices. The colloquia focus attention on individual projects and disseminate their results for application by others. In those forums and others, faculty and graduate students are now asking questions that serve as a foundation into research about teaching and learning, most of the time in addition to disciplinary research agendas.

Well over a hundred citations are included in a hyperlinked bibliography of SOTL and other teaching-related publications by Indiana University faculty. As more faculty members address more learning outcomes and explore more alternative learning environments, they use more diverse and increasingly sophisticated techniques to examine the effectiveness of their strategies. These projects and the presentations and publications emerging from them are a fundamental outcome of the SOTL programme (for more details see the Bloomington SOTL website www.indiana.edu/~sotl).

A key indicator of the synergy generated by the administratively fostered, bottom-up strategy is the number of these presentations and publications that have been authored jointly by faculty and administrators or by faculty and professional development staff (see, for example, Becker and Andrews 2004; Pace and Middendorf 2004).

Other pervasive changes in the campus teaching climate are attributable, at least in part, to the SOTL Program. Teaching development workshops, sponsored by Instructional Consulting offices around the campus, now include elements of assessment, literature review and scholarship that were not commonly featured before the SOTL initiative. Also, the number of departments offering pedagogy or SOTL courses for their own PhD. students has expanded considerably in recent years and now exceeds twenty departments (details at www.indiana.edu/~teaching). From these changes, it seems safe to infer that much teaching at Indiana University Bloomington is now more scholarly and approached as more of a public and intellectual endeavour.

Some confirmation of an improved climate for scholarly teaching has come from outside reviewers. In 2003, Indiana University's SOTL Program received the Hesburgh Award in recognition of the intentional synergy it creates by linking faculty development, faculty scholarship and student learning. Also, the Carnegie Foundation for the Advancement of Teaching and the Council for Advancement and Support of Education recognised an active Indiana University participant as the US Professor of the Year 2000 among research and doctoral university professors. In 2001, the University seconded that award by giving him its President's Medal for Excellence, a significant increment in institutional recognition for SOTL.

Obstacles

How scholarship of teaching and learning is acknowledged in rewards systems will be key to its lasting status and institutionalisation. As discussed above, two major factors resist significant change in teaching and learning in almost every research university in the USA. One is the tradition of faculty autonomy in teaching decisions. SOTL deals with this effectively by defining teaching challenges as parallel to research opportunities (Bass 1999) and by keeping faculty members entirely in control of any inquiry they do into teaching and learning. The second major impediment is the reward system for faculty members. Salary increases, tenure, and promotions at Indiana University are currently based almost exclusively on research. Measures of scholarly productivity emphasise peer-reviewed publications and grants. Peer-reviewed publication is also, arguably, the most important way that institutions such as Indiana University make knowledge available.

Some developments indicate that institutional structures can be changed to accommodate SOTL and evidence-based teaching within a research-intensive culture. In 1999, the annual faculty summary reports of professional activity were changed to include 'scholarly activity related to teaching and learning (e.g., investigation/research, dissemination/publication of results)'. And, in 2002, SOTL was made part of the expectations for some non-tenure-track and clinical faculty members. With teaching as their primary duty, their promotions are now based, in part, on 'research in support of teaching' and 'currency with pedagogical developments in their fields', with SOTL as at least one means for meeting these criteria (Bloomington Faculty Council 2002).

However, it remains to be seen how these top-down initiatives will be received by the general faculty and especially the department chairs. Collectively, these changes should make explicit the administration's support for treating SOTL as research, thereby making it more attractive for individual faculty. However, the power for initial decisions on salary, tenure and promotion are made at the departmental level, and the departments have substantial autonomy in deciding how to apply the criteria. While the centre-peripheral models of change management bifurcate the stakeholders at a university into the institutional administration and the faculty, our observation is that departments occupy a 'middle ground' in US institutions that is especially important in teaching initiatives, including scholarship of teaching and learning. The chairs have the responsibility of safeguarding the research excellence of their departments and, at research-priority institutions particularly, any emphasis on teaching may appear to dilute disciplinary research efforts and reputations. While the change principles employed by the Indiana programme foster dialogue among and accommodation for different constituencies and levels of commitment, the departments have proven to be difficult to engage. Thus, a significant challenge still exists in getting SOTL recognised as valuable by departments and 'counted' toward rewards, tenure and promotion.

In other words, such change as we have seen on the Bloomington campus has brought out tension among the stakeholders (Bennis *et al.* 1969, Trowler *et al.* 2003 and Clarke 1987). An important discussion continues as to what constitutes scholarship of teaching and learning, what constitutes good scholarship of teaching and learning, and how these fit within the mission of the institution. That debate reflects different approaches to the field of study that are based, at least in part, on disciplinary differences. Some emphasise the importance of accumulating evidence, developing models and practical understanding, and measuring impact; others are more concerned about asking better questions, developing a vocabulary, and understanding relationships that will vary according to context.

The success of scholarship of teaching and learning that is an interdisciplinary movement will likely rest not on one 'side' of this debate or the other. Rather, it may often take different forms for different people, depending on the disciplinary 'skills [faculty members have] spent their adult lifetimes learning', those that allow them to 'make judgments [usually good ones] about the nature of under-standing in our own fields' (Bernstein and Bass 2005). Key mediators in this discussion will be the disciplines and their representatives within university departments and on journal editorial boards. To some extent, then, the contours of the field will emerge inductively from the work that is published rather than from centralised assertions of what it should look like.

Conclusions: processes and practices to promote teaching and learning

Programmes to foster the Scholarship of Teaching and Learning are fundamen-tally distinct in three ways from many attempts to promote change in teaching and learning in higher education. First, rather than advocating a particular change in teaching, SOTL programmes seek to establish mechanisms that encourage indi-vidual faculty to ask what changes would be most appropriate in their own classes and then implement them. Second, they ask faculty to approach the improvement of teaching as part of their research or scholarly efforts. Third, because the locus of change is the individual faculty member, the processes of change almost auto-matically have key features advocated by Bromage (2006): collegiality, focus on high quality evidence, and direct responsiveness to the opinions of participating academics.

The attention to grassroots participation, administrative support and connec-tions to larger contexts in this case may be relevant to other institutions and to other changes. Indiana University has been successful in getting strong support from three vital groups of stakeholders: a critical mass of faculty, senior adminis-trators and effective staff. The institution's participation and leadership in national initiatives broadened and refined our ideas and added significantly to local credi-bility. Further, we strove both to provide support and to remove barriers to the researchers who undertook this kind of scholarship. Providing a variety of exam-ples of this kind of study, small research grants, bibliographic and other library assistance, facilitation of collaborative peer groups, and assistance with the approval process for using human subjects in research all helped researchers move their work forward. Finally, we aimed to engage a broad array of faculty members, ranging from those who were looking for more effective ways to teach to those who were already deeply engaged with educational scholarship.

Far from being a sure-fire recipe for transformation, the Bloomington case reinforces the importance of a contextualised strategy for change. Those directly involved in the scholarship of teaching will always be a subset of the entire faculty. But as a means of transforming broader faculty perspectives on teaching and allowing for public and evidence-based discussions of learning and teaching, scholarship of teaching and learning shows early success and great promise. The programme and the field will continue to grow organically and incrementally through administrative support that is responsive to genuine faculty interests.

Endnotes

1 The history and dynamics of the SOTL Program at Indiana University are described extensively by Thompson (2003), Robinson and Nelson (2003) and Robinson (2004). Additional information is available on the programme's website (www.indiana. edu/~sotl). Here we focus on the process of change in moving the campus culture from a private, how-to teaching orientation toward a climate in which teaching is increasingly understood to be more public, more researchable, and more open to development.

Bibliography

Angelo, T.A. and Cross, K.P. (1993) *Classroom Assessment Techniques* (2nd ed.), San Francisco, CA: Jossey-Bass.

Bass, R. (1999) 'The scholarship of teaching: What's the problem?' *Inventio* Vol. 1, No. 1. Avalable at <http://www.doiiit.gmu.edu/Archives/feb98/randybass.htm> (accessed 2 August 2005).

Becker, W. and Andrews. M. (eds.) (2004) *The Scholarship of Teaching and Learning in Higher Education: The Contribution of the Research Universities,* Bloomington, IN: Indiana University Press.

Bennis, W.G., Benne, K.D. and Chin, R. (1969) *The Planning of Change* (2nd ed.), New York: Holt, Reinhart and Winston.

Bernstein, D. and Bass, R. (2005) 'The scholarship of teaching and learning', *Academe Online* Vol. 9 No. 4. Available at <http://www.aaup.org/publications/Academe/ 2005/05ja/05jabass.htm> (accessed 2 August 2005).

Bloomington Faculty Council (2002) *BFC Circular B23–2002.* Available at <http://www.indiana.edu/~bfc/BFC/circulars/01–02/B23–2002.htm> (accessed 2 August 2005).

Boyer, E. (1990) *Scholarship Reconsidered: Priorities of the Professoriate,* Menlo Park CA: Carnegie Foundation for the Advancement of Teaching.

Bromage A. (2006) 'The management of planned change: An interdisciplinary perspective' in L. Hunt, A. Bromage and B. Tomkinson (eds.) *The Realities of Change: Interventions to Promote Learning and Teaching in Higher Education,* London: Taylor & Francis.

Carr, W. and Kemmis, S. (1968) *Becoming Critical: Education Knowledge and Action Research,* London: Falmer Press, quoted in A. Bromage (2006) 'The management of planned change: An interdisciplinary perspective', in L. Hunt, A. Bromage and B. Tomkinson (eds.) (2006) *The Realities of Change in Higher Education,* London: Taylor & Francis.

Clark, Burton R. (1987) *The Academic Life: Small Worlds, Different Worlds,* Princeton NJ: Carnegie Foundation for the Advancement of Teaching.

Elton. L. (1994) *Management of Teaching and Learning: Towards Change in Universities*, London: CVCP.

Feeny, D. and Ruddle, K. (1997) 'Transforming the organisation: New approaches to management, measurement and leadership', *Oxford Executive Research Briefings* No. 5, Oxford: Templeton College. Available at <http://www.templeton.ox.ac.uk> (accessed 15 May 2004).

Giroux, H.A. (1999) 'Cultural studies as public pedagogy making the pedagogical more political', *Encyclopaedia of Philosophy of Education*. Available at <http://www.vusst.hr/ENCYCLOPAEDIA/cultural_studies.htm> (accessed 2 August 2005).

Glassick, C.E., Huber, M.T. and Maeroff. G.I. (1997) *Scholarship Assessed: Evaluation of the Professoriate*, San Francisco, CA: Jossey-Bass.

Handy, C. B. (1993) *Understanding Organisations* (4th ed.), London: Penguin.

Hutchings, P. and Shulman, L. (2004) 'The scholarship of teaching: New elaborations, new developments', in L. Shulman (ed.) *Teaching as Community Property: Essays on Higher Education*, San Francisco, CA: Jossey-Bass.

Kogan, M. (2000) 'Higher education communities and academic identity', *Higher Education Quarterly*, Vol. 54, No.3, 207–16.

Lovell, R. (1994) 'Empowerment', in Lovell, R. (ed.) *Managing Change in the Public Sector*, Harlow: Longman.

Nelson, C.E. (2003) 'Doing it: Selected examples of several of the different genres of SOTL', *Journal of Excellence in College Teaching*, Vol. 14, 85–94.

Pace, D. and Middendorf, J. (eds.) (2004). 'Decoding the disciplines: Helping students learn disciplinary ways of thinking', *New Directions for Teaching and Learning*, No. 98.

Pettigrew, A.M. (1985) *The Awakening Giant*, London: Blackwell.

Rice, E. (1996) *Making A Place For The New American Scholar*, Washington, DC: American Association for Higher Education.

Robinson, J.M. (2004) 'Multiple sites of authority,' in B. Cambridge (ed.) *Campus Progress: Supporting the Scholarship of Teaching and Learning*, Washington, DC: American Association for Higher Education.

Robinson, J.M. and Nelson, C.E. (2003) 'Institutionalizing and diversifying a vision of scholarship of teaching and learning,' *Journal on Excellence in College Teaching*, Vol. 14, 95–118.

Rogers, E.M. (1995) *Diffusion of Innovations*, New York: The Free Press.

Thompson, S.B. (2003) 'From two box lunches to buffets: Fulfilling the promise of the scholarship of teaching and learning', *Journal on Excellence in College Teaching*, Vol. 14, 119–34.

Trowler, P., Saunders, M. and Knight, P.T. (2003) *Change Thinking, Change Practices: A Guide to Change for Heads of Department, Programme Leaders and Other Change Agents in Higher Education*, York: Learning and Teaching Support Network. Available at <http://www.heacademy.ac.uk/resources> (accessed 10 December 2005).

Trice, H.M. and Beyer, J.M. (1992) *The Cultures of Work Organisations*, Upper Saddle River, NJ: Prentice Hall.

Wenger, E., McDermott, R. and Snyder, W.M. (2002) *Cultivating Communities of Practice*, Boston: Harvard Business School Press.

Zahorski, K.J. (2002) 'Nurturing scholarship through holistic faculty development: a synergistic approach,' *New Directions for Teaching and Learning*, Vol. 90, 29–37.

Chapter 8

Phases in the development of a change model

Communities of practice as change agents in higher education

Milton D. Cox

Introduction

This chapter shows how communities of practice may be effective agents for change in higher education. The case study describes a professional learning community model that resulted in change at Miami University, Ohio, USA. Now, supported by national and state grants, the model is in the fourth year of testing at other institutions with positive results.

A community of practice may be described as a group of people working towards the same goal. These comparatively fluid groups develop, change and disband in accordance with need. They create opportunities for mutual learning and accord with learning organisation theory and practice, shown to by Tagg (2003) to be well suited to higher education. A learning organisation is defined by well-connected networks that enable reflective practice in relation to that organisation's mission, goals and challenges (Senge 1990). They are open to change and, therefore, well-suited to meet the demands of rapid change.

The Faculty and Professional Learning Community model, presented here, is a special type of community of practice (Wenger 1998). While it is described in detail in Cox and Richlin (2004), in broad terms, the development has occurred in three phases:

1   The initial Miami University years of local, one-dimensional, cohort development for junior faculty, 1978–88.
2   Local multi-dimensionality – the broadening of the model to other cohorts and to topic-based and professional learning communities at Miami, 1989–98.
3   State, national, and international extension of the model, 1999 to the present.

The purpose of this chapter is to show how the reflective practice that defines learning communities resulted in an evolutionary model of change that was structured as phases of development. It shows the strategies that worked and illustrates how local initiatives transform into global endeavour. The three phases of the development model evolved at Miami University – a public, state-supported, research-intensive institution in Ohio, USA. The sites for the international, third phase of development are the connected colleges and universities in Ohio, the USA, Sweden, Canada and Scotland.

A description of faculty and professional learning communities

At Miami University, the communities of practice are called Faculty and Professional Learning Communities. They are multi-disciplinary groups of 6–15 members (8–12 recommended), consisting of staff, or a mix of staff, graduate students, and administrative professionals. They work collaboratively on nine-month, scholarly programmes to enhance teaching and learning. Specific activities include retreats and bi-weekly seminars. These build capacity and develop the scholarship of teaching and learning (Nelson and Robinson 2006). Participants may select a course or project in which to try out innovations. They also assess outcomes, including student learning, and may prepare a mini-portfolio to chronicle results. They select and work with student associates to engage student perspectives. Finally, they present project results to their institutions and national conferences.

A Faculty and Professional Learning Community Programme is the system of learning communities that an institution has in place and the administrative structure that manages it. This is usually a teaching or faculty development centre. In this case study, the two levels will be referred to, respectively, as faculty learning communities (or simply learning communities) and the learning community programme.

Faculty learning communities may be cohort-based or topic-based. Cohort-based communities address the developmental needs of a group of staff with special needs. Examples include graduate students preparing to become lecturers, early-career staff, more senior staff, and heads of departments. The cohort curriculum is shaped by the participants and includes a broad range of teaching and learning matters. In contrast, a topic-based community has a year-long curriculum designed to address a special teaching and learning innovation, such as the introduction of problem-based learning. Once the topic or cohort is set, the learning communities programme management works to find committed participants, a qualified facilitator and funding. Their organisational tasks are underpinned by two national workshops, offered each year, to train facilitators and programme directors. Full details may be found at the project website: www.muohio.edu/flc.

A faculty learning community is more than a committee seminar, or action learning set precisely because it is a community – with everything that means in terms of bonding and support. However, the associated objective of developing a scholarship of teaching and learning does mean that the learning communities are more structured and scholarly than discussion groups or informal teaching circles. Faculty learning communities are based on a sense of community and they are multi-disciplinary. They work on trust, sharing and the cross-fertilisation of ideas. In short, they operate at Level Two of Ashwin and Trigwell's (2004) three forms of knowledge because they generate local knowledge, with the purpose of informing participants who decide what is important and the direction of learning. In fact, the participants become the teaching consultants (Cox 1999).

The phases of change

The first phase, 1978–88

The initiative that launched the faculty and professional learning community model at Miami University was funded by the Lilly Endowment – a private organisation that supports innovations in higher education in the USA. The Endowment began its Lilly post-doctoral teaching awards programme in 1974. Its purpose was to provide annual, year-long programmes of teaching enhancement for tenure-track junior faculty at each of six to nine research-intensive universities. At that time, such universities focused their expectations, efforts and rewards on encouraging junior staff to blossom as traditional researchers – that is, as producers of disciplinary research rather than pedagogical scholarship. In contrast, the Lilly Endowment provided a rare opportunity for junior faculty to develop their teaching interests and skills.

By invitation only, selected universities applied for three-year participation. Two to three new institutions were selected annually, so that six to nine participated each year. Each institutional applicant was asked to indicate how it would institutionalise its Lilly Program. The expectation was that, as Lilly funding decreased during years two and three, the participating university would pick up the funding and continue its programme. Applicants were encouraged to design their own approaches for use of the funds. This involved costs associated with meetings; time-release; mentors; projects; and retreats and conferences. The national Lilly program was reviewed by Austin (1990), who describes the failure of most universities to sustain momentum. This lesson was remembered when designing phase three of the change management described in this case study.

Miami University participated in the national Lilly program, 1979–80, and continued through to 1982. It institutionalised the programme, naming it the Alumni Teaching Scholars' Program. This has continued, essentially the same, for 27 years, with university funding and support contributed by Miami University alumni. Each member of that learning community receives release time from one teaching course and US$400 for a teaching project as well as student associate expenses. The programme received the 1994 Hesburgh Award, which recognises the best faculty development programme in the USA for enhancing undergraduate education. An important outcome is an increasing network of junior staff who became members and facilitators of subsequent faculty learning communities. There are currently 162 participating or graduated teaching scholars at Miami. This is 21 per cent of the current tenured and tenure-track staff.

The programme at Miami was housed in the Provost's Office – to signal its importance and to provide a home for its administration (there was no teaching centre until 2002). In 1980, the Provost invited the author, then director of under-graduate studies and chief departmental adviser in mathematics, to direct and institutionalize the programme. Before Lilly financing ended in 1982, we sought and won university senate endorsement for extending the programme. In 1981 we initiated the Lilly Conference on College Teaching to provide a forum for Miami University staff to present their teaching innovations along with those at nearby institutions. A new provost arrived, who provided alumni donations for financial support. The alumni teaching scholars programme was successfully launched. This was integrated with a teaching and learning grants programme at Miami University to become part of the Teaching Effectiveness Programs.

The phase one planning, strategies, outcomes and recommendations for insti-tutionalising a programme to enhance the teaching of junior faculty are in Cox (1995). Highlights include the pioneering engagement of the scholarship of teach-ing and learning (Cox 2003). Notably, this was 12 years before Boyer's (1990) now well-known naming of this scholarship. The programme included assessment of outcomes, in particular a study showing that junior staff who participated in the Alumni Teaching Scholars Community were tenured at a significantly higher rate than those who did not participate (Cox 1995).

The second phase, 1989–98

In the late 1980s, key outcomes of the Alumni Teaching Scholars Pogram were emerging. These included: multi-disciplinary networks; the scholarship of teach-ing and learning; and the level of support and interest shown to be provided by community. We decided that these key aspects of the community could be expanded to further address shortcomings at Miami – departmental silos, lack of curricular cohesion, little community, and teaching that was not scholarly. A national study (Massy *et al.*1994) showed that these problems were common even in departments. They found collegiality to be 'hollowed', with a sense of commu-nity usually absent from meetings, curricular planning and pedagogical work. The problems were ongoing in higher education; Palmer lamented (2002: 179):

> Academic culture is a curious and conflicted thing. On the one hand, it holds out the allure and occasionally the reality of being a 'community of scholars.' ... On the other hand, it is a culture infamous for fragmentation, isolation, and competitive individualism – a culture in which community sometimes feels harder to come by than in any other institution on the face of the earth.

The aspects of the Alumni Teaching Scholars Community were seen to be embry-onic features of a learning organisation. It seemed this faculty learning community had the potential to incubate a learning organisation approach at Miami University that might address some of the perceived barriers to teaching and learning development. Based on a scholarship of teaching and learning, such communities would provide an evidence base for teaching and learning development and facilitate connections across departmental and disciplinary boundaries. The idea for the development of Faculty and Professional Learning Communities beyond the original Alumni Teaching Scholars Communities sprang from staff rather than from administrative or governmental direction. In particular, it arose from mid-career and senior faculty who had not had the opportunity to experience the Alumni Teaching Scholars Program when they were junior staff. Further, it reflected the desires of former members, now in mid-career, who wanted, again, to experience community and support for pedagogical innovation – opportunities that were absent in their departments.

Thus a second cohort-learning community for senior staff began at Miami in 1991 (Blaisdell and Cox 2004), funded by the provost, also using alumni-donated funds. This initiative was confirmed by a study of mid-career faculty at a Canadian university: Karpiak (1997) reported faculty feelings of low interest and malaise due to isolation and marginalisation. To address this problem, she offered recommendations that included senior and mid-career professional learning communities to provide opportunities for them to be members of a team and to help each other grow as intellectuals as part of a support network.

In 1993, the first topic-based learning community was developed to improve the practice of teaching evaluation at Miami. Teaching portfolios (dossiers) were introduced as a means to broaden the summative and formative evaluation of teaching. A two-tier approach was adopted, resulting in a learning community in each participating department and an institution-wide community made up of departmental learning community facilitators. Participating departments designed and developed portfolio procedures that suited disciplinary and departmental cultures. This successful approach involved eleven departments, three academic divisions, one of the regional campuses, and University Libraries during 1993–6. Full details, strategies, and outcomes are described in Cox (1996). Different topic-based communities followed, with 30 different topics in ensuing years.

One significant development in phase two was the extension of the model as a system, with appropriate management structures. There were obstacles in this phase of the project, including resistance from some department chairs, concerned about staff time committed to an intensive year spent in learning and teaching. This was addressed by the study showing that junior staff who participated in learning communities were tenured at significantly higher rates than those who did not (Cox 1995).

In phase two, similarities between staff and student learning in student learning in communities was noted. For example, students, especially those at risk, fared better, academically, than those who were not in learning communities. In short, learning communities increased retention rates. Similarly, tenure-track staff in learning communities fared better at earning tenure than non-participants: also a factor in retention. Other parallels included faster intellectual development (Cox 2003) and greater civic contributions, for example through participation in university governance, for both staff and students.

Two significant developments occurred in phase two during the late 1980s. These were motivated by the need to provide a broader venue for presentations and for publications arising from the scholarship of teaching and learning. In their disciplines, faculty members are oriented to larger, disciplinary networks where they present and publish research outcomes. In this context, we felt that we would get buy-in from faculty if the learning community experience could provide a larger network. As a consequence, the Lilly Conference on College Teaching was expanded to regional conferences to enable more staff to share their teaching and learning innovations.

The second significant development was the 1990 inauguration of an internationally refereed journal, the *Journal on Excellence in College Teaching*. This addressed a gap because there were few avenues in the US for publication of cross-disciplinary scholarship of teaching and learning. The *Journal*, like the Lilly Conferences, was not requested or funded by the administration. Rather, it was an entrepreneurial effort by staff of the university. However, it was important that the administration supported these efforts. Four regional conferences were developed during this time.

The third phase 1999–present

The third phase comprised two parts, intended to disseminate the model as well as test its feasibility at other institutions. This initiative was funded in 1999 by an US$80,000 grant from the Ohio Board of Regents, the state higher-education governing board. It began with workshops for teaching centre directors. By 2001, seven Ohio institutions had successfully initiated Faculty Learning Community Programs. As a consequence, a new state-wide consortium was established for teaching centre and faculty development directors. Next, the Ohio Learning Network, a state-wide agency designed to infuse technology into established courses and programmes, adapted the faculty learning community model for its initiatives. It generated 31 learning communities in 23 institutions during 2002–3, and 25 more in 2004–5. The change strategies for this state-wide effort are elucidated in Hansen *et al.* (2004).

The ongoing second part of phase three is national. It started in 2001 with five universities and is funded by a four-year US$324,800 grant from the Fund for the Improvement of Post-Secondary Education, of the US Department of Education. The objective of this initiative is to test the feasibility of fast-track development of faculty learning communities. The task is to have each of the five universities design and implement two learning communities the first year, four in the second year, and six in the third year, giving a total of 12.

Again, workshops for the directors and site visits were effective. One obstacle, though, concerned the funding needed by teaching centres to start a learning community programme. As a consequence, the grant facilitated funding of professional expenses, books and meals for participating staff. An obstacle at one institution was the term 'community'; the director said it would sound ludicrous at a university with thousands of staff and students. Another obstacle was the absence of trained facilitators. To overcome this obstacle, a handbook for facilitators and directors was prepared.

The project has been successful: over the three years of the grant, 60 learning communities of 30 different types were designed and implemented at the five universities. The term 'community' is now used seriously at the large institution. For a list of cohorts and topics, see Cox (2004). The initiative has now extended beyond US research-intensive universities to institutions of various types, including community colleges, four-year liberal arts colleges, comprehensive colleges and medical schools. In a national survey of US and Canadian institutions in 2003–4, 308 learning communities were identified at 132 institutions. The results are reported and analysed in Richlin and Essington (2004). Finally, there is now international engagement with communities of practice, for example the Breakthrough Project at Lund Institute of Technology in Sweden (Roxå 2004).

Summary of the phased change process

The change management processes described in this case study may be described as bottom-up and incremental-organic (Bromage 2006). A double-loop process that engages assessment and reflection during each step (Argyris 1993) has been employed. In brief, the process deployed has practiced what it preaches in terms of collegial and reflective approaches. Reflective practice has given rise to an evolutionary process in which the outcomes of each phase illuminated the way forward. Further, the learning communities built high levels of trust through participative decision-making. The ensuing sense of community and the scholarship of teaching and learning provided the social dynamics and the intellectual linkage between theory and practice for successful change management. The capacity-building inherent in learning communities fed off itself because successful graduates of the programme are now facilitators of subsequent learning communities. They also serve as members of advisory groups.

This case study highlights the need for cultural change to enhance learning and teaching in higher education. This means addressing the values, attitudes and behaviour of individuals, as well as the context that supports a particular culture. When working with individuals, the processes in this project honoured different learning styles, valued individual contributions and respected differing disciplinary cultures. Further, the project created opportunities for supportive and challenging dialogue. It also provided mechanisms for change such as mentoring and opportunities to learn new ideas. Context has been addressed through the use of evidence to show that the learning community model works. While top-down approaches have not been used, administrators have been apprised of change management processes, which were modified to include their perspectives.

The many innovations, assessments, presentations and changed practices, as well as the adaptation of this model for use at a wide variety of institutions, attest to its success. Faculty and professional learning community programmes can contribute to transforming higher education institutions into learning organisations. Cox (2001) details how the phased process addressed systems thinking, personal mastery, mental models, building a shared vision and team learning (Senge 1990).

Analysis

This case study gives rise to a number of insights into managing change in higher education. It is clear that change must be appropriately resourced. Further, not all resources are monetary. For example, the capacity-building inherent in a learning community approach feeds off itself so that graduates of the programme become a resource for its future development. Learning communities are networks and their growth and development is enhanced when they network with each other. Conferences provided a venue for inter-community networking, and mentoring at institutional level has ensured the development of learning communities nationally and internationally. The processes described in this case study acknowledged and respected institutional culture. The scholarly and professional approach articulated successfully with university culture. In similar vein, the change process should itself model expected outcomes. In this case, student-centred, facilitative and participative models of learning were exemplified.

In brief, supporting fundamental change represents not the power to direct but the symbolic power to 'model, to be the change you are seeking to create' (Senge 2000: 286). The inclusion of junior staff and professional, non-academic staff shows how learning communities can capture new and fresh perspectives. Further, the evolution of the project to include mid-career staff indicates that change is multi-levelled and multi-layered. In this context, the inclusion of senior staff is important.

According to Palmer (2005), the approach adopted in this case study extends beyond the higher education sector. His account of the new professional as community organiser has resonance with many of the processes in learning communities. These include the power of the inquiry model and emotional engagement that can motivate people to take responsibility. He notes the power of one, and the need to expand this to community power, and he advocates the use of significant outsiders in the change process. The Miami case study of community of practice initiatives encapsulates these features in an approach that seeks a change in the culture of universities.

Bibliography

Argyris, C. (1993) *Knowledge for Action: A Guide to Overcoming Barriers to Organisational Change,* San Francisco: Jossey-Bass.

Ashwin, P. and Trigwell, K. (2004) 'Investigating staff and educational development', in D. Baume and P. Kahn (eds.) *Enhancing Staff and Educational Development,* London, Routledge Falmer, 117–131.

Austin, A.E. (1990) *To Leave an Indelible Mark: Encouraging Good Teaching in Research Universities Through Faculty Development: A Study of the Lilly Endowment's Teaching Fellows Program, 1974–1988,* Nashville, TN: Vanderbilt University, Peabody College.

Blaisdell, M. and Cox, M.D. (2004) 'Senior faculty learning communities: learning throughout faculty careers', in M. D. Cox and L. Richlin (eds.) *Building Faculty Learning Communities,* New Directions for Teaching and Learning, No. 97, San Francisco: Jossey-Bass.

Bromage, A. (2006) 'The management of planned change: an interdisciplinary perspective', in L. Hunt, A. Bromage and B. Tomkinson (eds.) *The Realities of Change: Interventions to Promote Learning and Teaching in Higher Education,* London: Taylor & Francis.

Boyer, E.L. (1990) *Scholarship Reconsidered: Priorities of the Professoriate,* Princeton, NJ: The Carnegie Foundation for the Advancement of Teaching.

Cox, M.D. (1995) 'The development of new and junior faculty', in W. A. Wright and Associates (eds.) *Teaching Improvement Practices: Successful Strategies for Higher Education,* Bolton, MA: Anker, 283–310.

Cox, M.D. (1996) 'A department-based approach to developing teaching portfolios: Perspectives for faculty developers', *To Improve the Academy,* Vol. 15, 275–302.

Cox, M.D. (1999) 'Peer consultation and faculty learning communities', in C. Knapper and S. Piccinin (eds.) *Using Consultation to Improve Teaching,* New Directions for Teaching and Learning, No. 79, San Francisco: Jossey-Bass, 39–49.

Cox, M.D. (2001) 'Faculty learning communities: change agents for transforming institutions into learning organizations', *To Improve the Academy,* Vol. 19, 69–93.

Cox, M.D. (2003) 'Fostering the scholarship of teaching and learning through faculty learning communities', *Journal on Excellence in College Teaching,* Vol. 14, No. 2/3, 161–198.

Cox, M.D. (2004) 'Introduction to faculty learning communities', in M. D. Cox & L. Richlin (eds.) *Building Faculty Learning Communities,* New Directions for Teaching and Learning, No. 97, San Francisco: Jossey-Bass.

Cox, M.D. and Richlin, L. (eds.) (2004) *Building Faculty Learning Communities,* New Directions for Teaching and Learning, No. 97, San Francisco: Jossey-Bass.

Hansen, S., Kalish, A., Hall, W., Gynn, C.M., Holly, M.L. and Madigan, D. (2004) 'Developing a statewide faculty leaning community program', in M. Cox and L. Richlin (eds.) *Building Faculty Learning Communities,* New Directions for Teaching and Learning, No. 97, San Francisco: Jossey-Bass.

Karpiak, I.E. (1997) 'University professors at mid-life: Being a part of ... but feeling apart', *To Improve the Academy,* Vol. 16, 21–40.

Massy, W.F., Wilger, A.K. and Colbeck, C. (1994) 'Overcoming "hollowed" collegiality: departmental cultures and teaching quality', *Change,* Vol. 26, No. 4, 11–20.

Nelson, C. and Robinson J.M. (2006) 'The scholarship of teaching and learning and change in higher education', in L. Hunt, A. Bromage and B. Tomkinson (eds.) *The*

Realities of Change: Interventions to Promote Learning and Teaching in Higher Education, London: Taylor & Francis.

Palmer, P.J. (2002) 'The quest for community in higher education', in W.M. McDonald & Associates (eds.) *Creating Campus Community,* San Francisco, CA: Jossey Bass, 179–92.

Palmer, P.J. (2005) *The New Professional: On Thinking and Acting Like Community Organisers,* paper presented at the 25th annual Lilly Conference on College Teaching, November 2005, Oxford, OH.

Richlin, L. and Essington, A. (2004) 'Overview of faculty learning communities', in M. D. Cox and L. Richlin (eds.) *Building Faculty Learning Communities*, New Directions for Teaching and Learning, No. 97, San Francisco: Jossey-Bass.

Roxå, T. (2004) *How to Change a Teaching Paradigm: An Example,* paper presented at the Lilly Conference on College Teaching, November 2004, Oxford, OH.

Senge, P.M. (1990) *The Fifth Discipline,* New York: Doubleday.

Senge, P.M. (2000) 'The academy as learning community: contradiction in terms or realizable future?' in A. F. Lucas and Associates (eds.) *Leading Academic Change: Essential Roles for Department Chairs,* San Francisco: Jossey-Bass, 275–300.

Tagg, J. (2003) *The Learning Paradigm College,* Boston: Anker Publishing.

Wenger, E. (1998) *Communities of Practice,* Cambridge, UK: Cambridge University Press.

Chapter 9

Dynamics of planned change

When participants talk back

Wim H. Gijselaers and Sigrid Harendza

Introduction

The present chapter describes a case study of top-down curriculum change in a German medical school that was stimulated by extrinsic pressures in the form of new legislation of the German Federal Government concerning curriculum content. It illuminates how medical teachers and academic leaders face potentially contradictory requirements and how difficult it is to deal effectively with extrinsic pressures for change.

The difficult nature of bringing about organisational change is not restricted to medical schools, as the following quotation illustrates:

> More than 70 per cent of the change programs in organisations either stall prematurely or fail to achieve their intended result. Goals are not achieved, policies are not implemented, customers do not experience improvement in service and quality, and employees, supervisory staff, and middle management are confused by all change efforts.
>
> (Boonstra 2004: 1)

While there are certain features of this case study that distinguishes it from other settings, there are commonalities in the processes of change across the contexts in which it occurs. A key point is that, be it in products, services or medical curricula, individuals and organisations have to come-up with new ideas to develop creative responses to changes in the outside world (their operating context).

From an organisational perspective, medical schools hold the final responsibility for producing graduates equipped with specific skills, knowledge and attitudes in the context of limited resources and a range of regulations by government. However, they do this within the framework of academic and professional views about required competencies (Meyer and Land 2003). In brief, the values, beliefs and perspectives of professionals (professional culture) must be considered as a reality of change. Professionally trained academics have enormous responsibilities in designing the medical curriculum and managing curriculum renewal – processes that must attend to staff empowerment, and the appropriate arrangements for quality management that are discussed in this case study.

Calls for change in medical education have been expressed since the publication of the early Flexner Report (1910). As medicine took on professional status in the early twentieth century, a need to ground clinical education in the basic laboratory sciences emerged. Flexner recognised that, due to the advancement of medicine, clinical practice should be connected to theoretical laboratory sciences. Once basic sciences were mastered, students should learn to apply these in clinical practice. This model remained predominant in Germany until recently. In other countries it lost importance twenty years ago, especially in Anglo-Saxon countries, where it was acknowledged that medical problems should serve as the organisational principle of curricula instead of the traditional, disciplinary framework (Harris 1993). Curriculum change was based on the premise that disciplinary knowledge should be made functional to understand and learn medical problems as encountered in medical practice (McGuire 1996). Hence far-reaching curriculum reforms have been developed in the medical domain, such as problem-based learning (Wilkerson & Gijselaers 1996).

The inherent nature of producing competent graduates in medicine may not differ markedly from delivery of any higher education graduate. However, variations emerge because the constraints differ. To illustrate this, the case study adopts a production metaphor from the business world. It is true that universities differ from business organisations, and graduates are certainly not comparable to cookies (products) or summer vacations (services). However, the development of successful graduates may still be considered a production problem with certain production constraints to provide insight into the issues that arise for German medical schools in adapting to new legislation of the German Federal Government.

Professional and academic values and expectations are significant features of curriculum change. For example, a 'production constraint' in German medical schools has been adherence to Flexner's discipline-based views of curriculum design. Only through recent government interventions (enforced by law in 2002) has this model partly been discarded as a curriculum guideline. A second constraint originates from general, academic 'ways of thinking', such as deeply rooted beliefs that students should have the right to select from a wide variety of courses or so-called principles of 'academic freedom to teach'.

Beyond professional values and beliefs, the strongest production constraint is the German government's impact on curriculum governance. It has legislated detailed laws concerning required curriculum content, pedagogy and assessment. As a consequence, the history of curriculum change is one dominated by top-down decision-making with few options for individual medical schools interested in developing unique curriculum profiles.

This case study of a case of top-down curriculum change in a German medical school will examine obstacles to change by connecting curriculum design problems with the change process that affect patterns of work between individual teachers, departments and committees. The analysis is based on the emerging view that change processes are essentially interactive learning processes within an organisation (Evans 1996; Bland *et al.* 2000; Boonstra 2004). It deviates from the dominant view that curriculum change is essentially a matter of changing organisational structures. Researchers, such as Quinn (1997), have questioned this view and pointed out that, although it makes sense for organisations to focus on structure, it does not explain why organisations become stagnant over longer periods of time when they are preoccupied with structure.

According to Quinn (1997), individuals possess knowledge, values, assumptions, rules and competencies. However, as the world changes, this knowledge loses sense, resulting in problems, because those individuals do not learn from what happens outside their organisation. Incremental changes are no longer sufficient to cope with emerging problems. Denial and resistance to change are the inevitable outcome of this scenario. A key point in this chapter is that organisations sensitive to changes in the outside world address stagnation and resistance by stimulating debate between individuals and by encouraging learning processes that allow modifications in knowledge, values and competencies, resulting in the capacity to initiate and cope with change.

The focus on educational change has now shifted from structure to culture, from top-down decision-making processes (structure) to the creation of faculty-wide commitment (culture), from hierarchy to development of leadership, and from delivering products to coaching change processes (Evans 1996; Boonstra 2004). These new views on change processes allow participants to develop a shared vision on curriculum standards, pedagogy, and the skills necessary for change. This case analysis shows the importance of communication, social practices and leadership that engages participants in and outside the change process.

Changing views about change management

Change is often described as a rational process, managed by changing rules and procedures. Changed behaviour and outcomes are considered the result of new rules or new procedures. According to Evans (1996), the traditional model of educational change finds its basis in three elements of Taylor's scientific management model: stability, rationality, and structure. In the early twentieth century, new industrial developments, such as mass production, resulted in developing management procedures based upon standardisation, mechanisation, specialisation, and bureaucratisation. In this model, an organisation and its environment are predictable and stable entities. For example, an educational organisation may be understood in terms of official roles, a formal hierarchy and clear procedures. Organisational problems may be understood in terms of imperfections in the organisational structure. Change takes place through clear-cut, top-down decision-making. Evans (1996) defines this view as the rational-structuralist approach to management of change.

This recipe seems doomed to failure at universities. In the case of Weatherhead School of Management (Cleveland, USA) presented by Boyatzis *et al.* (1994), the school followed the traditional model of curriculum change. Attempts to change the MBA programme were made in 1979, 1984, 1987 and 1988; all of these attempts failed. In each case, the proposals for change were not supported by the faculty. According to Boyatzis et al. (1994) the typical remark of faculty members was: 'Let's not tinker. The proposal is not a sufficiently dramatic change'. This happened despite the fact that MBA programes were heavily criticized by corporations and professional bodies, and colleges of business were experiencing decreasing enrolments.

Evaluations of the change process at Weatherhead School of Management identified six factors causing this lengthy preparation period. First, it was their first attempt in the history of the school to engage the entire faculty in the change process. Second, faculty questioned the need to make a transition from a discipline-based organisation to a faculty-wide organisation. Third, it was difficult for faculty to commit themselves to revolutionary change instead of evolutionary change. Fourth, an insufficient number of staff members were available to take leadership in the change process. Fifth, the planning process was limited to a number of 'in-crowd' faculty (position-related); teaching staff perceived the problems as something for the administrators or faculty leaders, and not as their own problems. Sixth, no stakeholders from outside the organisation were involved.

The key to understanding this case lies in the fact that members of the organisation were not convinced that change was necessary, and that no attention was paid to the balance of power, individual psychological factors, and the culture of the organisation. Recently, Boonstra (2004) cast doubt about planned change efforts. When changes are initiated and controlled by the top, people feel pushed away from existing work procedures, and not invited to participate because no one asks for their input, ideas or opinions. Boonstra's view aligns with that of Bromage (2006), who emphasised the importance of ownership of those involved in the change process.

Management researchers have shifted their views on change management from structure to the importance of organisational culture, from top-down decision-making to the creation of faculty-wide commitment, from organisational hierarchy to development of leadership, and from planned change to encouragement of learning processes. Evans (1996) calls this new approach 'the strategic-systemic paradigm', which is the opposite of the 'rational-structural paradigm.' This paradigm does not deny the need to change structures; instead it argues that:

> Structure, though important, is not a sufficient focus for change. Centring innovation on formal tasks and procedures and moving directly to how-to-do-it training ignores much about the process of how people actually change (especially how they alter their beliefs).
>
> (Evans 1996)

Recent management research pays more attention to participation and commitment building. Learning is considered to be the key for organisations. Adaptation to changes in the environment, and the development of strategies that allow continuous modification of organisational processes is essential for successful change (Gardiner and Whiting 1997). Ramsden (1999) shows that academics working in institutes for higher education face similar issues in their daily work as researcher/teacher. Academics' beliefs and perceptions drive their motivation and readiness for adapting to change, and should not be ignored.

Medical educators have become aware that they can learn from industrial management research and transfer knowledge about change processes from organisations to their medical schools (Bland *et al.* 2000; Armstrong 2004). Bland *et al.* found good leadership to be essential for success. However, leadership should not be considered in traditional hierarchical terms: rather, good leaders are able to articulate and advocate an organisational vision, build opportunities to develop a shared vision, give practical guidance, and allow that change is a learning process in which feedback is essential.

Background to the case study

The present case study took place at the Medical School of Hamburg University, Germany. This school decided on radical changes in its clinical curriculum after the Federal Council in Germany passed a new law (Approbationordnung für Ärzte) for medical education in 2002. Through this law, the German government wants to improve medical knowledge and skills in all medical subjects. This new law had a substantial impact on the design of clinical education in Germany. The following major changes were required.

- The number of mandatory national exams was reduced from four to two. This implied a substantial change, because current curriculum practices were based on detailed content guidelines from the National Institute for Medical and Pharmaceutical examinations.
- Integrated, theme-based courses should cover a substantial part of the curriculum.
- The medical school became highly responsible for assessment of required medical competencies.
- The number of teaching hours in hospitals was substantially increased.
- A substantial amount of instruction time should be dedicated to small-group work (three to six students), with a special emphasis on the pedagogy of problem-based learning.
- Group size in seminars should not exceed twenty students.
- Medical schools are allowed to develop different curriculum profiles as long as they fit within the general legal framework.

Medical schools also had to change their curriculum governance because this law required changes in:

- pedagogy (introduction of problem-based learning), organisation of curriculum contents (multidisciplinary courses)
- assessment practices (increased responsibility for medical schools), increased orientation to professional practice (bedside teaching, learning at clinical wards, emphasis on skills training)
- course schedules (reduced group sizes).

The following organisational changes needed to be explored to make radical reform possible.

- The traditional departmental-driven and discipline-based organisation focused on cooperation within departments; reform required an organisation that fostered and rewarded cooperation between departments.
- Multidisciplinary teacher teams were required for organising new clinical courses.
- Staff development became a necessity for the acquisition of new pedagogical skills.
- Traditional evaluations focused at the course level. Reform required evaluation at the curriculum level as well.

How was the change process planned and managed?

Hamburg Medical School had hardly any experience of effective curricular change. The previous major change had taken place over twenty years before those that are the subject of this case study. As a consequence, innovation remained focused at the mono-disciplinary course level. The current initiative involved the implementation of a new curriculum framework organised around academic years, and not around semesters. Each year consists of rotating thematic blocks that address certain clinical issues from an integrative perspective. Blocks are offered as modules, which may be taken in free order. Each block aims to foster student-centred learning, and offers course content from a multi-disciplinary and integrated perspective. For our analysis, we adopt a framework based upon Bland *et al.* (2000), who identify three political components most salient for curricular change in medical schools: internal networking; resource allocation; and the intstitution's relationship with its external environment.

One of the key issues is whether the school 'owns' or 'controls' the curriculum. In this case, individual faculty or departments, and not the medical school, controlled the new curriculum. Hamburg Medical School decided that the new organisation should reflect the new curriculum framework. A curriculum committee, with twelve members, was installed to develop a curricular strategy and structure in weekly meetings. The committee defined a competence profile for graduates and the overall educational goals of clinical education, which include active learning, problem-based learning, clerkships, self-study and new forms of assessment.

The committee appointed one, multi-disciplinary teacher team for each thematic block. Departments were invited to nominate faculty staff to participate in the weekly meetings. These teams became responsible for the development of a common catalogue of learning objectives for the new clinical curriculum (KliniCuM), selection of course contents, course design and course assessment.

Communication took place in various ways. News about the new curriculum was published in the university newspaper on a regular basis. Faculty meetings were organised to inform the heads of departments about the change process. Training units were planned for faculty members to become tutors for problem-based courses, design multiple-choice questions or organise exams for practical skills.

Concerning 'regular resource allocation', nothing changed. However, a special budget from the office of the Dean of Education was set aside to pay for the work of the curriculum committee, faculty development courses, participation in a medical education programme, invitations of educational experts, and for setting up a skills lab.

In regard to establishing 'relationships with the external environment', links with other institutions were sought in various ways. For example, since further planning required broad support from staff, a teacher training course was offered for 32 faculty members of Hamburg Medical School in cooperation with Heidelberg University (Germany). This course prepared staff with detailed knowledge of educational strategies and skills in learning and assessment methods. Curriculum committee members received training and feedback from external experts in medical education. During two, two-day sessions they discussed the development of the curriculum, worked on course outlines, and assessed possibilities for establishing curriculum change. A few members of the committee took part in a two-year postgraduate Master of Medical Education (MME) programme at the University of Bern (Switzerland).

Evaluation of the change process

Participation in the change process is the core factor in developing shared visions. Members acquire a voice in the change process, develop an understanding of the current situation, and learn to see solutions. They meet faculty from other departments, learn about the rationale of the innovation, and profit from faculty development, meetings with curriculum experts, and visits to external partners (Levin 2004). In our case, several different groups of faculty were involved in the change process in Hamburg. Their engagement in the change process differed substantially depending on their position in the institutional hierarchy. The curriculum committee members met external experts and participated in external faculty development programmes or postgraduate programmes. It will be seen that other faculty were less well-connected.

We investigated how various faculty members felt about the change process depending on their degree of linkage with the curriculum change process

(Harendza 2003). To find out how the curricular reform process was judged by the different groups and to decide how further faculty development should evolve to improve the change process, four groups of faculty were identified:

Group 1: The curriculum committee (6 members)
Group 2: Thematic block groups participating in the 'teach the teacher' programme (10 members)
Group 3: Thematic block groups not participating in the 'teach the teacher' programme (8 members)
Group 4: Faculty staff not actively involved in the curriculum reform process (6 members)

The groups reflected differences in the degree of involvement in the change process. From each group, a random sample was chosen to collect judgments about the change process.

Research into curriculum reform processes has identified several factors that influence the success of curriculum change. In their review of the process of planning, implementing, and institutionalising curricular change efforts Bland *et al.* (2000) identified ten factors that seem important for change efforts:

1   cooperative climate
2   politics (internal networking, resource allocation, relationship with external environment)
3   strong leadership
4   good communication and information
5   shared vision and goals
6   faculty development (training, reward structure)
7   history of change in the organisation
8   active participation of faculty in the reform process
9   evaluation as quality control of the reform process
10   need for change.

All participants were asked to rank these factors from 'most important for curricular change' to 'least important for curricular change' using a matched-pair analysis. Each factor had to be compared individually with every other factor from the list in a table modified according to Thomas (1992).

The table featured a list of the ten factors in the same order both across its top and down its right hand side, giving a grid of 100 boxes. Each box in the main grid represented the comparison of a factor from the vertical list with a factor from the horizontal list. The participants were briefed to allocate a total of 10 points across each pair of boxes in the grid that compare the same two factors (e.g. vertical factor one with horizontal factor two and vertical factor two with horizontal factor one). These points express the relative importance of the two factors to each other. If, for example, the horizontal factor one is judged more important than the vertical factor two, the respective box will be filled with a number higher than 5 (6–9, depending on 'how much more important' the factor one is) and the respective other box in the other lane will be filled with the difference to 10 (1–4). Factors that are equally important receive 5 points in both boxes.

This main grid was appended by two columns on its left hand side, one for the sum of each row of ten scores, and one for the rank of these sums relative to each other. When all factors are compared individually with each other, the points for each factor are added horizontally, row by row, and the total number of points is recorded in the corresponding box in the 'sum' column. Ranks are then assigned to all of these sums: the highest sum is ranked as 1; the lowest score is ranked as 10.

Every member of each group assigned a rank for all ten factors individually, and so a ranked sum score was made for every group for all ten factors. This technique enables a better understanding of the group members' overall mental model about processes that take place in a particular situation or organisation. The results are summarised in Figure 9.1, which shows the different rankings as provided by the four groups.

Outcomes of the analysis

Figure 9.1 shows that the curriculum committee attributed great importance to 'cooperative climate' and 'shared vision and goals'. These factors are related to interaction with participants in the reform process. This may be explained by the way in which this committee, the group with the longest participation in curricular development, worked as a group. They experienced a cooperative climate from the very beginning. The curriculum committee had 4-hour meetings on a weekly basis. The meetings were characterised by open discussions and humour. Conflicts were addressed openly and all members of the committee volunteered for additional tasks, if necessary. They showed great interest in reaching consensus when making decisions and commented on the good group climate.

The importance of 'shared visions and goals' may be attributed to the start of the curriculum committee's work with a two-day workshop on curricular development. Since the medical school had almost no history of curricular change, the committee members needed to learn about management of these processes, and how to cooperate with people from different disciplines. After the workshop, the curriculum committee developed visions and goals for the curricular reform process in Hamburg, the foundation for all further developments.

Interestingly, 'good communication and information' is ranked fairly low by the curriculum committee, while both sets of thematic block groups put this factor on rank one. This discrepancy might highlight that good communication and information are inseparable from the 'cooperative climate' that the curriculum committee had already experienced for quite some time in the process (rank one for this group). Thematic block groups not participating in the 'teach the teacher' programme depend on what has been decided by the curriculum committee and

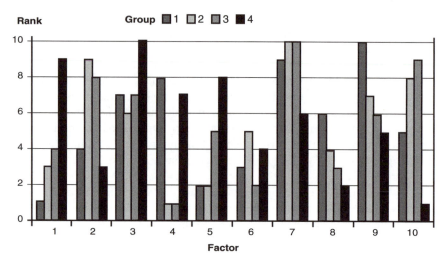

Figure 9.1   Rankings of different factors

need to understand the decisions. These observations are consistent with the literature showing that need for information and communication depends on the rank of a person within a reform process (Weiss 1995). The lower one is in the hierarchy, the more one perceives the need for such communication.

'History of change in the organisation' appears to be relatively unimportant to our participants. It appears on rank nine for the curriculum committee and on rank ten in both sets of thematic block groups. This is understandable, since hardly any participants had had experience in curricular reform in the past. In contrast, for faculty staff not actively involved in the curriculum reform 'history of change in the organisation' appears on rank six, which might have to do with the fact that these teachers still remember the problematic experiences with the development of a problem-based curriculum as parallel track in 2001. Also, they did not share the mutual visions of the other three groups when the study took place. The mutual experience during the faculty development week of the thematic block groups participating in the 'teach the teacher' programme seems to have had a major impact on their perception of the reform process. This confirms Evan's theory (1996) that systematic change cannot take place mechanically in prescribed, developmental steps, but rather it happens at a deeper psychological level, which influences attitudes and actions.

Experience of innovation arising from top-down decisions may cause a feeling of detachment. Our results seem to confirm this assumption. Faculty staff not actively involved in curriculum reform, those with the lowest engagement in the change process, put 'need for change' on rank one. For all other groups this factor is far less important. This may be explained by the fact that they are already involved in the reform process. It seems likely that staff who are not actively involved in the curriculum reform do recognise that change is needed, despite their lack of involvement. This could also explain why 'cooperative climate' is relatively unimportant to them (rank nine), while the other groups put this factor between ranks one and four. Faculty not actively involved in the curriculum reform, having not yet participated in the process, thus perceive a cooperative climate to be important. At the same time, this group wants to participate in the curricular reform process, because they placed 'active participation of faculty in the reform process' on rank two. Comparing these ratings and those of the other groups suggests that factor eight is ranked lower by groups whose members are active participants in the change process.

'Evaluation as quality control of the reform process' was put on rank five by faculty not actively involved in the curriculum reform, which is, in fact, the highest rank for this factor across all groups. This difference could indicate a wish for quality control and prevention of inappropriate developments by the latter group, whereas the curriculum committee is occupied with its involvement in the planning and implementation steps of the change process. It suggests that some participants interpret 'importance' in terms of personal relevance.

The influence of 'politics' on the reform process is ranked fairly highly by the curriculum committee and faculty not actively involved in the curriculum reform (ranks four and three respectively). In contrast, both sets of thematic block groups rank this factor on rank nine and eight respectively. This could be due to the timing of this study. At the beginning of the committee work, the resource allocation and distribution of rooms and personnel seemed a great worry. Discussions about these issues were interrupted in the beginning because they blocked creative thinking and the development of a curriculum strategy. The ranking of this factor arguably shows different groups at different stages of their learning process and attributes the importance of certain factors to the state of learning and engagement.

'Faculty development' was consistently highly ranked by all groups. This could reflect a strong wish to gain competencies for participation in the change process. Another consistent finding across the groups was that 'strong leadership' was perceived to be of importance. Two explanations seem possible for this counterintuitive finding. One is in line with Boonstra's observation (2004) that top-down decisions result in low engagement. It might be the case that the former experiences of faculty with 'strong leadership' are mostly based on 'autocratic' management, and not on leadership based on providing guidance (Ramsden 1999). This results in the perception that leadership is a negative factor and has to be put on a low rank. The second explanation may be that leadership has worked quite well during the reform process so far. As consequence, faculty did not experience leadership as 'strong' in the sense of 'pushy', explaining the low rank of this factor.

Facilitating factors and obstacles for change

Independent of current personal involvement in the curricular reform process, 'faculty development' was nominated the most important factor for a successful curricular reform. The least important factor was perceived to be 'strong leadership'. These findings are intriguing, given that the Dean of Education showed strong leadership from the very beginning of the reform process. His strategy was to engage individual faculty by establishing a curriculum committee, and a teacher team for course design. Special attention was paid to building a shared vision by participating in workshops. It is, thus, arguable that his strong leadership was not necessarily salient to our participants, in that it did not draw attention to itself.

Groups with different roles and degrees of engagement in the change process developed different views on the importance of factors for the change process. Their perceptions reflect substantial differences in the learning processes of participants. By contrasting the curriculum committee and faculty not actively involved in the curriculum reform, it becomes evident that belonging to the core of the change process results in substantially different perceptions of what is important. This is in line with observations from management research (Boonstra 2004, Evans 1996), which highlights the importance of engagement in the change process.

An obstacle to change lies in the incentive and reward structures of Hamburg Medical School. At the time our research was conducted, these structures were not aligned with the requirements of the curriculum reform process. However, since the new curriculum requires the development of new teaching competencies, participation in faculty development programmes and financial rewards for high-quality teaching are presently being established.

Conclusions

The case study reported in this chapter shows that organisational change is influenced by the design of the associated learning processes for faculty. Academic institutions flourish on debate and discussion. This implies that existing academic mechanisms for exchange of information should be used as part of the change management process, which gives rise to the question: To what extent does faculty engagement in the change process facilitate development and the implementation of new curricula?

In this study, insights from management research were used to analyse the needs of individual, faculty staff. It is often thought that only new (medical) schools can implement educational innovations because of the associated radical changes that are needed in the organisational structure and culture (Bouhuijs 1990). However, as shown here, change may occur even within established schools. In our case, the pressure for change was external, arising from the legislative environment in which the medical school operates. The relative importance of factors in the change process differed according to the degree of engagement of groups of academics in the change process. It may be concluded that these differences can be accounted for in terms of individuals' perceived learning needs in relation to the process of change.

Our findings imply that the key to successful change is a careful consideration of the learning needs of different groups in relation to the proposed changes. In an academic context, this would mean considering how to develop processes that encourage engagement, vitality and competence. Centralised planning of learning experiences to satisfy these needs will be problematic, as what is perceived as important by the planners will tend to differ, in many cases substantially, from the perceptions of more peripheral groups.

These findings are consistent with an existing body of literature that emphasises change as a learning process. For example, Bromage (2006) indicates that both Trowler's (1998) and Hopkins and Ainscow (1993) reach broadly similar conclusions, as does Elton (1994) in his 'new collegiality' model, which also has the long-term, strategic aim of developing a change-ready 'learning institution'. Similarly, Errington (2001) addressed the provision of learning opportunities in a way that closely fits our conclusion that people, perceptions, engagement and organisational culture form a significant part of the reality of change in higher education.

Bibliography

Armstrong, E., Mackey, M. and Spear, S.J. (2004) 'Medical education as a process management problem', *Academic Medicine,* Vol.79, 721–28.

Bland, C., Starnaman, S., Harris, D., Wersal, L., Moorhead-Rosenberg, L., Zonia, S. and Henry, R. (2000) 'Curricular change in medical schools: how to succeed', *Academic Medicine,* Vol. 75, 575–94.

Boonstra, J. (ed.) (2004) *Dynamics of Organisational Change and Learning,* Wiley Handbooks in the Psychology of Management in Organisations, Sussex: John Wiley.

Bouhuijs, P.A.J. (1990) 'The maintenance of educational innovations in medical schools', in Z. Nooman, H.G. Schmidt and E. Ezzat (eds.) *Innovation in Medical Education: An Evaluation of its Present Status,* New York: Springer Publishing Company, 175–88.

Boyatzis, R., Cowen, S. and Kolb, D. (1994) *Innovation in Professional Education,* San Francisco: Jossey-Bass.

Bromage, A. (2006) 'The management of planned change: an interdisciplinary perspective', in L. Hunt, A. Bromage and B. Tomkinson (eds.) *The Realities of Change in Higher Education: Interventions to Promote Learning and Teaching,* London: Taylor & Francis.

Elton. L. (1994) *Management of Teaching and Learning: Towards Change in Universities,* London: CVCP.

Errington, E.P. (2001) 'The influence of teacher beliefs on flexible learning innovation in traditional university settings', in F. Lockwood, and A. Gooley (eds.) *Innovation in Open and Distance Learning: Successful Development of Online and Web-Based Learning,* London: Kogan Page.

Evans, R. (1996) *The Human Side of School Change: Reform, Resistance, and the Real-Life Problems Of Innovation,* San Francisco: Jossey-Bass.

Flexner, A. (1910) *Medical Education in the United States and Canada, A Report to the Carnegie Foundation for the Advancement of Teaching.* Bulletin No. 4, Boston, MA: Updyke.

Gardiner, P. and Whiting, P. (1997) 'Success factors in learning organisations: an empirical study', *Industrial and Commercial Training,* Vol. 29, 41–8.

Harendza, S. (2003) *Process Analysis of the Development of a New Clinical Curriculum at the Medical School of Hamburg University (Germany)* [Prozessanalyse der Entwicklung eines neuen klinischen Curriculums (KliniCuM) an der medizinischen Fakultät der Universität Hamburg], unpublished Masters Thesis, Master of Medical Education Program, University of Bern, Switzerland.

Harris, I.B. (1993) 'New expectations for professional competence', in L. Curry and J.F. Wergin (eds.) *Educating Professionals: Responding to New Expectations for Competence and Accountability,* San Francisco: Jossey-Bass, 17–52.

Hopkins, D. and Ainscow, M. (1993) 'Making sense of school improvement: an interim account of the "Improving the Quality of Education for All" Project', *Cambridge Journal of Education,* Vol. 23, No. 3, 287–304.

Levin, M. (2004) 'Organizing change processes', in J. Boonstra (ed.) *Dynamics of Organisational Change and Learning,* Sussex: John Wiley & Sons, 71–84.

McGuire, C. (1996) 'Contributions and challenges of medical education research', *Academic Medicine,* Vol. 71, No. 10, 121–26.

Meyer, J. and Land, R. (2003) *Threshold Concepts and Troublesome Knowledge: Linkages to Ways of Thinking and Practising within the Disciplines,* ETL project Occasional Report 4. Available at <http://www.ed.ac.uk/etl/publications.html> (accessed 12 December 2005).

Quinn, R.E. (1997) *Deep Change: Discovering the Leader Within,* San Francisco: Jossey-Bass.

Ramsden, P. (1999) *Learning to Lead in Higher Education,* London: Routledge.

Thomas, B. (1992) *Total Quality Training,* London: McGraw-Hill.

Trowler, P. (1998) *Academics Responding to Change: New Higher Education Frameworks and Academic Cultures,* Buckingham: Society for Research into Higher Education and Open University Press.

Trowler, P., Saunders, M. and Knight, P.T. (2003) *Change Thinking, Change Practices: A Guide to change for Heads of Department, Programme Leaders and Other Change Agents in Higher Education,* York: Learning and Teaching Support Network. Available at <http://www.heacademy.ac.uk/resources>.

Weiss, C.H. (1995) 'The four "I"s of school reform: how interests, ideology, information and institution affect teachers and principals', *Harvard Educational Review,* Vol. 65, 571–92.

Wilkerson, L. and Gijselaers, W.H. (1996) 'Bringing problem-based learning to higher education: theory and practice', *New Directions in Teaching and Learning,* Jossey-Bass Quarterly Sourcebooks, number 68. San Francisco: Jossey-Bass.

Chapter 10

Technology and change in higher education

Conor Vibert and Craig Place

Introduction

There is no question that changes in educational technology have influenced learning and teaching in higher education. In past decades, technological agents of change have included open concept architecture, new forms of visual and audio presentation, the internet and dramatic innovations in computing and communications technologies. However, what counts is not the technological tools themselves, but how they are used. Technology merely opens possibilities: the outcomes are dependent on decisions made. For example, which change processes will result in the effective introduction of new technologies? What pedagogies will inform the introduction and development of new technologies: how will notebooks, pocket PCs or smart phones be incorporated into students' learning environments? Should wireless networks be incorporated? Should support be provided for Apple and Microsoft Windows operating environments?

This chapter will explore the process of technology-led change management at Acadia University, Canada. It will also analyse the usefulness of industry partnerships to advance teaching and learning in higher education. The Acadia Advantage was an academic initiative designed to integrate information technologies into the undergraduate curriculum, with the aim of providing new learning experiences. This case study will describe the 'change' process from the perspective of the senior administrators, who were the change agents, as well as those charged with implementing the initial change, those providing support for change from a teaching and learning perspective, and those affected by the change.

The chapter will begin with a review of the organisational change literature that is relevant to understanding the processes of change. A methodology is then presented that describes the case of Acadia University, the research participants, the survey instrument, and the analytical strategy underlying the case study. A discussion of the outcomes is followed by a conclusion that summarises the realities of change and suggests a number of implications for change management in higher education.

The process of planned change

Innovations in information and communications technologies such as smart phones, digital video cameras, web-based searching and translation software are becoming more deeply embedded in daily life. While the long-term impact of such technological advances may not yet be fully understood, the change dynamics associated with their uptake by organisations can be discussed because these are well documented in a diverse change management literature. The analysis of The Acadia Advantage project is eclectic and includes reference to concepts such as chaos theory, population ecology, life cycle perspectives, punctuated equilibrium, and models involving decay and death (Van de Ven and Poole 1995).

Whether intended or unintended, change occurs when a 'difference exists between two (or more) successive conditions, states or moments in time' (Ford and Ford 1995: 543). These conditions and circumstances exist within broader contexts, which may be conceived as 'sequences of change events that are driven by different conceptual motors and operate at different organisational levels' (Van de Ven and Poole 1995: 510). Van de Ven and Poole argue for the existence of four different basic types:

> A life-cycle model depicts the process of change in an entity as progressing through a necessary sequence of stages ... A teleological model views development as a cycle of goal formulation, implementation, evaluation and modification of goals based on what was learned by the entity ... In dialectical models of development, conflicts emerge between entities espousing opposing thesis and antithesis that collide to produce a synthesis which becomes the thesis for the next cycle ... An evolutionary model of development consists of a repetitive sequence of variation, selection, and retention events in a designated population
>
> (Van de Ven and Poole 1995: 520)

Citing Porras and Silvers (1991), Ford and Ford (1995: 541) suggest several conditions and circumstances that influence individuals to produce new behaviours. These include: a shift in the balance of forces for and against the change; the level of top management commitment; the type of intervention used; individuals' readiness for change; the level of resistance; and the organisation's culture. They also adopt a social constructivist stance, suggesting that the process of change is facilitated by 'intentional communication'.

Implied in these conditions and consequences is the idea that intended organisational change efforts are complex and necessitate focused efforts. Insights from Dunphy and Stace (1988; 1994) suggest the existence of several generic change programmes; developmental transitions, task-focused transitions, charismatic transformations and turnarounds. Developmental transitions place an emphasis on managers' attempts to alter the overall organisational values and beliefs towards one where 'change is considered a normal way of life'. In this programme, teams represent the locus of direction and persuasion, with executives providing insight and contributions in a collegial and consultative manner. Task-focused transitions represent attempts to improve overall structures and systems by emphasising cultures of continuous learning dictated and directed from the executive level, with consultation and input from business unit managers. Charismatic transformation is one form of planned alteration undertaken on a much larger scale than any of the two transitions noted above, the focus being on a fast, radical makeover of the overall firm at both the division and corporate levels. In this case, executive leadership seeks to sway or convince staff members through the high-quality or inspirational nature of their new ideas. A turnaround shares the need for quick action with charismatic transformations; however they are usually more drastic in nature, involving significant and occasionally frequent downsizing, selling off of non-essential divisions, workplace restructuring, and a recentralising of decision-making authority. Such tumultuous upheaval is usually held together by a strong chief executive officer, who guides a management team charged with the design and implementation of a radically new understanding of the corporation's core business.

So, aside from a plan, what facilitates effective organisational change? It is clear from the descriptions above that the social dimensions of change are crucial. Hopkins and Ainscow (1993) argue that '... change is typically facilitated by organisational cultures that are characterized by a consensus of values, willing collaboration and an orderly secure environment where stakeholders are encouraged to take on leadership roles'. Bromage (2006) also suggests 'consensus can never be assumed and a certain amount of resistance is regarded as unremarkable'. Recognised in these thoughts is the idea that conflict between stakeholders with different points of view is a normal part of any change process and must be planned for (Bennis *et al.* 1969).

A second key component is the role of change agents. Referring to organisational leaders, Bromage (2006) argues that:

> There is wide agreement that such leaders should recognise that stakeholders' motivations are likely to differ ... managers must understand and take account of stakeholders' adaptive behaviour during organisational change ... those leading ... the management of planned change must be able to understand and deal with stress, both their own and that of other stakeholders. Similarly, educational change leaders should 'walk the job' to understand the work environment and demonstrate their commitment to change ... Effective communication at all levels is held to be crucial to the success of planned change.

The following case study shows how technology-led change at Acadia University demonstrates the explanatory value of some of the concepts advanced in the literature.

The case study: the Acadia Advantage

Acadia University provides a liberal education to 3800 students in a rural setting in Wolfville, Nova Scotia, Canada. In 1996 Acadia University changed the teaching and learning environment on its campus by integrating notebook computers, leased by the university, into the undergraduate curriculum. This major long-term academic initiative, called The Acadia Advantage, was explained in 1996 by former Acadia University President Dr Kelvin Ogilvie as:

> ... moving the classroom into a new, dynamic, and exciting environment that brings students and faculty together in a fashion that has never before occurred. The dynamism of the classroom is unprecedented. The possibilities are limited only by the imagination.

The Acadia Advantage had a long gestation. Development of the core ideas and planning started in 1987 when Dr Ogilvie became Acadia University's Vice-President Academic. He was looking for ways to provide the quality and quantity of library resources and information available at large universities to Acadia University's comparatively small community of learners, in particular the undergraduate students. Technology-led change provided the answers.

The initial planning stage involved the university librarian and the director of the Computing Centre, who visited leading centres with regard to the collection and dissemination of information in both North America and Europe. Their report concluded that information technology would transform distribution, storage and access to information. In 1991, after review by all academic and support units on campus, a recommendation was made to, and approved by, the Senate and Board of Governors that Acadia University should 'move as quickly as possible to provide access to the world's information at the users' preferred location on campus'. This shows the value of gaining high-level support in change management. It also illustrates that a vision of the future is also important, even if that vision is as yet unformed, though mobile computing was clearly a goal.

The President led a second round of consultation that began in earnest in August 1995. Starting with several keenly interested persons, he sent most of them on site visits to bring back information on the current state of networked and mobile computing. They were invited to present their findings to a larger group of around 20, and then others were sent to find answers to any remaining questions. This group returned and reported to an even larger group. The process was repeated until no new major questions emerged. By October 1995, very large groups of both faculty and students had been involved, and in early 1996 the President held an 'open mic' forum where the key elements of The Acadia Advantage were presented and the community at large was able to ask questions. An estimated 700 persons attended. These consultations, which the President called the 'expanding universe', were extensive and an important feature of the change management process that helped shape the implementation of The Acadia Advantage.

In February 1996, with technology and costs well worked out, the President called an open meeting to plan the implementation strategy. A key element of The Acadia Advantage, was that every student and professor would be issued the same model of IBM ThinkPad(tm) notebook computer. The university would lease the laptops, which would be renewed every two years. A project budget of CA$15 million was raised outside of the university's operating budget. These processes show that key features of change included not only high-level support but also planning, implementation strategies, appropriate resources and a sustainable outcome that would keep technology evergreen.

Timing was important and the plan was to phase in The Acadia Advantage over a five-year period starting in September 1996. Piloting the initiative was also wise because it enabled the project managers to address emergent problems. It also facilitated the use of an early adopters approach that engaged staff in the excitement of a new venture that would benefit their students and their own careers. In the first instance, all new students in Business Administration, Physics, and Computer Science participated in the initiative and 37 professors (early adopters) were issued with notebook computers. Participation was optional for new students in Psychology, French and English. Subsequent to the 1996–97 academic year, when only 350 students participated, all incoming students in all programmes across the university were required to participate in the programme.

Managing the implementation phase

Although The Acadia Advantage was bringing to fruition a recommendation made five years earlier, the final decision to undertake the initiative left only eight months to plan and organise the implementation phase. Such a tight timeline meant good planning, communication and strategic partnering was absolutely critical. An implementation committee was formed that comprised the project coordinator, academic deans, representatives from the university Development Office, Library and Educational Technology groups, Directors of Computer Science and Continuing and Distance Education, the President of the Student Union and an alumni and parent. In the months leading up to September 1996 improvements were made to the university's local area network; there was installation of network access points (data drops) in the library, in classrooms and across campus, while in classrooms, an instructor podium, laptop computer docking station, document camera, video cassette recorder (VCR), sound system and data projector were added. Faculty and staff were trained, new policies and procedures for the use of information technology were developed, and preparations for the distribution of notebook computers to incoming students got underway.

The President guaranteed full support to faculty to help them adapt to this new environment through an expanded information technology help desk (the User Support Centre), and the creation of a faculty support centre, (the Acadia Advantage Academic Development Centre), … now called the Acadia Institute for Teaching and Technology (AITT)). Exemplifying the innovation that was encouraged at the time, the AITT was also fondly known as the Sandbox, a place where faculty, alongside staff and students, could play and build solutions to teaching and learning challenges, try them, then tear them down and start again if they did not work.

In the summer of 1996, just prior to the first year of The Acadia Advantage, the AITT employed three full-time academic computing specialists and 13 summer student assistants. Students and staff helped faculty develop materials and applications for that first year and also gave workshops on the use of various software applications. As no one had experienced this before, it was a time when professors, staff and students were all learning from each other. This model of students working alongside faculty members continues to this day in the AITT. In this sense the project itself became a part of students' learning experiences.

The introduction of notebook computers at Acadia University was a catalyst for discussions about teaching and learning, with professors questioning the pedagogical soundness of computers in the classroom. It was understood that the technology would not in itself make someone a better teacher; however it provided new opportunities to those willing to use it. Acadia Advantage promotional materials highlighted the possibilities for transforming the learning experience and used terms such as student-centric, active and collaborative learning, interactivity and multimedia. Although it was suggested that technology should be used only when appropriate, there was limited research on the benefits of a mobile computing environment, so it was left up to individual professors to make this judgement call – no different from the implementation of any other technology into their classroom, whether overhead projectors, television or chalkboards.

Having outlined the initiative, we will now briefly explore its broad impact on Acadia University, before evaluating the process of change underlying The Acadia Advantage.

A brief evaluation of the impact of Acadia Advantage

There has been no systematic institutional evaluation of The Acadia Advantage; however, there exist a variety of sources indicative of its effects. One aspect is the impact of the initiative on the esteem of Acadia University, and another its impact on the student experience at Acadia, and they will be dealt with in turn.

In the late 1990s, academic institutions from around the world were interested in the new opportunities offered by mobile computing. In December 1996 the first tour by other institutions wanting to experience The Acadia Advantage was organised. As a consequence, Acadia University's name, along with that of a few other institutions, became synonymous with mobile computing. The Acadia Advantage programme was recognised by, and incorporated into, the Permanent Collection of the Smithsonian Institute in Washington, DC in 1999. The programme has also been recognised through the Pioneer Award of the Ubiquitous Computing Society in 2001, and a Canadian Information Productivity Award (CIPA) in 1997. Every year *Maclean's,* a popular magazine in Canada, asks 'opinion leaders', for example, university officials, corporate recruiters and school principals, to rank universities according to a variety of criteria. In their 1996 ranking, Acadia University was judged Canada's 'best overall and most innovative primarily undergraduate university'. Acadia's ranking in *Maclean's* continues to be one of the highest in Canada.

Turning next to the student experience, every year since the start of the initiative, Acadia University has surveyed the student population on aspects of the initiative and produced an internal report. Typically, up to 20 per cent of the student body respond to the survey. The survey of 2004 (Centre for Organisational Research and Development 2004) attempts a comparison with the findings of earlier surveys since 1997, where equivalent data exists. When asked what they felt stood out most about The Acadia Advantage, 58 per cent of the respondents responded positively, mainly in terms of the convenience of having a laptop (12.2 per cent), the ease of communication with classmates and professors (9.7 per cent) and the academic value in and out of the classroom (8.6 per cent), making comments such as 'It has helped me with my school work, and has kept me organised'. It also appears that student computer use depends upon their academic programmes, in terms of the challenges and opportunities they present, of which more will be said later.

The majority of respondents felt that computers were a useful tool (23.8 per cent) and that they increased their computer skills (17.5 per cent). On the other hand, those who judged that their expectations were not met felt there was not enough classroom use or hookups (36 per cent) and that the programme was too expensive (30.7 per cent). On average, 47.2 per cent of students took their computer to class two or fewer times per week: indeed, it has been seen that students called for more classroom use of computers. However, the majority (66.3 per cent) agreed that their instructors had an adequate computer knowledge.

When asked what they felt would improve The Acadia Advantage, the students tended to call for better computers (17.6 per cent), and lower costs (15.7 per cent); however, compared to the 2003 survey, the latter proportion has approximately halved. In 2004, the students also called for 'more classroom use/teach professors more about computers' (13.8 per cent).The majority of students (54.6 per cent) either agreed or strongly agreed that their experiences matched their prior expectations of The Acadia Advantage. This question also featured in the 2002 and 2003 surveys, and it appears that the proportion who agree or strongly agree has tended to increase over this period.

In terms of long-term benefits of the Acadia Advantage, approximately 89 per cent of respondents reported knowing a fair amount or having extensive computer knowledge after attending Acadia University, compared to 67 per cent before. They also tended to agree that The Acadia Advantage prepared them to use technology effectively in their career and that they would have an advantage over non-Acadia students when applying for jobs.

The 2005 survey has not at the time of going to press been made publicly available. However, early indications are that the majority of respondents agreed with the statements 'I would recommend the Acadia Advantage programme' and 'my laptop is an integral part of my day-to-day life as a student doing academic work'. These findings again indicate that the initiative is continuing to embed information and communication technologies in the day-to-day activities of students at Acadia.

There are also some external data sources that provide an insight into the impact of the initiative. In the first Maclean's Graduate Survey of 2004, 82 per cent of those Acadia graduates who responded rated their educational experience as 'very good'. These diverse sources are indicative of how the technology-led innovation raised the status of the university, making it attractive to prospective students and rewarding senior staff with sustainable and marketable outcomes.

An evaluation of the technology-led change process

To understand the transformation process underpinning The Acadia Advantage, an open ended survey was developed and administered to four individuals who participated in its implementation. These included the university President who had served from 1993 to 2003, the Project Manager for The Acadia Advantage initiative, a manager employed with the AITT, and a tenured Business School faculty member, who had commenced his teaching career in September 1996. The survey instrument was designed to gain insights regarding four areas of interest: the factors for change, the change process, the obstacles to change and other important factors. Each participant was asked questions related to each of these four areas.

The design and implementation of The Acadia Advantage initiative was complex and involved extensive change across the university. Interestingly, the President and the Project Manager viewed the implementation of The Acadia Advantage as the mid-point of a planning process begun in the late 1980s: however, many at the university, including some academic support staff, considered it to be just the beginning. The following analysis offers insight into the changes that took place by highlighting the factors, processes and obstacles to change as revealed by the results of the qualitative evaluation.

Change is effective when it is relevant and meaningful. One respondent noted that a primary motivation for moving to a mobile computing environment was a societal shift to the everyday use of information technology. The expectations of teenagers already using these new computing technologies would have to be met when they reached university. Another respondent took a more pragmatic perspective, citing ongoing government cutbacks as well as the advent of the internet. One of the responses was eclectic, noting that impetus for The Acadia Advantage arose from government funding cutbacks, a need to change how teaching occurs, a perceived need for intuitive use of technology by students, as well as a need for evergreen technology. Whether educational considerations led the technological change or vice versa was an arguable point but, in considering why the changes actually occurred, it was suggested that the vision and personality of the President were quite important. In brief, educational leadership matters.

The broad educational motivators for change, as noted in The Acadia Advantage promotional materials, were that computers would 'change the way professors teach and students learn', and that students at Acadia University should expect 'a dynamic experience in their classes as they explore new ways of learning with their professors'. Although difficult to articulate at the onset, the President expected the improved access to information to empower students, to change the student–professor dynamic, and to increase the communication skills of students. When it came to the importance of improving education, the President's comments were telling:

> If I couldn't have seen the educational benefits, it would have been improper of me to have moved forward on Acadia Advantage. Just computers and software, that's not Acadia Advantage, it's how it changes the way you interact with your students.

One respondent to the evaluative survey suggested that expected learning and teaching outcomes included '... a better use of time in and out of the classroom, improved communication and enhanced interaction with course materials. New opportunities were expected to materialise'. Another considered Acadia Advantage to be a tool to provide access to information at the user's preferred workplace. He anticipated many outcomes, including the creation of an even playing field for faculty and students in terms of technology access, an evolution away from the lecture style of teaching, and classrooms that are more engaging for students. Only one respondent suggested that the enhancement and improvement of teaching was not the primary objective. He suggested that consistency and affordability of hardware and software were far more important determinants.

The respondents were asked if the intention of The Acadia Advantage was to change the culture of the University. One suggested that a goal of the transformation was the development of a 'culture of collaboration' brought about by the ubiquitous presence of technology. A second respondent focused more on the specific attributes of any intended cultural change, suggesting a goal of technically literate faculty and staff along with improved communication. Another suggested that it was more of the same because 'there's a culture of innovation at this institution that has existed for decades and I think we accept innovation as part of our culture – we expect it. So it was an important aspect of Acadia Advantage.' Ideas and a vision of themselves were seen to be important: 'innovation is the successful implementation of new ideas, and if you look at Acadia Advantage it was chock-a-block full of the successful implementation of new ideas'. In fact innovation was so important to the success of The Acadia Advantage that it was promoted by the university President, who created the President's Award for Innovation, itself another source of motivation.

Key strategies to promote change included a vision, benchmarking teams and large consultation circles. Effective change has top-down and bottom-up dimensions. In the case of The Acadia Advantage, it was conceived at the top of the organisation, and driven from the bottom in a learning-by-doing or ad hoc manner.

The four respondents differed slightly in who they identified as early change agents, but the consensus was that the President and the Project Manager, the Head Librarian and the Director of the Computing Centre were key change agents, as were some students, in particular the Student Union President.

What enhanced communication of the initiative once implementation had begun? One respondent suggested a strategy of 'the CEO as the organisation' whereby the initiative was associated as much with the individual as the institution. Other notable strategies included a series of showcases, round tables, consultation circles, staff tours of facilities, faculty involvement in the design of facilities, meetings and emails as the primary communication strategies. Overall, the communication strategy was intended to ease fears of using technology. To some degree Acadia University developed its own change and implementation processes because, as the President suggested:

> In the early to mid-1990s wired campuses were few and far between. Even fewer were effectively integrating mobile computing into the classroom, so we had few examples to follow. However, after we implemented Acadia Advantage, many other institutions wanted to follow ... we went from a university primarily known to its own graduates, to the best-known undergraduate university [in Canada].

The Acadia Advantage involved several strategic partners, including IBM, MT&T, Marriot Corporation of Canada Ltd and American Express Special Teams. Addressing the question of the role of industry partnerships, three of the respondents cited the notebook computer partner's role as important, for both the legitimacy that they brought to this small university's efforts and the sharing of ideas about the physical hardware. The Project Manager, not surprisingly, emphasised the role of the telecommunications provider and its competence at building and maintaining a stable computer network in a timely fashion.

One of Acadia University's principal partners was IBM, a company chosen for its breadth of expertise and longevity. Not only did it have hardware and software, but it also had a true interest and commitment to education, as suggested by the President's comment:

> Khalil Barsoum, president of IBM Canada at the time, was excited about what we were doing and became one of our strongest supporters. It was a major commitment for IBM to partner with Acadia, but like all true partnerships there was a mutual benefit; Acadia University got a great deal and total commitment from IBM to help us succeed, and they had Acadia University as a test site [during the early days of academic mobile computing].

Although IBM Canada was to provide services and consultation on the integration of technology, it was imperative to maintain expertise on campus; therefore the Project Manager was appointed from Acadia University.

Threats to the change process and how they were dealt with

Turning next to the participants' insights regarding obstacles to change, the period 1993–2003 was rife with conflict between the university faculty union, national faculty union, and the University administration. There was certainly a need for the human resource dimensions of change to be addressed because of the potential impact of the change on tenure and promotion. Two respondents suggested the existence of an unnecessary but perceived fear among faculty members of repercussions if the technology was not adopted for classroom use. Other perceived sources of tension were a lack of teaching support for faculty members, who are not necessarily trained teachers, as well as a lack of research on the impact of technology on teaching.

All four respondents agreed that the adoption of a common technology platform was crucial to the success of the initiative, allowing technology to be supported and upgraded on a regular basis thereby enabling immense cost savings. The creation of the teaching support unit (AITT) was also seen as important for the overall success of the initiative. Broadly speaking, the AITT was created to eliminate barriers to the use of technology by the faculty, and was a source for funds, training and technical support. It became an important source and repository of ideas, a facilitator for the sharing of ideas and teaching innovations developed by faculty members and others, and also as a key link between the faculty and the information technology departments of the university.

With a number of potential obstacles facing the implementation of The Acadia Advantage, motivation to change was important at all levels. Personal drive to use the technology was the dominant motivator. Other factors in the success of the project included: the institution's status as an early adopter; student feedback; bureaucracy reduction; ease of information sharing and ongoing technology upgrades; financial savings for departments from centralised technology purchasing; staff enthusiasm for access to new technologies; and faculty knowledge that these tools, used appropriately, could benefit students academically. Offering faculty members their own notebook computer as well as the potential to improve teaching and research also proved important. Successful change has something in it for everyone and many faculty members became recognised and acknowledged both at the university and internationally for their expertise in using technology effectively in their teaching.

Discussion and conclusions

It is now nine years since The Acadia Advantage initiative commenced, and any judgement of its long-term impact on Acadia University depends upon a number of variables including not only the evaluation criteria but also who is asked. There are two key aspects: first, the impact of the Acadia Advantage on learning and teaching; and second, the impact of the process of innovation itself on Acadia. This chapter has briefly explored the former, but it is the latter aspect that is of particular relevance to this chapter. This concluding section seeks to explore the issues raised in more depth.

Arguably, the real challenge for The Acadia Advantage initiative was to ensure that the conditions were right for Acadia's innovative culture, established well before the initiative commenced, to survive Acadia's transition to the technologies of the information age. In these terms, The Acadia Advantage initiative has been a success. The decision to make use of a uniform technology platform was critical to this success, as was the provision and maintenance of a stable computer network. The teaching and technology support units played a crucial role in fostering collaboration, both among faculty and between the faculty and information technology units. Equally important were other human factors including the innovation of faculty, staff and students throughout the process.

There are important lessons for those who would lead change. Responses to the qualitative evaluation of The Acadia Advantage show that individual interpretations of the factors, processes and obstacles to change differ across hierarchical levels and functional areas of a university setting. In particular, perceptions of the key motivators that eased or enabled the transformation differed by respondent, and these differences seem related to their occupational role, day-to-day responsibilities and level of control in the change process. The implication is that the process of planning technology-led change must encompass wider issues than the technological infrastructure and, indeed, must be holistic in scope – that is, with parallel changes in an institutions' 'hard' and 'soft' infrastructure. This chapter also serves to demonstrate that such changes take time. The Acadia Advantage was phased in over a five-year period, and is arguably still developing, in the sense that it has become part of the pre-existing culture of innovation at Acadia university. Two very clear conclusions from this case study are first, that change takes time, and second, that it is crucial to have 'champions of change' who are at the top of the institutional hierarchy. Finally, The Acadia Advantage demonstrates what it means to champion rather than merely initiate change.

Bibliography

Bennis, W.G., Benne, K.D. and Chin, R. (1969) *The Planning of Change* (2nd ed.), London; New York: Holt, Reinhart & Winston.

Bromage, A. (2006) 'The management of planned change: an interdisciplinary perspective', in L. Hunt, A. Bromage and B. Tomkinson (eds.) *The Realities of Change in Higher Education*, London: Taylor & Francis.

Centre for Organizational Research and Development (2004) Acadia Computer use Survey, July 2004, Acadia University. Available at <http://aitt.acadiau.ca/research/technology/use_reports/ComputerUseSurveyReport2004part1.pdf> (accessed 12 February 2005).

Dunphy, D. and Stace, D. (1988) 'Transformational and coercive strategies for planned organisational change: Beyond the OD model', *Organisation Studies*, Vol. 9, No. 3, 317–34.

Dunphy, D. and Stace, D. (1994) *Beyond the Boundaries*, Sydney: John Wiley & Sons.

Ford, J.D. and Ford, L.W. (1995) 'The role of conversation in producing intentional change in organisations', *Academy of Management Review*, Vol. 20, No. 3, 541–70.

Hopkins, D. and Ainscow, M. (1993) 'Making sense of school improvement: an interim account of the "Improving the Quality of Education for All" Project', *Cambridge Journal of Education*, Vol. 23, No. 3, 287–304.

Institute of Management Foundation (1998) *Checklist 040: Implementing an Effective Change Programme*, Corby: Institute of Management Foundation.

Porras, J. and Silvers, R. (1991) 'Organisational development and transformation', *Annual Review of Psychology*, Vol. 42, 51–78.

Van de Ven, A.H. and Poole, M.S. (1995) 'Explaining development and change in organisations', *Academy of Management Review*, Vol. 20, No. 3, 510–40.

Chapter 11

Change, cats and complexity science

Mark Atlay

Introduction

Change isn't what it used to be. Many change management texts make the process seem simple – define what you want to do, communicate this to those involved, and support the implementation. Yet change is rarely simple. It is inherently messy, uncertain and problematic. This case study makes the point that 'messy is good' as it explores the implementation of two, sequential change initiatives at the University of Luton. It shows the University's changing attitude to change and compares the different approaches adopted in the development of students' graduate attributes, sometimes known as generic or transferable skills. The analysis of the case study points to the relevance of complexity theory and notions of a learning organisation to an understanding of the realities of change in higher education.

The significance of this case study is that it illuminates the iterative nature of change. It also shows the top-down, middle-out, and bottom-up nature of change in universities. In particular, it reveals the crucial role of staff and educational developers, who often serve as intermediaries between the 'demands' and expectations of senior management and the realities for staff on the ground. Competing demands put those in the middle in a difficult position. They must ensure that there is a response to institutional initiatives – yet they know that obtaining cooperation will be difficult and full engagement nearly impossible. Securing staff cooperation in a change initiative is often likened to herding cats; this case study will argue that this is a false analogy.

Institutional setting

The University of Luton was established in 1993. From its inception it has been committed to vocational education and providing educational opportunity for all who might benefit. The curriculum is fully modularised and programmes are organised within a common credit and regulatory framework. In the early years students could choose from single and combined awards at undergraduate level in most areas. Recently, there has been a move away from providing such flexibility and choice.

Rationale for change

This case study describes how the middle-out staff developers at the University of Luton managed two related changes at different times. The pressures that drove these changes arose from the need to respond to a diverse student population as well as the changing external environment that included a new national policy associated with Personal Development Planning and Progress Files.[1] In line with recent government policy, the University is committed to widening participation and the recruitment of students with latent potential but often poor academic and generic skills. British universities have used the economic benefits of higher education as a marketing tool to attract such students. This has imposed a moral responsibility to ensure that students are adequately prepared for entry into the labour market as well as for the wider demands of life. This chapter describes the development of systems and procedures designed to implement generic skills that respond to the needs of the University of Luton's diverse student population. It required a whole-institution approach and affected policies, procedures and practices, curriculum structures, and student support mechanisms. The processes also challenged the nature of academic roles and demonstrated the importance of developing relationships with all staff to produce effective change.

Phase 1: up to 2000

In the first phase, the University defined a set of 'transferable skills' and sought to embed these in the undergraduate curriculum. In order to ensure consistency across a modular scheme, the approach to change was one of a central curriculum policy with consistent, local implementation (see Atlay and Harris 2000). At this time, the development and embedding of transferable skills had strong guidance from senior management. The model of change adopted approximates to Kotter's (1995) eight stages:

1: Establish a sense of urgency

The sense of urgency was created to address the diverse needs of a rapidly expanding student body. Undergraduate student numbers increased from less than 1,000 to 8,000 over eight years, with many students coming from non-traditional backgrounds. The need to have a coherent framework for the identification and support of skills across a modular scheme was important in ensuring that learning needs were met at a time when traditional tutoring and other systems were being challenged by high student:staff ratios.

2: Form a powerful guiding coalition

The driving force for the change came from the senior management of the University who, despite some staff reticence, drove the development of the institution's transferable skills through the committee structure and into practice.

3: Create a vision

As the institution developed and was granted University status it was relatively simple to create a vision of a modern university with a unifying, modular scheme embracing skills development. This was at a time when modularity was being embraced by the wider academic community and the skills agenda was beginning to develop nationally.

4: Communicate the vision

The skills were communicated to all staff through a 'skills template', which became an important reference point and, together with descriptors about requirements at each year level, provided the core of the University's curriculum design.

5: Empower others to act

The intention of the changes was not only that the skills would be specified but that academic staff would ensure that the skills identified in the modules were taught, practised and assessed (formatively or summatively).

6: Plan for and create short-term wins

When implementing the skills agenda, the University built on its experience of Business and Technician Education Council (BTEC) common skills. Those curriculum areas that had recently had the more vocationally oriented BTEC Higher National Diploma provision found it much easier to understand and implement what was required than subjects where the concept was new.

7: Consolidate improvements and produce more change

Once established, some curriculum areas took the developments beyond the expectations of the University. In Biological Sciences, for example, students were given a detailed and assessed transcript showing the transferable skills they had attained and the standard reached.

8: Institutionalise new approaches

Eventually, the identification of the transferable skills developed and assessed became a requirement for the validation of new modules of study. However, at that stage, attempts to institutionalise the production of a skills transcript for all students were thwarted by the University's student record system.

Outcomes

The University made great strides over this period in supporting students' skills development, as evidenced by student attainment and the comments of external examiners. Indeed, the generally top-down nature of the change meant that the University was at the forefront of implementing the skills agenda. However, this also led to a minimal engagement with the underlying rationale among academic staff in some areas. Over time, staff forgot the reasons why skills needed to be identified. It simply became part of normal institutional processes. Thus generic or transferable skills were not fully embedded in the experiences of academic staff working at the coalface of teaching – and, hence, were not part of the experience of all students. There was a risk that the transferable skills had become so embedded that they ceased to exist. This indicates that there is a need to continually revise and refresh any change initiative and to ask 'is this still working for us?'. At the end of 2000 the University came to the conclusion that it was important to review its skills agenda and the future approach to be adopted.

Interlude: effecting change in higher education

The project

At this time the University became involved in leading a national project on effecting change in higher education (see www.effectingchange.luton.ac.uk). The aim of the project was to develop a 'toolkit' for change, drawing on tools that were already in existence in the public and private sectors. These were revised and refocused for higher education. The project explored how change was accomplished and looked at the developing theories and understanding of change. From the resultant analysis a number of issues became clear:

- There are many different types of change and the strategy to be adopted needs to recognise the nature of the change as well as the circumstances in which you are operating.
- Change is a complex process and most changes do not occur in isolation.
- The culture of the organisation is an important factor to be considered.
- The timescale for the change constrains the approach to be adopted.
- It is important to have an approach to change – and simple models of change rarely apply.

Change and complexity

The University's subsequent approach to revitalising the skills agenda was influenced by notions of a learning organisation (Senge 1990), and complexity theory and its application to change (see Stacey 1992, Fullan 1993, 1999, 2003 and Scott 1999). Many large-scale changes have 'unknowable' outcomes and the change process itself is largely uncontrollable. This is a problem if planned change is

Table 11.1 The traditional and complex views of change clarified and compared

Traditional model	Complex model
Few variables determine outcomes	Innumerable variables determine outcomes
The whole is equal to the sum of the parts (reductionist)	The whole is different from, and more than, the sum of the parts (holistic)
Direction is determined by design and the power of a few leaders	Direction is determined by the emergence and the participation of many people
Individual or system behaviour is knowable, predictable and controllable	Individual or system behaviour is unknowable, unpredictable and uncontrollable
Causality is linear: every effect can be traced to a specific cause	Causality is mutual: every cause is also an effect, and every effect is also a cause
Relationships are directive	Relationships are empowering
All systems are essentially the same	Each system is unique
Efficiency and reliability are measures of value	Responsiveness to the environment is the measure of value
Decisions are based on facts and data	Decisions are based on tensions and patterns
Leaders are experts and authorities	Leaders are facilitators and supporters

Source: Olson and Eoyang (2001)

expected, but also an advantage because it is through the dynamics of the change process that new learning and more effective ways of doing things emerge, leading to effective and lasting change. Olson and Eoyang (2001) compared and clarified the traditional and complex views of change (Table 11.1).

This understanding of change, acknowledging the inherent complexity of dealing with a whole-institutional approach, embracing different subjects and disciplines, a heterogeneous student population, notions of collegiality and both academic and support staff and at a time of multiple and complex changes, seemed an appropriate stance from which to approach the revised change agenda at the University of Luton.

Phase 2: 2000 and beyond

The goals of the project

In 2000, the University committed to reviewing and revising its approach to skills and at the same time national expectations for Progress Files and Personal Development Planning (PDP) were articulated (Quality Assurance Agency 2001). A review of the University's existing approach identified the following issues that needed to be addressed:

- The initial curriculum model, whilst valuable in explicitly addressing skills development, was often seen as mechanistic.
- The need to be able to recognise students' learning in a wider range of settings: the university, employment, volunteering, work experience etc
- The importance of placing greater emphasis on students' responsibility for improving their own learning.
- Increasing the employability of graduates in an increasingly competitive, graduate, labour market.
- Assisting students to recognise and appreciate the skills and attributes they had developed so that they could represent these to potential employers.
- Addressing student motivation and self-efficacy.

The changes the University of Luton sought to effect aligned with those identified by Fullan (1993), reporting on change in the school sector:

> Society expects its citizens to be capable of proactively dealing with change throughout life both individually as well as collaboratively in a context of dynamic, multicultural global transformation (p 4).

> One cannot make a difference at the interpersonal level unless the problem and solution are enlarged to encompass the conditions that surround teaching and the skills and actions that would make a difference (p 11).

The University opted for a dual approach that included working simultaneously on individual and institutional development. It saw personal development planning as being the means to link these two strands. Further details of the changes that have taken place in relation to skills (Atlay 2003) and personal development planning (Atlay 2005) are given elsewhere. In brief, the approach to change adopted had the long-term aim of making the change sustainable and self-renewing.

Applying the lessons of change

> Cultures get changed in a thousand small ways, not by dramatic announcements from the boardroom. If we wait until top management gives leadership to the change we wish to see, we miss the point. For us to have any hope that our preferred future will come to pass, we must provide the leadership.
>
> (Block 1987, quoted in Fullan 1993)

If change is complex in a whole host of ways (cultures, pace, unknowable outcomes, multiple change, external environment, technological developments, and staff turnover), is it possible to manage change? The answer has to be no – if 'manage' is understood to mean tightly controlling change. However, it is possible to manage the conditions that facilitate sustainable and renewable change. Fullan (1993) describes eight lessons of change, based on complexity, dynamism and unpredictability. These will be used as a framework for describing the complex change process adopted in the second phase at the University of Luton.

Lesson 1: You can't mandate what matters – the more complex the change, the less you can force it

All educational changes of value require new skills, behaviour and beliefs or understanding by those who have to implement them. Edicts do not work. Staff and students' learning are the same. It is not possible to force educational change or to compel staff to think differently or to develop new skills. Mandating change makes it undervalued, superficial and temporary.

Change initiatives may come from a number of sources and those involved in developing them may have spent years getting to grips with the issues and debating the proposals. It is unrealistic to expect those who have to implement them to grasp immediately the essentials of what is intended. They require time, help and support to embrace the proposed change. Even then, it is unlikely that everyone will fully understand or to want to fully understand. Real change happens alongside the commitment of those with the key responsibility to make it happen – those at the sharp end: the academics. The acid test is whether these individuals and groups develop the skills and deep understanding to implement and sustain the change.

So, what happened at the University of Luton to implement Lesson 1? First, we addressed the time factor. We were clear about the intended direction of change and the broad time frame, but more relaxed about the precise timescales for implementation. The rationale was that tight timescales lead to surface implementation.

Second, staff in the teaching development unit communicated consistently and via a variety of means (broad policy statements, staff development sessions, updates, and feedback analysis from staff and students). They also found a variety of mechanisms to encourage engagement. These included workshops, small-scale projects and informal discussions. Constant communication was the key. It made staff aware that change was happening. It also created a climate of, and for, change.

The third action to address Lesson 1 was to create a critical mass to coordinate and support change. This led to the need to create 'change agents'. Initially the University had 'volunteers' who broadly fell into two categories: those who embraced the change (sometimes after initial hostility), and those who went along with the change, doing what they thought was expected, but with limited engagement. It became clear that the key constituencies that needed to be engaged were the programme managers and heads of department. Targeted workshops and one-to-one sessions were held to help this process. Subsequently, the University appointed a number of PDP Fellows as key change agents to take forward the next round of development. What may be seen here is that the application of complexity theory is full of paradoxes – those at the forefront of developments need to be supported in moving forward and not held back by the 'laggards': yet those who are less slow can benefit from the enthusiasm and ideas of others. The message conveyed was that it was 'OK to be where you are – as long as you are moving in the intended direction'.

In the initial stages, those leading change initiatives, such as staff developers, needed to help and support those actively engaging in effective change. This gave the change initiative its own momentum. Later it became possible to support those who were less fully engaged.

Lesson 2: Change is a journey not a blueprint – change is non-linear, loaded with uncertainty and excitement and sometimes perverse

There are different types of change; a few have clear and attainable goals but, for many, the final destination is unknown. Those involved are often engaged in managing or coping with multiple changes. Many outcomes are unpredictable, as is the route taken to get there. There are always delays, amended priorities and the need to counterbalance the change you are trying to make, with the reality of day-to-day work. A single change is unlikely to be the sole pre-occupation.

The important thing is the direction of travel, and detailed planning is likely to be out of date shortly after implementation commences. In the case of the change considered here, the aim was to use personal development planning to develop students' skills and attributes and to frame their learning. The variables (for example, staff enthusiasm and understanding, subject requirements, professional requirements, and resources to support) meant that the precise way in which change was to be accomplished was unknown and largely uncontrollable.

This does not mean that planning is not important, but it has implications for the sort of plans required. Planning needs to be high-level, involving the identification of broad aims, objectives and general indicators of the effectiveness of the change. Detailed plans are not worth the paper they are written on. It is through energy and dynamism that change creates true and lasting innovation.

In responding to Lesson 2, the University set broad objectives for the implementation of the revised curriculum and left local teams to develop their own response. The result of this approach was that some areas were much further ahead than others in implementing change. Those responsible for coordinating change had to accept this as the norm. This had implications for the University's quality assurance systems, which had to encourage and support innovation whilst ensuring that institutional expectations, standards and quality were maintained.

The University of Luton sought to create the conditions in which ideas spark off each other. Key staff were drawn together, not just to listen to others making presentations, but actively to engage in discussion with others around the core themes of the changes. This process of dialogue was assisted by funding for small-scale projects to support the broad direction of change. These proved helpful in developing the local curriculum. At the same time, the staff developers were wary about the dissemination of 'good practice' – which is rarely simply transferable. Staff need to find solutions that work for them and their context. Sharing alternative approaches with discussion and genuine debate and reflective practice generally works much better than prescriptions for best practice. This being so, it is important to return to the overall aims of the change project to review progress, to challenge any changes that do not appear to be heading in the intended direction and to recognise that things may get worse before they get better.

Lesson 3: Problems are our friends. Problems are inevitable and you cannot learn without them

> People do not provoke new insights when their discussions are characterized by orderly equilibrium, conformity, and dependence ... People spark new ideas off each other when they argue and disagree – when they are conflicting, confused and searching for new meaning – yet remain willing to discuss and listen to each other.
>
> (Stacey 1992: 120, quoted in Fullan 1993)

Those embarking on major change initiatives often feel that everything needs to be foreseen and planned from the start. Problems are referred to as 'challenges' and are too often ignored, denied, or treated as an occasion for blame and defence (Fullan 1993). In complex changes all of the problems and issues cannot be identified at the outset. Indeed, if there are no problems with a major change, then it probably indicates that not much real change is happening.

Those with responsibility for managing change in higher education often complain about academics and others challenging what is being proposed and doing their own thing. 'It's like herding cats!' goes the cry. This is usually represented as an obstacle to change. Yet, the argument in this chapter is that these challenges need to be welcomed and embraced. They are an important part of the learning process that needs to be supported. Middle-out change agents, such as staff developers, should facilitate the emergence of the real nature of any problems encountered and explore alternative ways around each issue. This requires time and timing. For example, the University of Luton's intention of providing students with a skills transcript was, at first, incompatible with student administrative systems. Now it is being addressed through the new student record system, which is opening up alternative ways of documenting student learning outcomes.

Lesson 4: Vision and strategic planning come later (premature visions and planning blind)

Vision is a much misunderstood construct. In a complex and ever-changing world a vision of a future reality is possible – but this will be only one of a number of possible futures, with little chance of coming to pass in reality. Any notion of a vision created by senior managers and then passed down is likely to be, at best, ignored. It may also fuel resentment, being seen as imposed and management driven – a recipe for failure and disengagement and particularly problematic within an academic culture. What is important is to provide a pre-vision, a sense of purpose around which the academic community can unite. The vision can then be created from the bottom-up and will change and adapt as collective understanding develops.

The initial starting point for the last major change at the University of Luton came from a planning document in 2000. This was given impetus by the national guidelines on Progress Files (Quality Assurance Agency 2001), which meant that University policy needed to be revisited. The revised policy statement was a framework document setting out a broad and flexible structure within which staff were expected to operate. It allowed for local, discipline-based differences. The plan was implemented, and only in 2005 was this clearly articulated in the University's revised Education Strategy since, as a result of trialling and developmental implementation, there was then a much clearer vision. In fact, the Education Strategy was and is seen as a developing document – at each iteration there is greater clarity and sense of purpose. The application of Lesson 4 may be seen in the utilisation of e-portfolios to support the implementation of generic or transferable skills. At the outset the University was keen to explore their use but decided against adopting one (or developing its own) since it did not want the e-portfolio software to drive curriculum change. The University is now returning to this issue with a much clearer view of what might be achieved and how e-portfolios might help.

Lesson 5: Individualism and collectivism must have equal influence. There are no one-sided solutions to isolation and groupthink

> The professional isolation of teachers limits access to new ideas and better solutions, drives stress inward to fester and accumulate, fails to recognise and praise ... Isolation allows, even if it does not always produce, conservatism and resistance to innovation in teaching. ... For complex change you need many people working insightfully on the solution and committing themselves to concentrated action together.
>
> (Fullan 1993: 34)

Groupthink is the tendency to conformity and doing what is perceived to be required with the minimum of challenge. Whilst change might be seen to be happening, it may be superficial. As we have seen, challenge is a positive influence on change. In the context of the University's change programme, much has been learned from the challenges to the perceived norm that came from different subject areas. The University's approach permits, welcomes and celebrates diversity – provided that diversity can be shown to be working to the advantage of the students and that it is broadly aligned with institutional strategy. This has its down side. Hard-pressed staff will say, 'Just tell me what I have to do and I will do it'. This outcome provides no real engagement with the issues. For example, an easy route to developing career management skills, part of our aims, might have been to allow careers staff to deliver this element. However, this would not lead to sustainability. Academic staff have to engage with the change process and the role of careers staff is largely to support and develop the academics, rather than absolving them of their responsibility for delivering an employability-focused curriculum.

Ownership of change is attained through encouraging engagement and ensuring that the collective vision is moulded by the individual visions of those involved. Those leading institutional change will have different priorities and perspectives; their vision will necessarily be different from those at the frontline teaching and supporting students' learning. The change agents, in our case PDP Fellows, proved important in providing the link between the vision of those coordinating the initiative and those delivering at the frontline. Their role is not just to communicate the vision of those at the centre but to feedback the vision and realities of academics' teaching in order to limit both isolation and groupthink.

Lesson 6: Neither centralisation nor decentralisation works. Both top-down and bottom-up strategies are necessary

> Centralisation errs on the side of overcontrol, decentralisation errs towards chaos.
>
> (Fullan 1993: 37)

For real, long-term change there has to be support from the top of the organisation and a groundswell of opinion from the bottom. An important lesson here is the need for middle-out coordination. Those who sit in the middle with a responsibility for change, (often staff and educational developers), have a key role in passing messages up and down the management hierarchy and in making real change happen. Dynamic change is achieved when top-down, middle-out, and bottom-up influences are mutually supportive of the intended purpose. This is where change becomes more than just the sum of its parts because it will start to engage all areas of the organisation in a holistic process. Furthermore, change breeds more change. For example, departments at the University of Luton are already noting that embedding the changes will require different kinds of teaching and learning environments, and are beginning to consider what these might look like.

Lesson 7: Connection with the wider environment is critical for success. The best organisations learn externally as well as internally

> Learning organisations know that there are far more ideas out there than in here. Seeing our connectedness to the world and helping others to see it is a moral purpose and teaching/learning opportunity of the highest order.
>
> (Fullan 1993: 39)

It is important to be engaged in environmental scanning, to know what is going on outside the University and to reflect on this for the implementation of local change. For example, the implementation of Progress Files and PDP are national initiatives in the UK. Different institutions are approaching this in various ways and with varying levels of engagement and success (East 2005). The message for the University of Luton is that there are no simple solutions and change is not easily transferred. Even so, reviewing what is happening outside can move change along and help to crystallize ideas. Instances of how this worked at the University of Luton include the engagement of the PDP Fellows with their own subject networks[2] and the University's own involvement in a number of national groupings, such as the Higher Education Academy,[3] including the Academy's discussion of complexity and change and the Centre for Recording Achievement,[4] which help and support change initiatives.

Lesson 8: Every person is a change agent. Change is too important to leave to the experts, personal mind-set and mastery is the ultimate protection

> No one person can possibly understand the complexities of change in a dynamically complex system ... each and every teacher has the responsibility to help create an organisation capable of individual and continuous renewal or it will not happen.
>
> (Fullan 1993: 39)

Whilst the University has established its PDP Fellows as change agents, it recognises that this will not be enough. Sustainable change will be effected only when key staff have sufficient awareness and commitment to take action in their own teaching and curriculum development. Thus everyone involved in the change – academic and support staff – are change agents and need development and support to undertake this role – they also need time. Stacey *et al.* (2000: 87) note that the level of energy affects the outcome of any change process; the more energy the greater the creativity and the better the outcomes.

Conclusions

This case study of the implementation of graduate attributes at the University of Luton has demonstrated that the ideas of Fullan and other complexity theorists are useful in explaining the reality of change, and thus in framing our own thinking about how to implement change. Those considering educational change need not only to think of the 'what' and 'why' of change, but also of the more complex and problematic 'how'. 'Blue skies' thinking is the interesting and easy part; implementing change is the difficult and messy part.

Whilst the University of Luton adopted a thoughtful, considered and logical approach to the last round of changes it has sought to implement, this may not appear to be the case to staff on the ground. The complexity and uncertainty of change combined with peripheral engagement, resourcing, and conflicting personal priorities and inclinations combine to make change disorganised and 'messy' to those on the receiving end. This case study has argued that such 'messy-ness' is good. It is not only what should be expected of any change process: it is also what is required for change to be successful and sustainable.

As noted earlier, those with responsibility for effecting change within higher education – staff and educational developers, and senior managers – often compare engaging academics with change as being similar to herding cats. This is fundamentally true, yet is an inappropriate analogy. It is true in the sense that academics are independent thinkers who will challenge and seek to subvert institutional directives to change – like cats it is difficult to contain them in one place or coerce them into following a specific course of action. It is an inappropriate analysis because the dynamic of allowing academics to find their own path results in sustainable and creative change. Employing independently minded 'cats' as academics is likely to be of much more benefit to change and to the institution than employing sheep.

Endnotes

1   Available at <http://www.qaa.ac.uk/academicinfrastructure/progressfiles/guidelines/default.asp> (accessed May 2006).
2   Available at <http://www.heacademy.ac.uk/SubjectNetwork.htm> (accessed May 2006).
3   Available at <http://www.heacademy.ac.uk/1745.htm> (accessed May 2006).
4   Available at <http://www.recordingachievement.org> (accessed May 2006).

Bibliography

Atlay, M.T. and Harris R. (2000) 'An institutional approach to developing students' "transferable" skills', *Innovations in Education and Training International,* Vol. 37, No. 1, 76–84.
Atlay, M.T. (2003) 'Refreshing and revising – an institutional approach to skills development', *Staff and Educational Development International,* Vol. 7, No. 3, 181–90.
Atlay, M.T. (2006, in press) 'Skills development: ten years of evolution from institutional specification to a more student-centred approach', in P. Hager and S. Holland (eds.) *Graduate Attributes and Lifelong Learning: An Agenda for Better Learning and Employability,* Dordrecht: Kluwer.
East, R. (2005) 'A progress report on progress files', *Active Learning* Vol. 6, No. 2, 160–71.
Fullan, M. (1993) *Change Forces: Probing the Depths of Educational Reform,* London: Falmer Press.
Fullan, M. (1999) *Change Forces: The Sequel,* London: Falmer Press.
Fullan, M. (2003) *Change Forces: With a Vengeance,* London: Falmer Press.
Higher Education Academy (2005) *Understanding How We Accomplish Complex Change in Higher Education Institutions,* Higher Education Academy discussion papers. Available at <http://www.heacademy.ac.uk/2492.htm> (accessed August 2005).
Kotter, J. P. (1995) 'Leading change: why transformation efforts fail', *Harvard Business Review,* April–June.
Olson, E.E. and Eoyang, G.H. (2001) *Facilitating Organisational Change: Lessons from Complexity Science,* San Francisco, CA: Jossey Bass – Pfeiffer.

Quality Assurance Agency (2001) *Guidelines for Progress Files,* Quality Assurance Agency (UK). Available at <http://www.qaa.ac.uk/academicinfrastructure/progressfiles/guidelines/default.asp> (accessed May 2006).

Scott, P. (1999) *Change Matters: Making a Difference in Education and Training,* Australia: Allen and Unwin.

Senge, P. (1990) *The Fifth Discipline: The Art and Practice of the Learning Organisation,* London: Random House.

Stacey, R. (1992) *Managing the Unknowable,* San Francisco, CA: Jossey-Bass.

Stacey, R. D., Griffin, D. and Shaw, P. (2000) *Complexity and Management: FAD or Radical Challenge to Systems Thinking*, London: Routledge.

Chapter 12

Angels in Concrete

Work-based learning and change in higher education

Frank Lyons and Mike Bement

Introduction

This chapter, through first-hand experience, emphasises that change takes time, and how an innovatory academic programme develops as its practical implications become clear. In 1989, Portsmouth Polytechnic (University of Portsmouth from 1992) won funding from Shell and the UK government for a degree programme for individuals who had left school at 16, gained Technical Vocational Educational Initiative (TVEI) and Youth Training Scheme (YTS) qualifications yet had not previously considered entry to higher education (Yeomans 2002). This was to build on preliminary work already done in investigating employer support for such a qualification (Claridge 1989: 1). The aims of the proposed Partnership Degree Programme were to 'attract capable students of 18+ who had not previously considered entry to higher education', provide 'work and study as a balanced integrated experience' with 'university attendance for selected classes' and learning from 'independent task-based learning'. The Partnership Degree Programme was seen as 'a way of retaining staff, providing career and progression routes, and increasing profitability' through degree programmes that 'respond in a broad and flexible manner to local employment needs'.

The Dean and Pro-Vice-Chancellor who signed the development contract in 1990 may not have recognised the full implications; they were committing a new University to a radically new programme managed by a small group of 'explorers' (Lovell 1994) highly motivated to initiate change. On an early draft paper on the practicalities of work-based learning, one of the two key co-explorers wrote of the programme: 'This is outrageous, we will never get away with it!'. As will be seen, the programme went ahead and over time became a model for work-based learning within the University and in other higher education institutions.

The present chapter reflects on the realities of this innovative curriculum development. It will be seen that the discussion illustrates the importance of the familiar requirements in change management for:

- risk takers
- inspiration and models of good practice

- understanding the change context
- reflection in change management
- dissemination and marketing.

Each of these will be discussed in terms of a case study that spans the inception, development and institutional embedding of the programme.

The case study

Risk takers: the development group

At the earliest conceptual stage, the Head of Educational Development brought together a group of five teachers who were also enthusiasts for change, with a pro-vice-chancellor as champion. The members of the development group were no strangers to change, both in their personal lives and in their jobs. Drawn from across the University, the team had a range of experiences: an engineer with a doctorate in education and another who was involved with development work on the accreditation of prior learning (APL) and credit accumulation and transfer; a sociologist who had developed access programmes and learning skills materials; a computer scientist who had been innovating with study skills and careers management tutorials; and a business studies lecturer who had extensive industrial experience and knowledge of training at work.

At this stage in the development of the programme, the group members gave their own time to work on the programme because of their personal commitment to active, student-centred learning and the principle of widening access. Apart from the enthusiasm for change, the common factor in that early group was that, with the exception of the Head of Educational Development, none of the enthusiasts was employed in a post with managerial responsibility and all were visualizers and risk takers who saw education from the students' perspective. Interestingly, despite the latter, they were often surprised by the implications of the vision and the changes this required of the emerging programme.

Inspiration drawn from models of good practice

Like many others in the 1980s, the programme development group turned to the inspirational work of an American organisation, the Council for Adult and Experiential Learning (CAEL), and the UK Learning from Experience Trust. Ideas on ways to accredit learning from experience were blended with notions of the learning contracts and the self-managed learner found in the work of the Empire State College and the School for Independent Study at North East London Polytechnic. Particularly important was work on the four key elements in the design of deep learning programmes: intrinsic motivation; active learning; interaction with others; and a structured knowledge base (Gibbs 1992). This work helped to shape the students' learning support programme as well as the overall

Partnership curriculum design. The programme team interacted from the outset with other practitioners in the 70 work-based learning development projects funded by the UK Government (Brennan and Little 1996).

Working in context

Even at the earliest stages in the development of the Partnership Programme it was obvious that if the project were to be accepted by the University, some level of collective ownership was necessary. The course team wrote 'first draft' programme documentation that indicated the vision behind the scheme and its component parts: component parts: the accreditation of prior experiential learning (APEL), work-based learning and learning contracts through which students would propose and manage their own degree programmes. The documentation was circulated widely within all faculties, the registry and in student support services, asking for comment and suggestions about how to overcome the potential pitfalls.

Two strategies were being adopted. First, by asking colleagues to offer and write about solutions to the perceived problems, material was produced for a second draft validation document that included contributions from across the University. Second, the issues raised established the agenda for the validation event, and answers could be ready for the anticipated criticisms. The Director of the programme edited the contributions and suggestions received into a final validation document, presenting the work-based scheme as a programme to which the University had already committed itself, and including reference to international practice in many of the contested issues.

Anticipating potential objections became a central strategy as the programme developed. In the early stages of the programme, the University had not yet moved to a unitised, credit-rated curriculum with a semester-based timetable. The Partnership team was able to work with relative freedom in this locally undeveloped field, pioneering quality assurance methods in relation to level and volumes of learning, the nature of 'graduateness' and the writing of learning outcomes, outstripping the rest of the University. The legitimacy of Partnership procedures was reinforced when it became known that the key members of the team were working at a national level with the Higher Education Quality Council (HEQC) on graduateness (HEQC 1995) and with the Southern England Consortium for Credit Accumulation and Transfer (SEEC) on levels and learning outcomes (SEEC 2003). Thus, by the time the University as a whole had moved to a unitised and credit-rated curriculum, experiential and work-based learning was more readily quality assured, because the Partnership model had now been nationally authenticated, and because of the University's acceptance of the learning outcomes approach central to the writing of learning contracts.

Managing through reflection

In the original feasibility study, Claridge (1989: 36–7) had identified 55 potential candidates promised from local companies including 'engineer technicians with Higher National Certificate qualifications' and 'trainees on Youth Training Scheme apprenticeships with minimal or no formal educational qualifications'. The targeted recruitment of 18 year olds with technical education did not materialise, despite earlier promises, and it later became obvious to the Partnership team that such students were in any case not generally mature enough for a self-run and self-reflective learning programme. The pilot year enrolled just seven students, who were in their mid-twenties to mid-thirties, all having both formal qualifications at tertiary level and credit-worthy experiential learning. They fulfilled the general goal in that they were technical students who had missed out on higher education, and were from social backgrounds with no higher education traditions: they were the 18+ target group, but a little older.

As the lessons of the pilot year were learned, some members of the original development group could not continue to devote time to the emerging programme. Two academics, with administrative support in the Partnership Programme Office, took increasing responsibility for developing the programme. They adopted an organic and iterative approach that mirrored the same reflective learning approach that the first Partnership students were practicing. Two drivers of change were paramount: outsiders who were consulted for ideas and encouragement; and internal stakeholders whose concerns drove further innovation:

- the Partnership Steering Group – chaired by a series of senior industrialists with excellent educational credentials
- Partnership students – who fed back comments on the programme at tutorials, through their responses to questionnaire surveys and (after 1995) through the progress reports that were the assessment artefacts for their learning management unit
- external academic colleagues – who were working in staff and curriculum development, and as external examiners on the programme.

The external push to the professional curriculum

Experience with the pilot cohort led to the first of a series of incremental adjustments to the Partnership Programme that have impacted organically on the programme itself and work-based learning in general. Students and their employers were quick to alert the Partnership Office to problems. Models of good practice were all right in theory, but to meet fully the needs of students and their employers the Partnership scheme needed to evolve, often moving in unanticipated directions.

First to be changed was the programme's name. The name 'Partnership Degree Programme' emerged in the earliest work (Claridge 1989: 2). By 1991, the curriculum documentation used the name 'Partnership Degree Programme' but there was no mention of the titles of the degrees that would result. Responses from potential students and their employers suggested that something called a 'BA or BSc Partnership Studies' or 'Work-based Learning' would have little worth. The idea of generic but subject-related titles such as 'Engineering and Management Studies', with a transcript showing learning included in the degree, was eventually accepted. This marked a significant recognition by the University of the value of work-based learning and the standard of the award.

Similarly the curriculum model itself was to move as the Partnership team became sensitised to the real needs and aspirations of the students and their employers. The Deputy Director of the Programme interviewed two potential Partnership students at Fairey Microfiltrex. One had been identified as the right person to be Chief Designer and the other for promotion to lead the Technical Engineering Services team. After meeting the students, he told the Board that he foresaw no problem in getting both students through the BSc (Hons) Engineering and Management in two years. Instead of the appreciation he expected, he was told by the Managing Director (later to become Chair of the Partnership Programme's Industrial Steering Committee and a University Governor): 'I don't think you understand – we're not interested in degrees, only that they get the right skills and knowledge to do the job! Degrees are just a by-product.' External members on the Steering Committee further clarified this professional curriculum element when they placed greater emphasis on 'soft' transferable skills than University academics would have done.

The Steering Committee at this early stage was an invaluable sounding board, allowing the Programme team to validate practical developments as they occurred. During scrutiny of proposed developments, the industrial members exposed the senior academics on the Committee to the nature of a curriculum that would be commercially valued. In fact this exposure had such telling effect that it was these same senior academics who insisted that Partnership regulations be sufficiently flexible to cope with the pressures mature learners in employment and with family and personal commitments might experience. Principally, there had to be freedom to design degree programmes that were fit for the specific careers of the students and the interests of their employers. It had to be possible to suspend or extend studies (perhaps because of a posting overseas, or pregnancy), or to change the direction of studies because of new job responsibilities.

Students were developing similar arguments. For an example of the pilot student group, one particular student's experiences illustrated the important point that every job creates its own subject coherence and hence a study programme. He developed a personalised learning programme including computing, people skills, journalism and marketing to suit his employment in public relations work at IBM. The Partnership team and the University were forced to recognise this as the professional curriculum in action: the learning programme arises from the unique setting of the individual and his or her work.

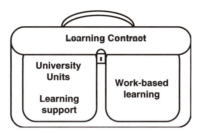

Figure 12.1 'The Bag'

With this vision of professional learning, much else became clear, not least how much employers value learning achieved through work-based projects. In fact, the Partnership Programme's definition of work-based learning grew directly from it – *the achievement of planned learning outcomes using workplace resources based on a given task or function.* In this model, each student must:

> ... show that the work planned forms a unified and achievable package, that the work based learning and University courses are complementary, and that they provide sufficient opportunities for the assessment of progress and achievement.
>
> (Bement 1993)

As the Partnership team began to feel more comfortable with its view of how the work-based learning element could fit together with other emerging elements, the learning contract was envisioned as a briefcase or 'the Bag' (see Figure 12.1) containing work-based learning projects, together with formal studies ('units' in University of Portsmouth parlance), and the all-important learning support needed by independent learners.

This model of learning with the student filling and carrying his or her bag became a useful metaphorical tool for explaining the Partnership Programme to potential stakeholders. It helped the Partnership team recognise the importance of exemplars and imagery to help the stakeholders (students, their sponsors, new partnership tutors and mentors). It was possible to explain the Partnership Programme as a means for students to identify the bag of learning needed to equip them for their own jobs – with the University being asked to provide facilitation and quality assurance.

Quality management concerns about the Bag

Within the University concerns were being raised about Partnership APL practice, the starting point for students designing their own learning contracts. Although portfolios demonstrated often extensive and relevant learning from experience, many in the academy believed that this blend of APL together with work-based learning credits and some university taught learning was not 'fit for award'. There were questions as to whether there were limits on the amount of general credit that could be awarded for the learning of general transferable skills, whether credit would be given for learning that could not be matched or mapped to the learning that a conventional student of the University might attain, and whether the degree programmes would be of sufficient depth and coherence.

The Partnership team had to argue convincingly that credit would only be awarded for prior learning that was relevant to the work of the learner and therefore to the proposed studies. Similarly they made the case that it would be discriminatory to disregard learning relevant to the student that did not match learning in the University yet was of equivalent worth. In relation to depth, the case was made that learning contract proposals were submitted for scrutiny both by University academics and company mentors before being approved as appropriate for degree level. The team recognised that the programme was being challenged on quality grounds, and that a case against the standard of the Partnership awards could not be answered with traditional appeals to 'excellence' and 'custom and practice'.

With this in mind, the team developed another visual image, firstly to understand the issues themselves, and secondly (drawing on experience with 'the Bag') to explain them to others. In order to plan, manage or measure learning from experience, work-based projects or, indeed, traditional classroom instruction, three sets of tools are required. These are: means by which *volumes of credit* may be standardised; means for establishing the *level* of learning; and criteria by which learning may be *assessed* and graded. Naturally enough this was seen as a three-legged stool. It is interesting that in kinematics, three points of contact between a body and a surface supporting it represent the necessary and sufficient conditions for stability. The model is thus stable metaphorically and pedagogically, and it underpins and informs all that the Partnership, and its learners (students and staff) do. As with 'the Bag', the stool provides a convenient image to help stakeholders understand the underpinning principles of learning design and measurement, useful also in the design of study units, and as a tool for use when acting as a consultant or external examiner elsewhere (Lyons and Bement 2001).

Managing the mature programme: from the Bag to Angels in Marble

The introduction of a Master's route in 1994 led to new insights into what the Programme team and the students were doing. The Master's scheme allowed a student up to 135 credits for work-based learning out of the required total of 180, creating the space in which professional learning could be more readily achieved. Although some students have seized the opportunity to attend as many University units as possible, most have seen the project as the most important element – for them, learning support, University units and other courses were there only to provide input to the project. The instrumentality of this approach was resisted by colleagues expressing 'rhetorical preference' (Rothblatt 1976) for the academic pursuit of knowledge 'for its own sake'; however for the programme team this insight was transferred to the undergraduate Partnership Programme and critically to the team's understanding of the nature of education and enquiry.

As the quality arguments were won, the Programme team were to reject the bag metaphor with its suggestion that the student came shopping for learning that they then took away. The team recognised that the learning was coming from the students' needs, and became attracted to the metaphor used by Trowler (1996) when he wrote of the background to APEL, taking his title of Angels in Marble from Michelangelo's notion that the angels he carved were already present in the rock, and that he merely set them free[1]. Trowler's paper elaborates on what were then seen as two contrasting approaches to APEL – the credit exchange and developmental models – arguing that they should be seen as the poles of a continuum rather than essentially dichotomous approaches.

Whilst the Partnership team agreed with this analysis, it was thought that 'marble' seemed a rather arty and exclusive material, and that there were overtones of agency that clashed with the student-centred and student-mediated ideals of the Partnership. So the Partnership Programme came to the idea of Angels in Concrete as a more appropriate metaphor, placing the student at centre stage during the process of identifying areas of learning already achieved and learning desired, thereby locating the centre of gravity of the Programme firmly in industry and the real world.

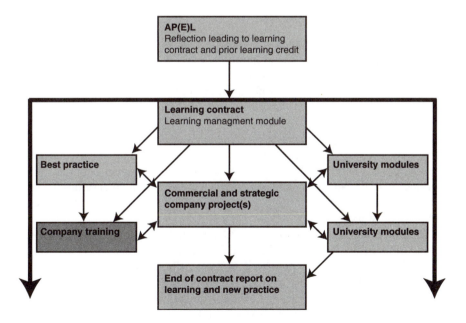

Figure 12.2 The curriculum model

By the mid 1990s, the Partnership team had developed the curriculum model illustrated in Figure 12.2 in order to find their Angels in Concrete.

At that time, Hants & Sussex Aviation, seeking advice and help with staff development, approached the Partnership Programme. The company services aircraft gas turbine engines, and their staff must be trained in accordance with Civil Aviation Authority requirements. The company wanted to develop 'Ian', a laboratory technician, to be their materials scientist. He was already educated to Higher National Certificate level (equivalent to the first year of a British University degree).

The APEL process allowed Ian to locate exactly where he was in relation to the output statements he and Hants & Sussex had developed. Working with his tutor (an engineer working in the Chemistry Department), he designed a programme incorporating units in metallurgy and materials science from the Mechanical Engineering Department, and inorganic and surface chemistry from his tutor's department. His major work-based projects were in the redesign of the laboratory facility to meet the requirements of a new range of engines serviced by Hants & Sussex, and the development of a novel process to remove ceramic coatings from turbine blades prior to reapplication. The removal process developed by Ian won approval from both engine manufacturers and airworthiness authorities, and was eventually licensed to other repairers. His first-class degree in Applied Science and his proven track record in delivering projects established him firmly in his professional field.

Managing Angels in Concrete

From the beginning, the Partnership team recognised that student support would be central to the success of the programme, given a student cohort with limited educational experience and the innovatory nature of the programme. It will be seen that in both APEL guidance and learning support, the team was to evolve its practice in response to what was learned from the students and what was understood about the professional curriculum.

Originally APEL guidance was presented in a workshop programme including 'time line' exercises, guidance on reflective writing, and individual counselling from APEL advisers. This was found to be time-consuming and impractical for working learners, and was replaced with a holistic distance-learning approach that started with application forms that contained questions designed to stimulate reflective answers.

The process followed on with the APEL guide (Lyons 1998). The guide was based firmly on the student establishing the authenticity, recency, relevance and sufficiency of the learning presented in the portfolio. In later iterations of the guide, the original academic language has been softened and supported by various exemplars of good practice. It also encouraged new claimants to seek help from previous learners on the programme on how to write prior learning claims. Most applicants now produce good-quality first drafts that need little tutorial support from Partnership tutors and no further revision.

The first Learning Support Group programme included workshops on, for example: learning styles; reflective writing and academic essays; learning contract regulations, design and management; reading and writing skills, the meaning and practice of work-based learning; and on groups and group work. The very first cohort taught the Partnership team to make materials more industry-relevant, and so transformations were made: from group work to chairing meetings; from writing styles to company versus academic writing. The ritualistic inclusion of learning styles was dropped – 'interesting but not much practical use'. The revised programme was designed to meet the needs of each separate cohort of students.

As the Partnership team's understanding of the Angels in Concrete metaphor grew, the Learning Support Group workshops were dropped and replaced by a credit-rated Learning Management study unit where tutors taught less and facilitated more. As with the APEL guidance, the learning management material was replaced by exemplars of good practice derived from the work of previous students. The assessment artefacts for the new unit include the student's learning contract and three progress reports covering students' reflective evaluations on their progress, a recommendation on their final degree award in their end of degree report, and constructive criticism on the Partnership Programme. The model has thus developed into one of educational project management.

In parallel with this developing approach to student management, the role of the Partnership Office was evolving from administrative support to account management. Office staff answered more and more of the student's day-to-day queries and helped students articulate with University systems. The Partnership academic tutors were taking a back seat and a more developmental role.

Marketing and dissemination

Discussion will turn next to what has worked well in generating student applications. It is notable that there are very few referrals from any publicity materials produced by the University as part of its general marketing strategy, such as the general prospectus and website. However, good results have been obtained with news stories in the local papers, and with flyers in local libraries. At one time a 'finder's fee' was paid to anyone introducing a new student who eventually enrolled, a cost-effective way of spending the advertising budget. Despite the success of this businesslike approach, the University did not approve, and stopped the practice. The most effective approach has been word of mouth, where the students act as champions – a real work-based learning method, in which students who have done well and gained both the learning and the degrees they wanted are active in spreading the word among colleagues.

External dissemination

The greatest advocates among employers were Partnership students and their commercially and strategically valuable work-based learning projects. One of the many examples used to market the programme is a work-based project completed for Yarrow Shipbuilders. The project involved learning about electromagnetic and mutual interference theory through application of the principles in a real evaluation and redesign of the topside arrangements during the refit of the Royal Navy's flagship HMS *Illustrious*.

Most significantly, with the support of the then chair of the Programme's Steering Committee (the MD of Fairey Microfiltrex) the Partnership team contributed to the British government's enquiry into higher education, presenting their insights into the University–Company partnership and the work of three graduates who had benefited from the programme. In the National Report (Dearing 1997), the Portsmouth Partnership Programme is cited as an appropriate mode of study in a society committed to lifelong learning:

> The University of Portsmouth, for example, offers a degree programme for people who work in local companies, which incorporates credits towards the degree based upon the individual's learning at work and his or her previous qualifications, organized and delivered in a way that fits in with the individual's employment.
>
> (Dearing 1997: Chapter 12, paragraph 23)

The Report endorses this as a way that universities can meet the local and regional economic needs of both individuals and companies, going on to say:

> Such partnerships between organisations and institutions will be an increasing feature of higher education. The employers responding to our survey told us that they envisage their links becoming both more focused and more exclusive.
>
> (Dearing 1997: Chapter 12, paragraph 23)

Consultation and change

Within the University, best practice in work-based learning has spread from the Partnership Programme to degrees in all faculties. Similarly the Programme's approach to APL has informed that of the University as a whole, and the Partnership APL guide is the recommended model. This dissemination at the level of practice has been managed through a consultation approach. Partnership guidance material is offered freely to others, as is advice on how to tailor and adapt this material and staff development is provided where requested. The same model has been used in spreading the work-based learning and APL approaches to other universities in the UK, most notably at Liverpool John Moores and Glamorgan

Universities. Furthermore, Partnership staff taking on the role of external examiner on work-based programmes have been able to support development elsewhere.

Post Dearing: managing in a changed context

The post-Dearing agenda for higher education and the success of work-based learning degrees at Portsmouth have changed the institutional context. This is reflected in a headline aim of the University's mission:

To be the first choice provider of skills development, enterprise, innovation, knowledge transfer and support for private, public and voluntary sector organisations of all sizes in our region and more widely in appropriate sectors of the economy.

In the space created by these developments, the University's industrial curriculum (Lyons 2003) has expanded with the introduction of new work-based programmes, including:

- professional doctorates that include teaching of the latest theory and practice combined with high-level work-based projects
- degrees for Royal Naval personnel, giving credit for naval training, and allowing them to achieve Masters awards through work-based projects
- corporate degrees including private sector training programmes that have been reformed to include assessed components and then accredited
- foundation degrees, introduced in 2001 that are 'employment-related higher education qualifications, designed in conjunction with employers to meet skills shortages at the higher technician and associate professional levels' (DfES 2005, Homepage). The University has emerged as a major provider of HEFCE funded foundation degrees, with around 17 per cent of foundation degree students in the south-east region.

In this climate of change, management in relation to work-based learning has moved to a new transformational level. In 2004 the University put together a team that made a successful bid to the Higher Education Funding Council (England) (HEFCE) for funding to develop a Centre of Excellence in Teaching and Learning (CETL) to support foundation degree students. A proven record of excellent practice in work-based learning, careers management, student support provisions and existing foundation degree programmes supported the bid. The award of CETL status has resulted in £4.5 million extra funding from HEFCE to establish 'Foundation Direct'. This Centre will provide a 'state of art' drop-in centre and online support services for foundation degree students and their in-company mentors. This developmental work will be thoroughly evaluated and the pedagogic research findings will be disseminated internationally.

The CETL project, supported by development and research teams, is operating in an environment that is a step change away from that in which the Partnership

Programme was originally situated. However, the teams managing the CETL and the Partnership Programme will continue to use the methods that have been so successful in the past.

Conclusions

In a sense, the Partnership initiative has come full circle, not least because the small team that started teaching reflection to Partnership students 15 years ago learned how to become reflective managers. Where the explorers were striving to enunciate the principles governing successful work-based education, the University is now confident in their application in programmes of study that incorporate student-mediated content in many different fields.

Reflecting on the case study that is reported within the present chapter, it can be seen that the most important predictors of successful change in the higher education sector are the five enunciated at the beginning of the chapter: change agents who are risk takers, inspiration and models of good practice, understanding the change context, reflection in change management, and dissemination and marketing.

The success of the Partnership initiative reinforces the message that taking risks can lead to significant incremental outcomes. However, it is important to stress that risk taking within a supportive institutional context is more likely to lead to step change. Indeed, it is arguable that the most significant learning has been in the contextual aspect of change management.

Time and again, the importance of metaphor in conveying the message has been highlighted as with the use of 'the bag' and 'the stool'. Similarly the presentation of exemplars of good practice and sample APEL portfolios are used as means by which key concepts and practices can be established within the minds of others. Furthermore, living metaphors are often used to assist new students, by arranging for them to make contact with past students from similar working backgrounds; this has been particularly effective with postulants overcome by the sheer scope of what is offered to them.

Endnotes

1   *Non ha l' ottimo artista alcun concetto, / Ch'un marmo solo in se non circoscriva / Col suo soverchio, e solo a quello arriva / La man' che obbedisce all' intelletto* (Gustati 1863).

Bibliography

Bement, J.M. (1993) *Learning in the Workplace – the Portsmouth Partnership Experience,* in Proceedings of the 2nd East West Congress on Engineering Education, Lodz, Poland.

Brennan, J. and Little, B. (1996) *A Review of Work Based Learning in Higher Education,* London: Department for Education and Skills.

Claridge, M. (1989) *Partnership Degree Scheme: A Report on Feasibility, Structure and Development,* Portsmouth: Portsmouth Polytechnic.

Dearing, R. (1997) *National Committee of Inquiry into Higher Education: Higher Education in the Learning Society,* London: NCIHE publications.

DfES (2005) *Welcome to foundationdegree.org.uk,* Department for Education and Skills. Available at <http://www.foundationdegree.org.uk/> (accessed 09 September 2005).

Gibbs, G. (1992) 'Improving the quality of student learning through course design', in R. Barnett (ed.) *Learning to Effect,* Buckingham: SRHE/Open University Press.

Gustati, C. (1863) *Le Rime di Michelangelo Buonarroti, Pittore, Scultore e Architetto, Cavate Dagli Autograf,* Firenze: Felice le Monmer.

HEQC (1995) *What Are Graduates? Clarifying the Attributes Of Graduateness,* The Higher Education Quality Council: Quality Enhancement Group. Available at <http://www.lgu.ac.uk/deliberations/graduates/starter.html> (accessed 9 September 2005).

Lovell, R. (1994) 'Empowerment', in R. Lovell, R. *Managing Change in the Public Sector,* Harlow: Longman.

Lyons, F. (1998) *How to Claim Credit for Prior Learning toward Learning at Work Awards,* Portsmouth: Partnership Programme, University of Portsmouth.

Lyons F.S. (2003) 'Customer led learning environments: university–industry partnerships', in *Learning for an Unknown Future, Proceedings of the Annual HERDSA Conference, Research and Development in Higher Education,* Vol. 26.

Lyons F. S. and Bement J.M. (2001) 'Setting the standards: judging levels of achievement', in D. Boud and N. Soloman (eds.) *Work-based Learning: A New Higher Education,* SRHE/Open University, 166–83.

Rothblatt, S. (1976) *Tradition and Change in English Liberal Education: An Essay in History and Culture,* London: Faber and Faber.

SEEC (2003) *Credit Level Descriptors for Further and Higher Education.* Available at <http://www.seec-office.org.uk/SEEC.%20FE-HECLDs-mar03def-1.doc> (accessed 9 September 2005).

Trowler, P. (1996) 'Angels in marble? Accrediting prior experiential learning in higher education', Studies in Higher Education, Vol. 21, No. 1.

Yeomans, D. (2002) 'Constructing vocational education: from TVEI to GNVQ', *Education-line,* University of Leeds. Available at <http://www.leeds.ac.uk/educol/documents/00002214.htm> (accessed 9 September 2005).

Chapter 13

Engaging higher education in the global challenge of sustainability

Charles E. Engel and Bland Tomkinson

Introduction

Change is not without difficulties. In fact, Burnes (2004) suggests that two-thirds of the changes that he surveyed were unsuccessful. In spite of this, case studies regularly focus on success rather than on the inhibitors to change. To redress the balance, this chapter explores some of the structural factors that can inhibit the change process. The case study deals with curriculum change, set against a background of major organisational change. However, broader organisational change issues are addressed only where they affect specific curriculum matters. For a fuller reading on some of the organisational issues, see Tomkinson (2005). Among other things, the curriculum change in question involves introducing a greater focus on the management of change into the experience of all graduates. The initial concept of interdisciplinarity for societal responsibility led to the Ultimate Challenge – an initiative to develop, promote and embed the concept – but it will be seen that this has been affected by considerations of sustainability. In brief, this is a case study of the management of change to introduce a curriculum that is, in part, focused on change management. The change process is still active. Indeed, the process of change is itself still subject to change.

Background

The Victoria University of Manchester and the University of Manchester Institute of Science and Technology (UMIST) united in October 2004 to become the largest higher education institution in the UK. Such a time of change and upheaval is an opportunity to look afresh at the synergy between research and teaching and to foster an environment open to new ways of thinking. For several years, the combined Teaching Research and Development Network (TRDN) of the two universities sought to promote new initiatives in curriculum innovation and professional development (see, for example; Kahn *et al.* 2003).

The Ultimate Challenge was delivered to staff by one of the authors (Charles Engel) at the May 2002 Teaching Research and Development Network Symposium. As a result of the enthusiasm engendered among staff, the concept of interdisciplinarity with societal responsibility became an element of the embryonic Teaching, Learning and Assessment strategy for the new university. However, this was in the context of interdisciplinarity becoming a unique selling point of the curriculum of the new university, and those involved were asked to keep the idea secret until the formation of the merged university.

The Ultimate Challenge arises from a concern to embed an interdisciplinary approach to societal responsibility within higher education. Major global developments affect human welfare internationally and they are increasingly influenced by worldwide changes, such as: reduction of biodiversity; pollution of air, soil and water with detrimental influences on the global environment; continuing growth of the world's population, accompanied by increasing poverty in the developing world; and growing competition for limited water supplies, resulting in threats of armed conflict (see, for example, Brundtland 1987). These developments arguably stimulate economic and social turmoil, extremism, terrorism and migration, which affect social stability.

Thus the world will require a new generation of leaders in the various professions who are able to adapt to, and participate in, the management of change – not only within their own sphere of activities, but also in society at large. This will involve interprofessional and intersectoral collaboration in global research and long-term remediation of the many interdependent, global problems. Interprofessional collaboration calls for familiarity with the various professions, their 'language' and their ways of thinking.

To meet this challenge, higher education will need to devise new curricula and enable its educators to facilitate such interdisciplinary learning. Interprofessional collaboration in education and training is not new, but, so far, this has been on a small scale and essentially concerned with local affairs. In the UK, various government agencies have encouraged interdisciplinary education, but essentially this has been in an attempt to achieve greater 'efficiency' in various sectors, notably the health service. The challenge is to focus on the problems rather than the techniques, and on societal responsibility where interprofessional collaboration is a means to an end. Elsewhere, notably in North America, higher education for 'citizenship' has been developed mainly with a focus on local conditions and needs (for example, Colby *et al.* 2003).

Some of the ideas behind the Ultimate Challenge stem from work undertaken by one of the authors (Engel 2002), in conjunction with the UK Centre for the Advancement of Inter-professional Education (CAIPE), on education for societal responsibility in the health professions. This produced a European consensus of ideas about the graduate skills and attributes required to achieve interprofessional outcomes and the educational interventions, as well as the conditions needed to produce them. Among the key skills and abilities for graduates identified in the CAIPE report were those of adaptability to change and participation in interprofessional and intersectoral management of change.

Meeting the challenge

As a result of the Teaching Research and Development Network Symposium in Manchester, the authors, together with a colleague from the university, Rosemary Warner, put forward a ten-point plan for implementation. The proposed steps were as follows:

- introduction
- fostering a climate of informed opinion and a sense of ownership
- defining the abilities and skills to be developed
- designing appropriate educational interventions
- designing supportive formative and summative assessments
- designing an interdisciplinary curriculum
- experimenting with educational interventions and formative and summative assessments
- planning and implementing a pilot curriculum
- monitoring and evaluation of the implementation with students
- organisation.

Effective collaboration between disparate disciplines for coordinated planning, implementation, assessment and monitoring requires a novel administrative approach to interdisciplinary education. Matrix management (Clarke 1979), which was seen as a useful prospect, has proved successful in many instances. The provision of incentives for students and academics was understood to be central to the change management process. Both need to be reassured that additional commitment to learning and teaching will be recognised in some tangible form (Mårtenson et al. 1998). A structure of collaborating working parties was to be established, each with a specific remit. Recruitment was to be based on skill: working party members would not be discipline representatives. Rather, they were to be knowledgeable in the tasks of the respective working parties.

The ten-point plan outlined above could itself be considered a model of change. Indeed, it does accord with Burnes' (2004) model of organisational change, though the sequencing is not always comparable:

- create a vision
- develop strategies
- create the conditions for successful change
- create the right culture
- assess the need for, and type of, change
- plan and implement change
- involve everyone
- sustain the momentum
- commit to continuous improvement.

The presentation to the Teaching Research and Development Network Symposium, the equivalent of the creation of the vision in Burnes' model, was the initiation of the change process. This led to further activity directed at wider promulgation of the idea. For example, the Teaching Research and Development Network set up a special interest group to foster interdisciplinarity with societal responsibility. Initially an evening workshop was arranged, focusing on the topic of migration. This event was largely for teaching staff but included other staff and also a few students. It was organised on the basis of small-group discussions in interdisciplinary groups that explored processes involved in migration and how study of these might be incorporated into the curriculum.

This was followed by a one-day event focusing on 'Water', where the larger constituency included staff of Manchester Museum, of public utilities and of UNESCO. A third profile-raising event, to foster the climate of informed opinion, was given a 'trigger' by the Deputy High Commissioner for New Zealand to look at the issues of aspects of life on small Pacific islands and potential problems due to posited climate change.

In parallel with these two events, aimed mainly at staff, a residential summer school was held with a small group of participants from a wide variety of programmes and levels. This also looked at issues of migration, using a collection of newspaper cuttings as the trigger and, separately, at the processes of interdisciplinary working.

At about the same time, the two universities were in the throes of planning a full merger that involved an examination of all aspects of policy and strategy as well as organisation and structure. Stemming from the discussions held to that date, the idea of 'interdisciplinarity with societal responsibility' was one that gripped the imagination of some of the planners of teaching and learning strategy, and was consequently written into the vision for teaching in the merged university.

Changing course

The high hopes held at the beginning of this change management process began to unravel in a number of ways. Perversely, the first of these was an opportunity to bid for substantial funding. The Higher Education Funding Council for England (HEFCE) issued invitations to universities to bid for 'centres of excellence in teaching and learning' (CETLs). Because of the moves towards systemic merger, UMIST and the Victoria University of Manchester were invited to submit joint bids. One of these was for interdisciplinarity, building not only on the ideals emphasised in Charles Engel's keynote address, and the subsequent development events, but also on some smaller-scale, interprofessional and interdisciplinary projects.

A panel was set up to prepare the bid document. Since one of the major aims in preparing the bid was to establish a track record in this area, individuals with contiguous interests were invited to join the panel. This introduced a wide range of examples of good practice, and power struggles within the group between rivals for ascendancy in obtaining the funding. The unfortunate result was a dilution of the original aims. There were also uncertainties arising from changes in the university structures, which created insecurities for staff and an increased imperative to focus on meeting individual needs. Partly as a result of these internal tensions, the bid for funding was unsuccessful.

Two major changes, one internal the other external, subsequently influenced the development of Ultimate Challenge. Internally, as the merger loomed closer and key figures were put in place, it became apparent that many of the priorities of the initial planning teams had been overturned, and the moves to establish interdisciplinarity as a keystone of the curriculum were eroded. At the same time, there were moves nationally within the UK to promote sustainability within the curriculum. The Higher Education Active Community Fund was used as a vehicle not only to promote sustainability, but also civic responsibility through student volunteering. The strands of sustainable development and global civic responsibility are contiguous with, indeed overlap, the idea of interdisciplinarity with societal responsibility. This forced a more pragmatic approach to alignment with these strands (see Figure 13.1).

Internally, the moves to promote the initiative became stifled by uncertainties in the organisational structure and by parallel developments. The prime organisational barrier was a strongly devolved power model, which meant that a cohesive cross-university approach was difficult to achieve, particularly in the light of different faculty priorities and nuances. Although somewhat defeating, the original object of supporting students from a wide-ranging span of disciplines in interdisciplinary working, the efforts began to focus on a single faculty, though other faculties started to undertake projects that were superficially aligned to the model but, practically, targeting different missions.

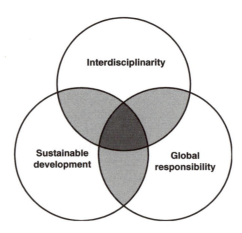

Figure 13.1 Aligning the strands

The University committed itself to the Talloires Declaration (University Leaders for a Sustainable Future 1990) in 2005, thus endorsing the sustainable development approach. The University also initiated the Manchester Leadership Programme, which supports a small number of students in developing leadership skills and involves them in 'out of hours' activity, including volunteering in the local community, thus endorsing the citizenship agenda. This proved slightly problematic in that the initial ideas became expanded and more diffuse, with excursions into the sustainability of the university campus and an emphasis on local student volunteering impacting on the concepts of sustainability and of global citizenship.

The prime concern, here, was that the direction of the project could easily set off down a sidetrack – focusing on broader issues of citizenship or of sustainability without the clear focus of interdisciplinarity directed towards mitigation and resolution of complex global problems. There was also a concern that some individuals were keen to jump to an end point of running a course or designing a syllabus without going through the intermediate analytical stages.

Externally, the ideas began to be promoted at relevant meetings and conferences on sustainable development and global citizenship, for example, the International Conference on Civic Engagement and Service Learning, held in Galway, Ireland, and the Education for Sustainable Development Conference, held in Bournemouth, UK. Furthermore, discussions were held with other universities and agencies around the world, with a view to exploring the scope for international collaboration in interdisciplinary education for societal responsibility.

The emphasis, of late, has been twofold: first, the move to use a single-faculty springboard to foster the development internally; and, second, the establishment of greater international links with a view to taking a global view of global issues. Part of this has also involved the seeking of funds because, within universities, particularly research-intensive universities, there is a temptation not to value initiatives unless they attract external support. In this present case, the funding for projects relating more directly to sustainable development has proved both an opportunity and a hurdle. The basic concept has achieved wide acceptance around the world, but, though many deem it a worthy objective, the money has so far failed to follow.

Discussion

There is a considerable literature on change, its processes and how institutions, managers and individual members react to the prospect and introduction of change. However, as this case study reveals, change does not always go as planned and there can be a range of reasons for this. One of the authors (Tomkinson 2005) has dealt with things that can go wrong in managing change, particularly sources of resistance to change, but here the analysis focuses on some of the structural factors that can inhibit the change process, causing delay and modification.

The setting of the case study is probably unique, yet the types of problem encountered are similar to those arising in many other situations. Generalising from some of the inhibitors that we have found, these can be grouped under five headings:

- too many changes at once
- mission creep
- power shifts
- slow pace of change
- personal insecurity

Too many changes at once

The incidence of a major change taking place might be seen to be the ideal opportunity to implement other changes: fear that staff may become change-weary suggests that rolling two changes into one might seem an easy way out. In our case, there were both internal and external changes that affected what we were trying to do. Changes in the operating environment will often cause planned changes to be modified, because that environment cannot be controlled, but hitching one change on to another, in our case aligning the introduction of the interdisciplinarity with a societal responsibility project with the teaching and learning strategy of the merging institution, can be a high-risk strategy. Dauphinais and colleagues (1996) in the Change Integration Team at Price Waterhouse suggest that positive change needs significant stability, and this reinforces the point of avoiding times of other major change when seeking to introduce your own change.

Mission creep

The external policy changes were difficult to foresee, but their arrival caused some rethinking of tactics. Where there is a major external (or even internal) realignment, the change aims and process have to be reviewed, but this can lead to the original mission being subverted. The original objectives can also multiply and become more diffuse: this can be as a result of others trying to achieve their own objectives by linking them to the original proposal or even by trying to link the proposal to the changes being wrought by others.

Power shifts

The internal organisational changes, in this case, meant that the roles of the initial champions changed and left them less well positioned to influence the take-up of the changes. This can happen in any change where senior staff, or more junior staff who are 'change champions', subsequently move to different roles. There is also a danger that some individuals will attempt to use the change process itself to improve their own power base, subverting the institutional change agenda into one of personal gain. There would also be the additional aspect of 'killing with silence' – the almost total absence of acknowledgement or any discussion. In our case, there was no wider dissemination of the implementation document beyond a few who joined the conspiracy of silence. Dauphinais and colleagues (1996) not only point to the need to focus on organisational culture, although circumspectly, but also to the need for forceful and courageous leadership in change management if people are to be empowered.

Slow pace of change

The initial slow pace of change was predicated on the basis of developing the idea comprehensively before making it public: this necessarily ran counter to the idea of gaining widespread commitment. Subsequent development has been slowed by some of the other inhibitors, but also by a necessity to reflect on the programme of change to see where the original concepts were not being achieved; where those objectives needed to be realigned; and where they needed to be restated.

Personal insecurity

Insecurity can come from too many changes at once and can, in turn, influence power shifts, mission creep and pace of change. Where organisational structures were being completely rewritten, and power vacuums created, many individuals became wary of their own position and unwilling to 'put their head above the parapet'; conservatism became the norm. An additional factor in our case was the coincidence of the government-initiated Research Assessment Exercise (RAE), which not only put pressure on individuals of itself, but, taken with other insecurities and a more managerial style, led to individuals fearing that any association with the development of teaching and learning would be damaging to their careers. Dauphinais and colleagues (1996) suggest that, in order to build an enterprise, you need to focus on the individual: this underpins the need to provide a secure base for individuals in order to develop an initiative.

Implications

Overall, these five points, taken with many of the other points made, suggest that, just as there are factors that are important to the success of a change initiative, there are others whose presence or absence will cause a project to stumble or fail. These will also be dependent on the scale of change proposed; a change to the delivery of a single module may be subject to fewer influences than a wholesale rewriting of a university's approach to the curriculum.

The analogy here is to Lewin's (1951) *force field analysis* and his 'driving forces' and 'restraining forces'. His restraining forces are comparable to the inhibitors that we have elucidated above, but his driving forces are more akin to the effects of changes in the external environment – political, economic, social and technological advancement that may impinge on the organisation and force a need to change. Lewin is best known as a psychologist and for his involvement in action research, but his earlier training in mathematics led him to conceive a vector statics model for change, his postulation being that change occurs when the sum of the driving forces exceeds that of the restraining forces. We would suggest a more dynamic model than this, with a need to retain at least a balance in forces throughout the change process.

Conclusions

The case study of the Ultimate Challenge demonstrates that the ethos and traditions of an institution, as well as internal and external pressures, will play a major role in the change process; some may support the process of change while others may be serious inhibitors. This applies to whole-of-university change as well as the smaller-scale curriculum change described in this chapter. Indeed, it applies to larger-scale systemic change: the current UK government initiative for *sustainability* in higher education (HEFCE 2005) is an example. It will be clear that sustainability is intended to support the status quo, primarily within the home country and perhaps with the students' future profession in mind.

However, the present initiative addresses interprofessional and intersectoral collaboration in the context of worldwide problems with a much wider influence on the future of our planet. Sustainability is a component, though an important one, in this broader educational aim towards international, interprofessional and intersectoral collaboration on behalf of society at large. These pressures impinge on individual academics and administrators.

In the face of change, individual academics and administrators will be concerned with their personal uncertainties, which relate to questions such as:

- How will this educational change affect my status quo, and how will I have to rearrange my life?
- How will the change affect my power base?
- How will I be able to maintain my academic reputation as an effective researcher and teacher?
- Will I be able to manage unfamiliar educational requirements?

It may be seen that individual stakeholders' responses to change may be fraught with uncertainty. Those with the ultimate power within the institution, including heads of major units, have little to gain from an innovation, but much to lose in terms of reputation. They will, thus, prefer not to intervene and to await results – sit on the fence, as it were.

In order for change to succeed in this climate, there needs to be charismatic leadership, though not necessarily by chief administrators – who should lend their mantle of authority to the main agent for change. This individual and/or associated groups need to be able to devote sufficient time and energy to the task in hand – too intermittent an effort may represent no more than drips on the sand. The crucial point is to link individual and group initiatives to those with the ultimate power within the institution, including heads of major units. Senior staff must be kept closely informed in order that their inertia is addressed. This represents the best of top-down and bottom-up change.

Satisfactory change processes call for carefully planned, and sensitively implemented, programmes for the dissemination of information. Hands-on induction should be the starting point for growing familiarity, informed acceptance, involvement and recognised ownership of the new. Indeed, this curriculum change process within just a single faculty required considerable and sustained emphasis on staff development over a number of years (Des Marchais 1991).

In the present context, the exploration of the abilities and skills to be developed in relation to societal responsibility will constitute a necessary first step towards the creation of a sequence of interdisciplinary, educational interventions that are not related to any particular discipline but to the development of generic capabilities. This, in itself, constitutes a new challenge to higher education.

On a more pragmatic note, tangible evidence of progress may attract attention from beyond the university, together with financial support. This would support confidence within the university in this venture into the unknown, this educational change, in the present climate of pressure on performance in 'hard' research. Yet external funding can be difficult to secure.

What of the future – when the change has actually become part of the educational programmes of the University? The initial rush of adrenaline and the satisfaction of achievement will be unknown to newly appointed academics who replace the change initiators, the 'founding fathers'. Newcomers who do not own the original aims and concepts may come from institutions that might not have adopted similar educational changes. The risk is that there will be a 'return to the mean' (Maddison 1978) – a process cited in the context of developing a new medical school, but also well known to those who have studied the cycle of enthusiastic sectarianism and its subsequent progression to established religion. The reality of educational change may well be its cyclical nature.

Bibliography

Brundtland, G.H. (1987) *Our Common Future,* New York: United Nations.
Burnes, B. (2004) *Managing Change,* London, Prentice Hall.
Clarke, R.M. (1979) 'Organising delivery of educational programmes', *Programmed Learning and Educational Technology,* Vol. 21, No, 4: 301–5.
Colby, A., Ehrlich, T., Beaumont, E. and Stephens, J. (2003) *Educating Citizens: Preparing America's Undergraduates for Lives of Moral and Civic Responsibility,* The Carnegie Foundation for the Advancement of Teaching, San Francisco: Jossey-Bass.
Des Marchais, J. E. (1991) 'From traditional to problem-based curriculum: How the switch was made at Sherbrooke, Canada', *The Lancet,* 338, 234–37.

Dauphinais, B., Price, C. and Pederson, P. (1996) *The Paradox Principles: How High Performance Companies Manage Chaos, Complexity And Contradiction To Achieve Superior Results,* Chicago: Irwin.

Engel, C.E. (2002) *Towards a European Approach to an Enhanced Education of the Health Professions in the 21st Century,* London, CAIPE. Available at <http://www. caipe.org.uk/pdf/CEReport.PDF> (accessed 15 July 2005).

HEFCE (2005) *Sustainable Development in Higher Education,* Report 2005/28, Bristol: HEFCE. Available at <http://www.hefce.ac.uk/pubs/hefce/2005/05_28/05_28.doc> (accessed 14 November 2005).

Kahn, P., Renfrew, A., O'Connell, C. and Tomkinson, B. (2003) 'A scholarly approach to learning and teaching: a local perspective', in B. Tomkinson and B. Smith (eds.) *Critical Encounters: Scholarly Approaches to Learning and Teaching,* York: LTSN Generic Centre 5–15.

Lewin K. (1951) *Field Theory in Social Science,* London: Tavistock.

Maddison D.C. (1978) 'What's wrong with medical education?', *Medical Education,* Vol. 12, 97–106.

Mårtenson D., Dahllöf, G. and Nordenström, J. (1998) 'Competence portfolia for assessment of academic performance at the Karolinska Institute', *Education for Health,* Vol. 11: 297–303.

Tomkinson, B. (2005) 'Organisational change' in John P. Wilson (ed.) *Human Resource Development* (2nd ed.), London: Kogan Page, 44–57.

University Leaders for a Sustainable Future (1990) *Programs [Talloires Declaration],* Available at <http://www.ulsf.org/programs_talloires.html> (accessed 20 November 2005).

Index